D0847775

D. H. Lawrence's non-fiction

D. H. LAWRENCE'S NON-FICTION
ART, THOUGHT AND GENRE

DAVID ELLIS *and* HOWARD MILLS
Senior Lecturers in English, University of Kent at Canterbury

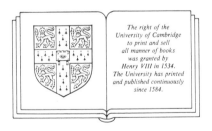

*The right of the
University of Cambridge
to print and sell
all manner of books
was granted by
Henry VIII in 1534.
The University has printed
and published continuously
since 1584.*

CAMBRIDGE UNIVERSITY PRESS
CAMBRIDGE
NEW YORK   NEW ROCHELLE
MELBOURNE   SYDNEY

Published by the Press Syndicate of the University of Cambridge
The Pitt Building, Trumpington Street, Cambridge CB2 1RP
32 East 57th Street, New York, NY 10022, USA
10 Stamford Road, Oakleigh, Melbourne 3166, Australia

First published 1988

Printed in Great Britain at the University Press, Cambridge

British Library cataloguing in publication data
Ellis, David, *1939–*
D. H. Lawrence's non-fiction : art,
thought and genre.
1. Lawrence, D. H. – Criticism and
interpretation
I. Title II. Mills, Howard
828'.91208   PR6023.A93Z/

Library of Congress cataloguing in publication data
Ellis, David, 1939–
D. H. Lawrence's non-fiction.
Bibliography.
Includes index.
1. Lawrence, D. H. (David Herbert), 1885–1930 – Prose.
2. Lawrence, D. H. (David Herbert), 1885–1930 – Knowledge
and learning. I. Mills, Howard. II. Title.
PR6023.A93Z6262   1988   824'.912   87–24990

ISBN 0 521 32739 3

GG

Contents

Acknowledgements

We would like to express our grateful thanks to Michael Black, Frank Cioffi, Edward Greenwood, Ian Gregor, Mara Kalnins, Mark Kinkead-Weekes, Molly Mahood, Laura Marcus, Christopher Pollnitz, Martin Scofield, Lindeth Vasey, Betsy Wallace, Jeff Wallace and John Worthen. We also thank the Harry Ransom Humanities Research Center in Austin, Texas for its helpful co-operation.

Chapters 4 and 5 contain material which originally appeared in the Spring 1977 number of the *D. H. Lawrence Review* and the Spring 1986 number of *English*.

We are grateful to John Martin, the present owner, for allowing us to reproduce on our jacket a page of the manuscript of Lawrence's 'Introduction to *Memoirs of the Foreign Legion* by M.M.', publishing rights for which lie with the Black Sparrow Press.

Introduction

I T was Catherine Carswell who in 1932 called Lawrence
'the most prolific writer our country has had since Sir Walter
Scott'.[1] Her own Scottish ancestry and the high critical standing Scott still enjoyed in her time must have made a comparison with that novelist seem natural. Nowadays one would be
more likely to think of Dickens or, moving somewhat down the
critical scale, the Trollope who so surprised Henry James — no
unproductive slouch himself — by being able to maintain his
large daily quota of words on a 'pitching Cunarder' steaming
across the Atlantic.[2]

The tone of James's remarks on Trollope warns us that quan-
tity means nothing without quality. But the most distinctive
feature of the remarkable amount of work Lawrence managed
to produce during his short life is not the very high proportion
of it which is good, but its diversity of form. None of the four
great writers just mentioned practised so many different kinds of
writing. As Carswell puts it, in reference to Lawrence's 'just
twenty years of writing life', 'in addition to a dozen full-length
novels he wrote short stories, essays, translations, pamphlets,
books of travel and of philosophy, plays and many poems. Over
the same period his correspondence, whether measured by interest or by bulk, bids fair to rival the correspondence of our
most communicative English men of letters.'[3] The passage of
time, and all the work done on Lawrence since Carswell's
biography, enable us to lengthen her list of the different kinds
of work Lawrence wrote whilst making it more precise; and they
also make it possible to confirm her guess as to the interest and
bulk of his correspondence. (In the new Cambridge edition, the
Letters will fill eight large and absorbing volumes.) But neither
time nor recent work can lessen the difficulty caused by the
way so much of Lawrence's astonishing output falls into the
category which, for want of a better term, it is usual to call non-
fiction. Towards the beginning of one of his non-fictional works

1

– *Psychoanalysis and the Unconscious* – Lawrence points out that 'The word unconscious itself is a mere definition by negation and has no positive meaning.'[4] Non-fiction is similarly a definition by negation and suggests how critically ill-equipped we are to deal adequately with that large part of Lawrence's work for which the methods and approaches developed during many years of novel criticism seem inappropriate. The difficulty is felt most perhaps when the non-fiction involved is (to use Carswell's terms) an essay, pamphlet or book of philosophy: a work, that is, in which Lawrence is likely to be tackling some familiar issue in intellectual life and competing with specialists in a specialist field.

One such instance is the examination of the Book of Revelation which Lawrence was writing in the last months of his life.[5] A friend from his Croydon days, Helen Corke, was so challenged by this work that she wrote a fictional dialogue in which she and Lawrence argue out their views on Revelation.[6] In 1933 she sent this publication to Jessie Chambers, whose response incorporated the two main charges which it later became common to level against Lawrence's non-fiction. She couldn't, Jessie Chambers explained, 'wax enthusiastic' about Helen Corke's book 'because it is concerned with that aspect of D.H.L. that I have always found least interesting. As an artist, when he is dealing with the immediate and concrete, he is superb, but when he assays to be a thinker I find him superficial and unconvincing, and quite soon boring.' The Book of Revelation itself, she went on, had never really attracted her.

> As a fragmentary and mutilated account of mankind's early attempts to understand his place in the universe, it *is interesting, but that was not really D.H.L.'s concern* with *Revelations*. His concern was to find some means of escape from the narrow prison of his own ego, and to do that he was prepared to assault the cosmos. So, whenever I read his almost delirious denunciations of what he pretended to regard as Christianity, I only see the caged panther lashing himself into a fury to find some way out of his strait prison.[7]

There are signs of both resentment and prejudice here, most of which Jessie Chambers succeeded in excluding from her moving *D. H. Lawrence: A Personal Record*. But the complaint that she voices – that Lawrence's concern with Revelation is really only a concern with himself – has had a long history and is still heard time and time again whenever his essays or travel writings are in question. The three or four recent monographs on the travel writings all take this alleged solipsism more or less for granted. The spirit of their authors' approach harks back to Rebecca West's pronouncement, in the year of Lawrence's death, that what he wrote was true 'only of the universe within his own soul' to express which he 'rifled the seen of its vocabulary', this or that place providing 'as good a symbol as any other'.[8] It is central to the purpose of our book to examine this issue, just as it must be to face Jessie Chambers's charge that Lawrence is a superficial and unconvincing thinker.

This second task is complicated by having been so often undertaken before, if not in relation to the formulation Jessie Chambers uses then to one of T. S. Eliot's which his opponents in this matter succeeded in making very well-known. One doesn't have to have read much in Lawrence criticism, or to be very familiar with the controversies which have always surrounded him, in order to know that it was Eliot who thought Lawrence had 'an incapacity for what we ordinarily call thinking'.[9] The reply to this indictment has taken two forms. In the 1950s, both Graham Hough and F. R. Leavis demonstrated that the working-class chapel culture which Eliot, in a strange fit of ignorance or snobbery, had characterized as beneath contempt was in fact a nourishing source of strength for Lawrence, and the provider of an environment from which he was able to emerge – according to all the conventional criteria one chose to apply (including the passing of examinations) – an exceptionally intelligent man and no less proficient at 'what we ordinarily call thinking' than Eliot himself.

This insistence was salutary and easily verified by reference to many episodes in Lawrence's life and hundreds of passages in his work. But it necessarily nudged to one side the occasional awkward presence in that work of what seem like manifest absurdities, and the associated phenomenon of Lawrence's deep suspicion of those processes of ordinary thought which he could be shown to have mastered. Early in his life he had learnt to mistrust the triumphant conclusions of a supposedly scientific cause-and-effect rationalism and the logical procedures which found themselves bolstered by it. The second form of reply to Eliot (not always easily reconcilable with the first) emphasized this mistrust and pointed out what we *ordinarily* call thinking was rarely Lawrence's chief concern. That argument is developed most impressively in Leavis's later work and is evident in remarks like these from *Thought, Words and Creativity*, where the issue is C. H. Rickword's contemptuous dismissal of 'Mr Lawrence's metaphysics' in a review of *The Plumed Serpent*:

> But the basic fallacy of this quotation from [Rickword's] review challenges us flatly in its first three words: 'Mr Lawrence's metaphysics'. As I tried to make plain in my opening chapter, his approach to his theme, and his mode of developing his thought, are nowhere a philosopher's, and his aphorism, 'Art-speech is the only speech', bears not only on those imaginative creations of his that are in the full sense creative works, but on his discursive writings too; it is a conclusion (with which I agree, and which I am undertaking to enforce) of the most important kind about the nature of thought.[10]

It was the challenge and stimulus of remarks like these which provided much of the motivation for this book. In the present instance challenge is the right word, since the aphorism of Lawrence's nearest to the one Leavis offers, 'Art-speech is the only *truth*', is found in a context not easy to associate with Lawrence's discursive writings. It occurs at the beginning of *Studies in Classic American Literature*, very near another well-known maxim, 'Never trust the artist. Trust the tale', and serves with it to mark a distinction, most obviously relevant to fiction, between a writer's conscious purpose or moral prejudice and all the elements in his work which transcend or evade them.[11] In the dozen essays on American writers which make up the *Studies*, Lawrence clarifies the nature of this distinction by applying it with great practical effect; but it is, in its initial formulation, too cryptic to allow ready transfer to a different context or easy resolution of its bearing on what Leavis calls 'the nature of thought'. No less difficult to decide is quite where to draw the line between Lawrence's discursive writings and those which are 'in the full sense creative'. Our solution to problems like these has been to try to emulate Lawrence's own characteristic procedures − his practical spirit in the *Studies* − and explore the issues raised by Leavis (and other critics who have stressed what is productively anti-rationalist in Lawrence) in close relation to a number of specific non-fictional texts. Our hope in doing so is to work some alteration in Lawrence's general 'profile': the sense one has about any writer of what matters most in his or her work and of how any one text stands in relation to the others.

The generally agreed view of that profile has changed very little in the last twenty or thirty years. An ever-increasing degree of attention devoted to Lawrence has meant that there is now a fair amount of critical writing on his non-fiction but, as the spate of centenary monographs showed, its place in his work as a whole is regarded very much as it was by the editors of *Phoenix II* in 1968:

> The essays and sketches of D. H. Lawrence take on a particular importance in any view of his imaginative, primary writings. Because his major achievements, his fiction and poetry, are so often prophetic − that is, closely related to Lawrence's passionately held beliefs − the secondary work is of greater significance than is the case with most writers. The material of the present volume, *Phoenix II*, offers special clues to Lawrence.[12]

This was prefatory to a volume which brought Lawrence's 'Introduction' to *Memoirs of the Foreign Legion* by Maurice Magnus before a wide public for the first time. Its editors are warm in their praise of this text but, in the passage above, they nevertheless offer a division of Lawrence's work into primary and secondary which is paradigmatic of the way his non-fiction has usually been treated. It is in the spirit of this division that Frank Kermode distinguished between the major novels as art and 'the unqualified, uninspected dogmas of the treatises and letters';[13] and it is largely as a result of it that the 'Study of Thomas Hardy' has become 'a recognised stopping-place for critics of Lawrence en route for *The Rainbow* and seeking some help with the "ideas" which inform that novel'.[14] It is no part of our intention to suggest that there should be a simple reversal of the priorities which the division implies − those which would make a mediocre novel inevitably and necessarily more worthwhile than the Magnus introduction (in Lawrence's own reported view, the best single piece of writing he had ever done[15]) − but we do want to suggest that what is primary and secondary cannot always be solved by an automatic appeal to traditional hierarchical notions of genre. It was because he was so convinced of poetry being 'the crown of literature'[16] that Matthew Arnold failed to recognize the full importance of

Dickens, Flaubert and Tolstoy. Yet in an essay where he first cited with respect Wordsworth's elevation of creative writing over criticism, he made what for our purposes is a significant sideways move by weighing Johnson's *Lives of the Poets* against his *Irene* and asking whether there was less profit for the world in the Preface to *Lyrical Ballads* than in Wordsworth's *Ecclesiastical Sonnets*.[17]

The texts discussed in this book illustrate how imprecise a term 'non-fiction' is. The established library categories with which they can be associated include travel writing, memoirs, literary criticism, philosophy and psychology, although the association is in practice often very loose. We also include a discussion of Lawrence's verse. This is made to seem surprising only by the traditional assumption that (to echo the editors of *Phoenix II*) poetry is, like fiction, a primary, imaginative mode from which a writer's secondary work needs to be distinguished. That way of thinking is one which we have set out to challenge but, even if we hadn't, there would be a case for a chapter concentrating mainly on Lawrence's late poetry. He himself thought that the poems he wrote after *Birds, Beasts and Flowers* (1923) marked a radical departure from his earlier, more 'lyrical' endeavours and by calling his last collection *Pansies* — from the French *pensées* — he suggested that its contents should above all be regarded as 'thoughts'. At the same time, he said that 'a real thought . . . can only exist easily in verse, or in some poetic form'.[18] How radical the departure really was and what relation there is between thought and verse are, we maintain, questions most conveniently approached by considering *Pansies* in the context of Lawrence's poetic career as a whole. But the main point is that to write about these later poems, in a book where the connections between Lawrence's thought and art must continually be at issue, is as appropriate as writing about any other of his non-fictional texts.

There is neither threat nor promise but mere illustration of the all-embracing nature of 'non-fiction' in saying that another book of equal length could be written under this one's title. It demonstrates how Carswell's list of Lawrence's writings could be lengthened to suggest that it would include chapters on *Studies in Classic American Literature*, 'Introduction to these Paintings', the essays on the novel written in the middle 1920s,

Apocalypse, the *Letters* and, possibly, *Movements in European History*. Although there is some reference to all these works in what follows, no one of them is treated at length. To regret or apologize for exclusions is pointless when there is so much else which might have been included and our intention has in any case never been to attempt a survey. There are certainly general questions which are raised by all of Lawrence's non-fictional works but it seemed to us that they could only be answered in relation to specific texts and that an answer which might work for one did not necessarily work for another. Since the very term non-fiction itself has — as Lawrence said of the unconscious — nothing positive in it, there can be no general formula applicable to all cases.

Carswell's admiration for Lawrence as a prolific writer only becomes meaningful if the non-fiction can be rescued from its automatically secondary status. But that is not to say that all the non-fiction is primary or that individual texts are free from disconcerting variations of quality. It is a mistake, however, to confuse the latter with the lack of rounded completeness which Paul Delany laments when he says that 'a definitive statement of [Lawrence's] principles always seemed to elude him'.[19] Certainly Lawrence felt the intermittent urge to achieve such a complete and theoretical formulation, reflecting what he called the need to 'fix it, and have a foothold, to be *sure*',[20] 'the absolute need which one has for some sort of satisfactory mental attitude towards oneself and things in general [which] makes one try to abstract some definite conclusions from one's experience as a writer and as a man'.[21] In the war years especially, no doubt partly to refute those who in anticipation of Eliot told him he couldn't think,[22] he strove to abstract from the 'Study of Thomas Hardy' some formal expression of 'a constructive, synthetic, metaphysical process'.[23] After a series of abortive attempts he wrote one text (since lost) which prompted him to tell his friend Koteliansky that 'I have written into its final form that philosophy which you once painfully and laboriously typed out [as the "Study"] . . . Now it is done'.[24]

Perfectum est . . . Lawrence's more characteristic attitude comes out in his own play on the words *perfect* and *done* in the original 'Study' which 'Kot' typed out in 1914. 'Turner is perfect' he says, in one of the chapters where he is discussing painting. The very word is like a bell that tolls Lawrence back to the necessary opposite, from light to substance, particularly to his own body, not least to his knees. 'But I cannot look at a later Turner picture without abstracting myself . . . if I look at the "Norham Castle", and remember my own knees and my own breast, then the picture is nothing to me.' Equally, in front of 'the completed symbol', the 'dead certainty' of Raphael, 'I know I am the other thing as well'. For 'whenever art or any expression becomes perfect, it becomes a lie. For it is only perfect by reason of abstraction from that context by which and in which it exists as truth.'[25] This same suspicion of the static and finished led him at the end of his career to admire the Etruscans for having built impermanent wooden temples and to suggest that paintings should be periodically taken down from the walls and burnt so that new ones could be put up.[26] His hostility to those notions of art which his Imagist friends popularized by so often relating the writing of poetry to sculpture means that, as his career progresses, there are in his works an increasing number which quite deliberately juxtapose the perfectly conceived with suggestions of the rough-and-ready.

Nonetheless, it would be foolish to deny real or inadvertent unevenness of quality in the non-fiction. On the intellectual plane, the more characteristic Lawrence justifies the wholly favourable implication in Leavis's insistence that his approach and procedure 'are nowhere a philosopher's'; yet one still has to recognize that passages of striking penetration and originality can often be succeeded by others which scarcely appear to make good sense. But then, as Dr Johnson said, 'good sense alone is a sedate and quiescent quality, which manages its possessions well, but does not increase them'. He contrasted with this faculty a definition of genius which suits Lawrence very well. What was involved, he said, was

> a mind active, ambitious, and adventurous, always investigating, always aspiring; in its widest searches still longing to go forward, in its highest flights still wishing to be higher; always imagining something greater than it knows, always endeavouring more than it can do.[27]

This definition is echoed in Lawrence's own dictum: 'Man is a thought-adventurer'.[28] All of the texts we discuss in the following pages are thought adventures. To be an adventurer means taking risks and, in art as in life, Lawrence was nothing if not a risk-taker. It was unavoidable that he occasionally came to grief, but these chapters would not have been written if we did not feel that the number of times this happens is insignificant in comparison with those when a supposedly secondary literary form becomes the vehicle for manifestations of great creative power and originality.

1 'Slightly philosophicalish, mostly about Hardy': 'Study of Thomas Hardy'[1]

'BOTCHED and bungled'; 'clumsy efforts to push events into line with his theory of being', a theory which is 'almost silly': so says Lawrence of Hardy (pp. 100, 93). In appraising the 'Study', however, many commentators have suggested that Lawrence should be beaten with his own stick.

'Rum stuff' was one of Lawrence's own phrases for the piece: 'queer stuff – but not bad' (*Letters* 2, pp. 210, 212). As for his calling it his philosophy, did he himself not come to dismiss philosophy, at least when split from fiction as it had been since Plato, as 'abstract-dry'?[2] John Worthen, in a spirited and comprehensive attack, accordingly dismisses the 'Study' as 'ideas in a vacuum'.[3]

We need to step back for a moment and consider the circumstances of composition, the occasion. The work exemplifies the way much of Lawrence's discursive prose, not least the handful of brief pre-war pieces, are occasional – rising to an occasion, taking up an invitation to write on something specific and for somewhere specific (with those earlier pieces, for a home-town discussion group, a Croydon literary circle, a magazine). In the summer of 1914 he was approached by a publisher to write what Lawrence called in a letter to his friend Edward Marsh 'a little book on Hardy's people' (*Letters* 2, p. 198); in reply Marsh sent him a late wedding present of Hardy's complete works, together with *Thomas Hardy: A Critical Study* written by Lascelles Abercrombie two years earlier, in opposition to which Lawrence formulated his own views. But as he got down to work the 'little book' became more ambitious, in length (ten chapters totalling, in the Cambridge Edition, 122 pages) but also in scope. He felt it taken over by that element of personal apologia or manifesto which had been strong but subsidiary in earlier pieces (the 'Foreword to *Sons and Lovers*', never intended for publication, was a special case). And he ended up prefer-

ring the title 'Le Gai Savaire' (something like The Cheerful
Wisdom), calling the piece 'mostly philosophicalish, slightly
about Hardy' (*Letters* 2, p. 292).

Lawrence's thought is always adventurous, always aspiring.
But this work is no exception to its own rule that there must be
'a reconciliation between the aspiration and the resistant' (p.
90). As the title to my own chapter shows, it is my contention
that Lawrence writes mainly what is promised by his more
familiar title: this is a study of Hardy. The more general stretches and the direct approaches to Hardy in chapters 3, 5, and
9 are not just interleaved, they interlock. More than this,
Lawrence's critique of the older novelist is legitimate in its approach, close in its reading and challenging in its conclusions.

I

The two opening chapters ostensibly answer to some such title
as 'Le Gai Savaire' or *Confessio Fidei* (*Letters* 2, p. 243).
Lawrence here throws his energies into countering the systole,
the overweening impulse to self-preservation, by 'the diastole of
the heart-beat' (p. 7), self-fulfilment. The former requires social
conformism, concern with money and offspring, and war is its
escape valve; this is the life of the self-enclosed, weakly flowering cabbage. The latter, expressing all that the cabbages of
the commonwealth call vanity and excess, is epitomized by the
poppy, 'the thing itself at its maximum of being' (p. 11), in its
'colour and shine' (p. 15) taking no thought for the morrow.

That summarizes baldly in a dozen lines twelve of the liveliest
pages Lawrence ever wrote. Another chapter, complementing
my present one, could dwell further on how immediately accessible and infectiously exhilarating Lawrence is here; how deftly
he varies the tone and focus; how richly his primary contrast
gathers further attributes, examples and figurative phrases; how
aptly he alludes to many of Christ's sayings and parables. But
something of these qualities as well as the substance will be conveyed by the peroration to chapter 2:

> He who would save his life must lose it. But why should he go
> on and waste it? Certainly let him cast it upon the waters. Whence
> and how and whither it will return is no matter, in terms of
> values. But like a poppy that has come to bud, when he reaches
> the shore, when he has traversed his known and come to the

> beach to meet the unknown, he must strip himself naked and
> plunge in, and pass out: if he dare. And the rest of his life he will
> be a stirring at the unknown, cast out upon the waters. But if he
> dare not plunge in, if he dare not take off his clothes and give
> himself naked to the flood, then let him prowl in rotten safety,
> weeping for pity of those he imagines worse off than himself. He
> dare not weep aloud for his own cowardice. And weep he must.
> So he will find him objects of pity.   (p. 19)

Most relevant to my purpose is the way this attack on loving
one's neighbour as evasion of one's self leads immediately into
chapter 3 on 'Hardy's people'. More accurately, it is adduced
from Hardy's people − including, as we will see, Hardy's own
comments on his Returning Native who features prominently in
that third chapter. Although chapters 1 and 2 make no mention
of the older novelist, clearly Lawrence had reread and absorbed
him before he ever put pen to paper. Hardy is present from the
outset, dictating topics and prompting images.

A sheaf of such images occurs just before that peroration,
when Lawrence juxtaposes his poppy with the biblical parable of
the rich man. According to the latter, the poppy should bow
down to help his poor neighbours; but 'the *truth* about him' is
that

> his fire breaks out . . . and there it hangs at the brink of the void,
> scarlet and radiant for a little while, immanent on the unknown,
> a signal, an out-post, an advance-guard, a forlorn, splendid flag,
> quivering from the brink of the unfathomed void, into which it
> flutters silently, satisfied, whilst a little ash, a little dusty seed, re-
> mains behind on the solid ledge of the earth.
>   And the day is richer for a poppy, the flame of another phoenix
> is filled in to the universe, something is, which was not.
>   That is the whole point: something is which was not. And I
> wish it were true of us. I wish we were all like kindled bonfires
> on the edge of space, marking out the advance-posts. What is the
> aim of self-preservation, but to carry us right out to the firing
> line, where what *is* is in contact with what is not. (pp. 18–19)

This draws on the War, which has been an explicit subject of this
second chapter; *Macbeth*, which will be contrasted with Hardy's
tragedies; those books of the Bible which Hardy himself constantly draws on;[4] but also *The Return of the Native* which will
be central to the 'Study''s third chapter. That Lawrence is
adapting that novel's imaginative landscape is confirmed when
in the opening to chapter 3 he speaks of 'men who have left the

walled city to live outside in the precarious open' (p. 21).
Lawrence would not have written as he did had not Hardy introduced his heroine using a bonfire as a signal, gazing out on
the heath from a home protected by banks topped by 'discon-
nected tufts of furze . . . like impaled heads above a city wall'
so that the scene resembled 'a fortification upon which had been
kindled a beacon fire'; the bank 'enclosed the homestead, and
protected it from the lawless state of the world without' (*RN*
pp. 81, 83).[5]

I will now reapproach by a more indirect route the opening
chapters' firm anchorage to Hardy.

In Lawrence's polarities, both sides are supposedly equal: this
is one point of his adopting, here and elsewhere, the image of
the heart-beat. But in the 'Study' the diastole of self-fulfilment
is much more equal, to a degree that we might call downright
unscrupulous if we did not recall the contemporary context, the
occasion. He is not beating his wings in a void and the 'Study'
should be judged (as Lawrence himself said of poetry) not 'in the
vacuum of the absolute' but in 'the penumbra of its own time
and place and circumstance'.[6] As he looked about, he could
reasonably see self-preservation and societal considerations as
an inert weight on one side of the scales. He had learned at college the influential Victorian Herbert Spencer's answer to the
question, 'What Knowledge is of Most Worth?'.

> Our first step must obviously be to classify, in the order of their
> importance, the leading kinds of activity which constitute human
> life. They may be naturally arranged into: − 1. those activities
> which directly minister to self-preservation; 2. those activities
> which, by securing the necessaries of life, indirectly minister to
> self-preservation; 3. those activities which have for their end the
> rearing and discipline of off-spring; 4. those activities which are
> involved in the maintenance of proper social and political rela-
> tions; 5. those miscellaneous activities which fill up the leisure
> part of life, devoted to the gratification of the tastes and feelings.
> That these stand in something like their true order of subor-
> dination, it needs no long consideration to show.[7]

As the grey eminences of educational theory, so the biologists
and anthropologists. Even Jane Harrison's 1913 book on *Ancient Art and Ritual*, which has its positive influences on the
'Study', lays down that 'the two great interests of primitive man

are food and children. As Dr Frazer has well said, if man the individual is to live he must have food; if his race is to persist he
must have children'.[8] With such heavyweights squatting in one
pan, and with such a provocatively complacent air of stating an
irrefutable commonplace, an emphatic compensatory jab of the
thumb in the other side of the scales is called for. So the free play
of mind in these opening chapters does not exactly entail what
the 'Study' later calls fair play all round (p. 89).

On the other hand, the 'Study' is hardly without congenial
precursors. It gives new impetus to several familiar currents of
Victorian exhortation. We have met its stress on a change at the
heart in Carlyle and Mill and Ruskin; or at very least, we have
read about it in Holloway's *The Victorian Sage*, Williams's
Culture and Society or De Laura's *Hebrew and Hellene in Victorian England* – which is a sign that we are very much less
close than Lawrence was, in years but also in spirit, to those
precursors. Lawrence also adapted the modal fluidity of
nineteenth-century discursive prose: in urging self-fulfilment,
Mill's *On Liberty* enlists post-Coleridgean organic metaphors
and feels free to move between the legally technical and
rigorously logical, the easy informal address of the essay and
(although restrained compared with Carlyle) the rousing voice
of the sage. One tone is this:

> But if it be any part of religion to believe that man was made by a good
> Being, it is more consistent with that faith to believe that this Being
> gave all human facilities that they might be cultivated and unfolded,
> not rooted out and consumed ... there is a different type of excellence
> from the Calvinistic: a conception of humanity as having its nature
> bestowed on it for other purposes than merely to be abnegated.
> 'Pagan self-assertion' is one of the elements of human worth as well
> as 'Christian self-denial'. There is a Greek ideal of self-development,
> which the Platonic and Christian ideal of self-government blends
> with, but does not supersede.[9]

Picking up the same terms, and pressing further the historical
contrast, Pater wrote that

> the broad foundation, in mere human nature, of all religions as
> they exist for the greatest number, is a universal pagan sentiment,
> a paganism which existed before the Greek religion, and has
> lingered far onward into the Christian world, ineradicable, like
> some persistent vegetable growth, because its seed is an element
> of the very soil out of which it springs.[10]

Such passages bring home to us that, on the evidence of the 'Study of Thomas Hardy', Lawrence concludes the nineteenth century as much as he helps initiate the twentieth.

But it was not Lawrence but his subject Hardy who heavily underlined those words in his copy of Mill; who copied into his notebook those words of Pater; and who after meeting Pater wrote in his notebook about 'the determination to enjoy':

> We see it in all nature, from the leaf on the tree to the titled lady at the ball . . . It is achieved, of a sort, under superhuman difficulties. Like pent-up water it will find a chink of possibility somewhere. Even the most oppressed of men and animals find it, so that out of a thousand there is hardly one who has not a sun of some sort for his soul.[11]

This is the writer who, early in *The Return of the Native*, which dominates the 'Study''s third chapter, cites the anthropological view that our November bonfires go back to Pagan rituals on which the Guy Fawkes pretext has been superimposed, and that

> Moreover to light a fire is the instinctive and resistant act of man when, at the winter ingress, the curfew is sounded throughout Nature. It indicates a spontaneous, Promethean rebelliousness against the fiat that this recurrent season shall bring foul times, cold darkness, misery and death. Black chaos comes, and the fettered gods of the earth say, Let there be light. (*RN* p. 45)

What my juxtaposition of excerpts has sought to indicate is one of the many ways (post-Darwinian thought being another important one) in which Hardy and Lawrence − and Lawrence's 'Study of Thomas Hardy' − emerge from what David De Laura has called the same 'complex contemporary matrix'.[12] However we may try to distinguish the direct Victorian descent of Lawrence's concerns, polarities and organizing images from the mediating influence of Hardy, the overriding point is that affinities of the kind I have indicated mean that the ostensibly general, Lawrence-orientated chapters 1 and 2 of the 'Study' are anchored throughout to Hardy, who comes forward as the explicit subject in the third chapter, and are anchored above all to what Lawrence calls Hardy's 'first tragic and important novel' (p. 23) which gets extended treatment in that chapter: *The Return of the Native*.

II

But if, in response to John Worthen's initial complaint that the

'Study' wrestles with 'ideas in a vacuum', one pointed out Lawrence's engagement with Clym Yeobright, Eustacia Vye and the novel's other people, then Worthen would make the further complaint that Lawrence snatches the pen from Hardy's hands, kidnapping his characters for his own different purposes. 'He tended to rewrite Hardy's books'; 'he makes them the novels he would have written had he been Hardy'. Worthen goes so far as to claim that one character is in Lawrence's account 'exactly the opposite' of Hardy's.[13]

The commonly-made caveats about the pertinence of the 'Study' to Hardy are, however, epitomized more accurately in the saying that 'no two novelists, in being so like each other, are in fact so different'.[14] So alike in preoccupations, in being 'embedded in the [same] matrix' (to use this time a phrase from the 'Study' itself (p. 45)), and alike in their pages's harmony of cultural reference if not of view;[15] so different in texture and narrative stance. In the latter respect, Lawrence, who was to warn that 'whoever reads me will be in the thick of the scrimmage',[16] is himself seen as always 'turbulently involved' in his own novels[17] – and equally so as a reader of Hardy's. By contrast, Hardy (so this common account continues) 'moves in and out of his fiction',[18] by turns in the thick of the scrimmage, scrum-half, referee and spectator now behind one goalpost and now the other. The implication is that the 'Study' is bound to be an extreme case of critic trying to nail down novelist, with Hardy an equally extreme case of novelist getting up and walking away with the nail.

My foregoing paragraph is a crude summary of two critical strands, which emerged fifteen or more years ago but which have come to dominate comment on Hardy (and, in large measure, on Lawrence) in the 1980s.[19] In particular I have given too univocal an impression of those recent critics who, in stressing Hardy's 'disjunction' and 'polyphonic' fictional discourse, have themselves been highly polyphonic and 'polysemous', claiming for their author a multitude of what may or may not be fictional virtues. John Bayley might be accused of offering it as a mode in which no fault is possible, an alibi for authorial responsibility. But Roger Ebbatson, whose key phrases in characterising Hardy include 'his shifty narrative stance' and 'the related instability of his style', is more wavering and hesitant if not shifty.[20] 'Wavering' and 'hesitation' are among Lawrence's words for Hardy, although he also speaks more strongly of 'contradiction', 'selfdivision', 'evasion' and 'cowardice': it is important to recognize that what Lawrence sees thus relates to what more recent critics of Hardy see, even while he often judges as severely as Bayley praises. Who, and in which instances, is the more persuasive?

In tackling that question, it will be important also to acknowledge that Lawrence's critique is not so 'turbulently involved' that it does not deploy a flexibility of discursive mode which is appropriate and effective in engaging with Hardy's own 'unadjusted impressions' under a mobile and 'idiosyncratic mode of regard'.[21]

I now consider Lawrence's treatment – and Hardy's – of two principal characters in *The Return of the Native* and, insofar as it relates to those characters, Egdon Heath.

Clym returns to his native heath; Eustacia Vye remains there in 'smouldering rebelliousness' (*RN* p. 90). The phrase links her to that fire of 'Promethean rebelliousness', the smouldering embers of which she stands by when we first meet her. She had 'lost the godlike conceit that we may do what we will', yet she 'foreswore compromise' – a state of mind 'dangerous to the commonwealth' (*RN* p. 93). 'She had advanced to the secret recesses of sensuousness, yet had hardly crossed the threshold of conventionality' (*RN* p. 116). (Hardy, like Lawrence, uses spatial metaphors strikingly for internal states.)

So Eustacia expresses what Hardy's notebook called 'the determination to enjoy'. And she relates as closely to Lawrence's introductory chapters which spoke of self-fulfilment in terms of 'the fire and flame of being' and 'kindled bonfires' and (especially at the start of chapter 3) linked 'the great self-preservation scheme' with community conventions.

But this is in some respects a small-minded and narrow-horizoned rebel whose sensuousness is epicurean, whose 'instincts towards social nonconformity' (*RN* p. 93) find such trivial outlets as housework on Sunday and reading the Bible in the week, and whose ambitions stretch to the nearby seaside resort. 'Every bizarre effect that could result from the random intertwining of watering-place glitter with the grand solemnity

of a heath, was to be found in her' (*RN* p. 91). 'Bizarre har-
monies' (Richard Swigg's phrase for the harp scene in *Tess*[22]),
which might be applied to this novel's registration of the sounds
of the heath, also describes what recent critics term Hardy's
multivocal account of Eustacia, not least in the early set piece,
the chapter entitled 'Queen of Night', which takes much further
the tone of our first formal introduction to her features as
hesitating between Sappho and Mrs Siddons (*RN* p. 79). If
'Queen of Night' swings *con brio* between extremes, much of
Eustacia's portrayal in the novel as a whole has the quality
which at one point Hardy attributes to another character: his
words 'retain their level tone as if by a careful equipoise between
imminent extremes' (*RN* p. 84).

In the 'Study', it is alleged, this Eustacia of Hardy's becomes
much too sympathetic a figure, 'released from ironies'.[23] But
although this is the first novel he can take seriously, never mind
be turbulently involved in, Lawrence's first paragraph on her is
not tonally remote from his playful plot-and-character summaries of earlier books. His attribution to Eustacia of 'novelistic
Italian birth' mis-states the exact Mediterranean whereabouts
but hits the circumspectly ironical note hit by Hardy himself
when he links her Pagan properties with her parentage (she was
daughter of a Corfiote bandmaster). Lawrence does not press
his advantage with his potentially lethal term 'novelistic', in
that he lets off lightly not so much Eustacia's novelistic notions
as Hardy's lapses into novelettish writing. Lawrence's account
of the novel has been called 'too skeletal, the bone-structure
without the play of expression across the face'.[24] But when, for
instance, Eustacia leaves her half-blind husband to join her old
lover at the village dance on the heath, Hardy himself makes his
thematic skeleton obtrude only too clearly: thus 'a whole village-
full of sensuous emotion', 'Paganism was revived in their hearts,
the pride of life was all in all, and they adored none other than
themselves', and to the couple the dance becomes 'like an ir-
resistible attack upon whatever sense of social order there was
in their minds' (*RN* pp. 269, 272). What of the fictional flesh on
this skeleton? Hardy describes well enough the play of expression across her literal face, and even better the play of light
across the faces and figures of all the dancers. But spoken expression amounts to this: 'No one shall know my suffering. I'll

be bitterly merry, and ironically gay, and I'll laugh in derision! And I'll begin by going to this dance on the green' (*RN* p. 267). Faced with Hardy's failure to create any characterising voice for Eustacia (or for Clym), admirers reach for that convenient version of the account of his 'multivocality' which has him drawing in turn on realism, folkballad and melodrama.

If Lawrence begins by oversympathizing with Eustacia's search for 'self-realisation', he promptly and trenchantly adds 'But she did not know how, by what means, so romantic imagination says Paris and the beau monde. As if that would stay her unsatisfaction' (p. 23); whereas she might have 'come to blossom', beside 'some strong-passioned, unconfined man, her mate' (p. 26). 'Which mate Clym might have been' (p. 26). But the irony of their mismatch which Hardy constantly dwells on is that she looks to him principally to 'take her away from all this' to Paris and the beau monde, while he has returned to the heath out of revulsion from that 'rookery of pomp and vanity' (*RN* p. 124). Hardy goes some distance towards endorsing the view of Clym's mother that, in the manner of George Eliot's Rosamond Vincy in *Middlemarch*, Eustacia drags Clym down. Lawrence's more charitable attitude stems from his characteristic perception that such a downfall requires a draggeree as well as a dragger-down; that equally Clym lets down Eustacia by not being 'strong-passioned, unconfined'; and that although both equally 'side-track from themselves' (p. 24), it is Clym and the novelist's indulgent attitude to him that invites the critic's stronger attack because the character's cowardice is 'excused by his altruism' (p. 24). To Clym I therefore now turn.

Eustacia first appears to us as a mysterious, ghostly figure before Hardy offers a full-length portrait. Clym remains a figure whose stature grows by force of her expectation, for nearly a third of the novel. But then Hardy is at pains to articulate the skeleton of the figure, to establish the main outlines of his conception. That he makes not one but three attempts to do so is indication that instead of the assured bravura double voice of 'Queen of Night', the Janus picture of Eustacia, we have with Clym an artistic ambiguity which reveals uncertainty, anxious wavering. Lawrence dogs Hardy's heels at each step – and effectively, because he responds appropriately to each shift in Hardy's manner as well as to his discrepant propositions.

The first of these attempts to establish a portrait of Clym (*RN* pp. 116, 155–7) begins pictorially, Clym being seen through Eustacia's eyes at the Christmas party as in 'Rembrandt's intensest manner', a study in chiaroscuro: 'a strange power in the lounger's appearance lay in the fact that, though his whole figure was visible, the observer's eye was only aware of his face'. Now it is a common complaint that in Lawrence's comments on all Hardy's characters there is too much of the judge's voice and too little of the observer's eye or (despite the 'Study''s own comments on art) the painter's eye. But in the present instance Hardy's indispensable observers themselves go much further than merely registering visual appearances: 'people who began by beholding him ended by perusing him. His countenance was overlaid with legible meanings'. The narrator first stands back diffidently to hear what they make of that face, but then intervenes to tell us what (in Hardy's words) 'it was really'. And the ensuing character-analysis takes its bearings by propositions about human nature in general and 'modern man' in particular. Thus

> Without being thought-worn he yet had certain marks derived from a perception of his surroundings, such as are not unfrequently found on men at the end of the four or five years of endeavour which follow the close of placid pupilage. He already showed that thought is a disease of flesh, and indirectly bore evidence that ideal physical beauty is incompatible with emotional development and a full recognition of the coil of things. Mental luminousness must be fed with the oil of life.   (*RN* p. 156)

Impatient readers might reach for *Middlemarch* (as Hardy here and elsewhere with Clym dares one to do) and say that this covers Casaubons but not Lydgates, or indeed that it sounds like Casaubon's own explanation of the matter to himself and to Dorothea. Or they might feel that it is a damn near-run thing whether Hardy is relying on generalizations to decipher a particular character or using him as a cipher in such general formulae. But my principal point is quite neutrally about the mode of writing which, after the brief initial painting, settles into discursive prose which might well occur in a psychological or critical essay rather than a novel. Although I have shown that it shifts over towards an omniscient stance, this is an instance of what Ian Gregor describes: 'whereas in a James novel we find the work has already found its finest reader in the author, in Hardy the reading is still in process, the narrator's reading being only as sharp and fitful as our own. The novel lies open before us'.[25] Lawrence simply takes up this open invitation. And he does so in the faithful and literalist mode of quotation and analysis:

> But did the face of Clym show that thought is a disease of flesh, or merely that in his case a dis-ease, an un-ease of flesh produced thought. One does not catch thought like a fever: one produces it. If it be in any way a disease of flesh, it is rather the rash that indicates the disease, than the disease itself. The 'inner strenuousness' of Clym's nature was not fighting against his physical symmetry, but against the limits imposed on his physical movement. By nature, as a passionate, violent product of Egdon, he should have loved and suffered in flesh and in soul from love, long before this age. He should have lived and moved and had his being, whereas he had only his business, and afterwards his inactivity . . .
>
> Yet he remained for all that an original, the force of life was in him, however much he frustrated and suppressed its natural movement. 'As is usual with bright natures, the deity that lies ig-nominiously chained within an ephemeral human carcase shone out of him like a ray.' But was the deity chained within his ephemeral human carcase, or within his limited human con-sciousness? Was it his blood, which rose dark and potent out of Egdon, which hampered and confined the deity, or was it his mind, that house built of extraneous knowledge and guarded by his will, which formed the prison. (pp. 26–7)

In introducing that quotation I sought to use 'literalist' as a compliment to the patient and lucid manner of comment. What I also had in mind is that Lawrence seeks to show that the passage of Hardy's which he inspects, while discursive and thereby open to discussion or objection, is not itself in a pure literal mode. While not qualifying as a form of 'art-speech', of imaginative evocation free from the ties of logic and exposition, it bustles with metaphors behind which lurk uninspected and questionable assumptions – whether or not Hardy had in-spected them, the authoritative manner seems to discourage readers from doing so. In drawing attention to this, Lawrence is neither transforming a Hardy character into one who would be at home in one of Lawrence's own novels, nor even offering to be a better reader of that character than Hardy here is. He simply detects a lack of rigour and coherence in Hardy's own reading of Clym – to be more blunt, he shows it doesn't add up.

'My Mind To Me A Kingdom Is' is the title of the chapter (book 3, chapter 1) which provides our second introduction to Clym. It attempts to consolidate the inchoate suggestions of the first, largely by making Clym now represent a type. In his face, Hardy now boldly begins, 'could be dimly seen the typical countenance of the future', expressing 'the view of life as a thing to be put up with, replacing that zest for existence' of Greek and other eras, as we 'uncover the defects of natural laws' (*RN* p. 185). Whereas Eustacia in her urge to self-fulfilment embodies the persistent and 'universal pagan sentiment' which Pater described in *The Renaissance*, Clym thus reflects Pater's diagnosis of what Hardy came to call 'the ache of modernism'.[26] We are not surprised to learn from Paterson's textual studies that the original Clym was less akin to Oedipus or Prometheus than Hamlet: Hardy first wrote that 'the humble way of life would have satisfied him, could he be free to think his own thoughts'.[27] Lawrence is justified in throwing this second introduction together with the first and seeing it as merely compounding the first's confusions of thought about the nature of thought.

But in the very next chapter Hardy replaces that notion of the pale cast of thought with the native's hue of resolution. In this third set piece of an introduction, his return is not now a would-be recluse's quietism but an act of initiative, of 'Promethean rebelliousness' – Promethean in seeking to help his fellow-creatures, rebellious against the gods, 'the general situation' and the vanities of conventional society. In this way Hardy now offers Clym's return as an act of self-fulfilment or at least of self-respect and, insofar as his impractical education scheme shows that he loves his neighbours not wisely but too well, an expression of *excess*.

Hardy avoids, wisely but not too well, explaining how the knowledge which Clym will teach in his school on the heath, to bring self-fulfilment and 'happiness' to the eremites, differs from that which has so severely marked him. What Lawrence detects in the altruism is an instance of the cabbage-pitying poppy in the parable of his second chapter, the coward who 'prowls in rotten safety, weeping for pity of those he imagines worse off than himself. He dare not weep aloud for his own cowardice'. When in the following chapter Lawrence now turns explicitly to

Hardy he passes a similar judgment on Clym, and in equally
figurative terms: 'What is Clym's altruism but a deep very subtle
cowardice . . . which makes him choose to improve mankind
rather than to struggle at the quick of himself into being' (p. 24).
The very first words of Hardy's third introduction of Clym show
that the 'Study' has not projected an alien Laurentian idea on
to the novel:

> Yeobright loved his kind . . . He wished to raise the class at the
> expense of individuals rather than individuals at the expense of
> the class. What was more, he was ready at once to be the first unit
> sacrificed.   (*RN* p. 190)

Lawrence's tone is severe, Hardy's is neutral-tinted or even inscrutable, but Lawrence's idea is, here, Hardy's own. And an
idea is what Hardy's passage offers: whatever the 'chequered
methods'[28] of the novel as a whole, this is in a cognitive mode
for which Lawrence's mode of comment is wholly appropriate.

Lawrence's severity is prompted by Hardy's explicit leniency,
his failure to create an admirable figure of Clym rather than
discursively excuse him. Thus part of the second introduction
(book 3, chapter 1) reminds us that the mass of men secretly
hope that the human exception will come a cropper. This point
insinuates by stealth the otherwise unsubstantiated idea that
Clym is 'an exceptional being'; and it deflects criticism from him
as the poppy that seeks to lift up cabbages by evoking its
unlikeable opposite, the cabbage's impulse to drag down the
poppy. Equally the third introduction of Clym, after its neutral
start ('Yeobright loved his kind . . .'), seeks to deflect more
drastic criticism by conceding that Clym's educational scheme
was impractical — and that his mind may not have been 'well-
proportioned' (*RN* p. 191). The tactic here is to provide a contrasting list of nonentities and mediocrities, such as West the
painter and Rogers the poet: by ridiculing these with poker-
faced faint praise, Hardy can defuse the actual word *ridiculous*
when he goes on to apply it to Clym: minds 'well-proportioned'
in that dismal way 'would have never allowed Yeobright to do
such a ridiculous thing as throw up his business to benefit his
fellow-creatures' (*RN* p. 191). And that last remark contrives to
exclude from consideration whether a mind and a scheme like
Yeobright's *would* benefit them. These chapters introducing
Clym also seek to control criticism by pitting Clym's defence of

his scheme only against the shrewd but limited opposition first of the yokels and then of his mother: in both conversations the terms in which Clym sees himself, that are broadly those in which Hardy sees him, remain intact and as unquestioned as those metaphors which Hardy leans on in our first introduction to Clym. Lawrence's response is, negatively, to question those terms and those metaphors; positively, to reintroduce into the consideration the terms which Hardy has omitted or even deliberately excluded.[29]

It is the degree to which Hardy shares Clym's confusion, his narrow terms of reference, that prompts Lawrence to quarrel with Clym's idea of himself when this is not reported discursively but conveyed symbolically. As Clym waits on the heath at night for his tryst with Eustacia (book 3, chapter 4), he thinks of the moon as limitless, uncharted and remote and so an image of aspiration beyond earthly pulls, 'social necessities' and 'personal ambition' (*RN* p. 210). A lunar eclipse begins – and Eustacia joins him. Lawrence, seeing a mind-forged restriction in Clym, thinks him incapable of a true vision of the beyond and the unknown, and guilty of projecting his own moral scheme and mental conceit. With the moon or the heath, 'a little of the static surface he could see, and map out. Then he thought his map was the thing itself' (p. 28). And, in Lawrence's reapplication of the imagery, Eustacia, far from blotting out aspiration and the beyond, is the 'sill of all the unknown' (p. 15) which Clym is too cowardly to cross. It is this which makes Lawrence exclaim, 'How blind he was' (p. 28). Hardy, on the other hand, does not dissociate himself from the view of Clym's mother who, just when he feels that 'his scheme had become glorified' because 'a beautiful woman had been intertwined with it', reminds him of 'the usual nature of the drag which causes men of promise to disappoint the world' (*RN*, p. 204). Immediately before he goes on to his eclipse she warns, 'You are blinded, Clym . . . It was a bad day for you when you first set eyes on her' (*RN* p. 209). When the wedding is fixed, Hardy clumsily underlines the moral: although 'they formed a very comely picture of love at full flush', Eustacia 'went with her head thrown back fancifully, a certain glad and voluptuous air of triumph pervading her eyes at having won' him (*RN* p. 221). And in this episode Hardy three times insists on the heath symbolically closing in on Clym, a weight of restriction and inertia 'which too much reminded him of the arena of life' (*RN* p. 222).

Hardy might equally with Lawrence have said that Egdon Heath 'is the great, tragic power in the book' (p. 25). But Lawrence offers it, not as the inert homogeneity which drags down the individual, but as the life-principle, 'strong and fecund', which Clym denies. Is Hardy's Egdon, as John Worthen claimed of his characters, 'exactly the opposite' of Lawrence's? It is, rather, that although Hardy more than once calls the heath monotonous, that word fits Lawrence's rhapsody about Egdon, whereas the novel sounds many notes. (Multivocality is the modern-dress term.) Some of these notes are finally related, can be harmonized; some remain discordant, even contradictory; but at least one of them shows 'harmony of view' with Lawrence's.

Hardy often startles us by sounding uncannily like Lawrence; as when Eustacia, overhearing the villagers linking her name with the expected native about to return, muses on this 'harmony between the unknown and herself', or when at their first meeting 'she was troubled at Yeobright's presence' (*RN* pp. 130, 157).[30] Equally, and especially because he rarely offers close commentary, Lawrence often startles us by the specificity of his recall. Even in the highest flights of his prose-poem about Egdon, his reference to a 'savage satisfaction' in the heath (p. 25) picks up the 'barbarous satisfaction' (*RN* p. 192) that Hardy tells us Clym feels at Egdon's dourly reassuming the land which humans have tried to reclaim and cultivate.

But this note of Hardy's which Lawrence registers is unadjustedly juxtaposed with others. It is at best in bizarre harmony with another note in the immediately preceding paragraph, which tells of Clym's love of the heath and his knowledge of it in loving detail. 'He was permeated with its scenes, with its substance, and with its odours'; 'his toys had been the flint knives and arrowheads which he found there . . . his flowers, the purple bells and yellow furze; his animal kingdom, the snakes and croppers' (*RN* p. 191). Although the description is here rather perfunctory, and the prose rhythm mechanical, its stress is on the subtle variety within the muted and the restricted which characterizes nearly all Hardy's evocations of Egdon and which calls out his characteristic delicacy of perception and language. (We think of Hardy's own prose when he says that the heath 'awakened . . . the attentiveness usually engendered by understatement and reserve' (*RN* p. 40).)

When Clym over-studies and makes himself literally half-blind, he takes up the humble work of furze-cutting. Although a deadening homogeneity rather than the delicate stirrings of life is, now and earlier, what Clym intermittently feels closing in on him, that is more often the view of the biased 'observers' Mrs Yeobright and Eustacia: the first biased about the second, and both biased about the heath or the natives remaining on it. But what Clym experiences as he cuts furze is community and intimacy with the non-human natives of Egdon, the lively diversity of which is conveyed by exquisitely distinguished sensations of touch, sound and sight. This is what prompted a recent critic to call the following passage 'one of the most contented Hardy ever wrote'.[31]

> His daily life was of a curious microscopic sort, his whole world being limited to a circuit of a few feet from his person. His familiars were creeping and winged things, and they seemed to enroll him in their band. Bees hummed around his ears with an intimate air, and tugged at the heath and furze-flowers at his side in such numbers as to weigh them down to the sod. The strange amber-coloured butterflies which Egdon produced, and which were never seen elsewhere, quivered in the breath of his lips, alighted upon his bowed back, and sported with the glittering point of his hook as he flourished it up and down. Tribes of emerald-green grasshoppers leaped over his feet, falling awkwardly on their backs, heads, or hips, like unskilful acrobats, as chance might rule; or engaged themselves in noisy flirtations under the fern-fronds with silent ones of homely hue . . . None of them feared him. (*RN* p. 262)

I have allowed Hardy's voice to be heard at some length here (even while economizing on space by omitting nearly half the passage) because it represents the novel at its strongest. My related reason is to give full weight to the fact that nothing of that passage or the whole aspect of the novel it represents is reflected in Lawrence's account of Egdon, although it was presumably in his mind when he praised Hardy's deep 'sensuous understanding' (p. 93) and although it reminds one of Lawrence's own linking of diverse life-forms in the 'Study''s opening chapters.

But then again . . . framing that contented passage of Hardy's come more negative suggestions which harmonize closely with Lawrence's view of Clym. Not only the positive sense of community but (and this is what Hardy explicitly comments on) the negative sense of 'a forced limitation of effort' becomes a satisfaction in itself to Clym: it 'offered a justification of homely courses to an unambitious man, whose conscience would hardly have allowed him to remain in such obscurity while his powers were unimpeded' (*RN* p. 263). In the dispute with Eustacia which ends the chapter he goes further: 'the more I see of life the more do I perceive that there is nothing particularly great in its greatest walks, and therefore nothing particularly small in mine of furze-cutting. If I feel that the greatest blessings vouchsafed to us are not very valuable, how can I feel it to be any great hardship when they are taken away?' (*RN* p. 265). Here, the vague phrase 'the greatest walks', when put in tandem with 'greatest blessings', seems to dismiss not only the vanities of diamonds and Paris but the vanity of all attempts to be original or to originate anything.

'Blessed is he that expecteth nothing, for he shall not be disappointed' runs one of Lawrence's mocking beatitudes.[32] (One thinks of Hardy's poem 'He Did Not Expect Much', and his taste for the Book of Ecclesiastes, as well as of Clym's stoicism.) We are familiar with Lawrence's temperamental impatience with any tragedy that did not give a kick at misery. Hardy by contrast is impassive; but not inscrutable. In one part of his mind he shares Lawrence's view of Clym as representing the impulse to rest rather than the impulse to motion, even though he avoids Lawrence's severity of tone. I believe that he planted one neutral-tinted word as a regular fingerpost. While he has half-advanced the suggestion that the native's return represents initiative, what Hardy recurrently stresses is rather that Clym *remained*. 'He had been a lad of whom something was expected'; he was expected to be 'original' in an unpredictable way – 'the only absolute certainty about him was that he would not stand still in the circumstances amid which he was born' (*RN* p. 185). Already as a boy he had distinguished himself as an individual around his native heath. He left for Budmouth, on to London and then Paris 'where he had remained till now' (*RN* p. 187). His return is, for him, to take an entirely new course, to fulfil honourably expectations of originality. But to his fellow-natives, and Hardy, it appears the opposite, inertia rather than initiative. After a few days they wonder 'why he stayed on so long'; the normal period of a holiday passed, 'yet he still remained' (*RN* p. 187). The word tethers him to the heath, of which it is also used repeatedly. 'The sea changed, the fields changed, the rivers, the villages and the people changed, yet Egdon remained' (*RN* p. 36).

'Yet he remained': the words this time are Lawrence's (p. 27). 'The established form of life remained, remained' (p. 21); 'he remained under cover of the community' (p. 24); 'remain quite within the convention, and you are good, safe' (p. 21); 'those remain who are steady and genuine, if commonplace' (p. 24). For all the difference in tone, Lawrence's equal insistence on the word is a further startling reminder of his close attention to Hardy. Although I have isolated a detail, a verbal organizing device, it indicates that the main burden of Lawrence's critique echoes one important ostinato in Hardy's novel. It further reinforces the point that, in Richard Swigg's words, 'the extent to which his discoveries issue from the substance and grain of a work has never been sufficiently recognised'.[33]

III

I chose to spend two-thirds of my pages on fewer than a third of the 'Study''s, because ample space was needed to demonstrate in one extended extract the work's qualities, cohesiveness and continuous relevance to Hardy. If the opening sequence of chapters 1–3 is arguably the finest, it is still characteristic in its interlocking of a direct approach to Hardy with apparently general chapters. In the same way the second critique of Hardy, in the second half of chapter 5, coheres to the sequence of chapters 4–5; and the third critique, forming the long ninth chapter, to chapters 6–10.

The sequences, however, overlap; most obviously, perhaps, the sixth chapter rounds off one sequence before launching the next. An appropriate image for the form of the 'Study' would be of waves of thought. A related point is that every stage in the 'Study''s thinking refers back as well as forward, refining or revising earlier ideas or earlier comments on Hardy as well as throwing proleptic light on novels to be discussed later.

The second sequence (chapters 4–5) exemplifies these points in its discussion of work. This aspect of self-preservation, part of the matrix goodness—good works—work that was attacked in chapters 1 and 2, and central to Clym's self-sidetracking in chapter 3, is now singled out as the prime target of chapter 4, which is entitled 'An Attack on Work and the Money Appetite and on the State'. The next chapter, 'Work and the Angel and the Unbegotten Hero', begins by rehabilitating work and linking it to a concept of knowledge. But its stress soon falls on backward-looking and 'extraneous' knowledge, pursued with mechanical effort analogous to physical hard labour – and so Lawrence works back round to Hardy's 'unbegotten heroes', not least Clym, who is diagnosed in this fifth chapter very much as in chapter 3, and contrasted with 'wonderful, distinct in-dividuals, like angels' (p. 43). This is also relevant to Angel Clare (of whom Lawrence is to say in chapter 9 that 'he must take to hard labour out of sheer impotence to resolve himself' (p. 97)), and to Jude Fawley, at both of whom chapter 5 gives forward half-looks. But in terms of the general topic of work and knowledge, these chapters (including the first half of chapter 6) mark time. Behind that ostensibly main subject, however, changes begin to emerge.

One change is both tacit and retrospective-corrective. In chapter 3 Egdon was for Lawrence a positive force originating and sustaining all life, somewhat like the sun. But chapters 4 and 5 draw very much on some of Hardy's strongest suggestions, and on his verbal colouring, when Lawrence posits a 'great, un-quickened lump', a uniform origin of life, which yet has 'some reaction, infinitesimally faint, stirring somehow through the vast, homogeneous inertia' (p. 42). This is Lawrence's version of Evolution, whereby the original stirring leads on to ever-multiplying differentiation and ultimately to individuals as distinct as angels. Now this is not only an extraordinarily acute recognition-on-the-rebound of Egdon, it is prospectively enabl-ing and, as a general idea, itself generative of several distinct thoughts.[34] But the most prominent component of the whole concept is conveyed by the phrases 'the matrix of his time' and 'the matrix of his nation, or community, or class' – the hinterland of assumptions in which the individual must not 'remain 'embedded', 'the womb of [one's] times' out of which 'ye must be born again' (pp. 43–4). And this is what propels the 'Study' forward, prompting the historical enquiry which occupies chapters 7 and 8 and through which Hardy is re-approached in chapter 9.[35]

Lawrence's earlier notion of Egdon directed his discussion of Tragedy at the end of chapter 3, dictating its spatial terms. The Heath bodies forth the 'great background' which Hardy shares with 'the greater writers', dwarfing 'the small action of his protagonists' and the 'smaller morality' against 'the vast . . . morality of nature or of life itself' (p. 29). But Sophocles's and Shakespeare's heroes are people to the fullest capacity who fight when faced, 'daggers drawn', with the very forces of life themselves (p. 30), whereas Hardy's are defeated by the smaller, social morality; as are Tolstoy's. This broad distinction is reiterated at the end of chapter 5, but the ultimate conflict of 'real' tragedy is now internalized when the 'eternal, immutable laws of being' are glossed as 'vital life-forces . . . set in conflict with each other' and more explicitly 'the action . . . between the great, single, individual forces in the nature of Man' (p. 50). Most emphatically, 'when Macbeth killed Duncan, he divided himself in twain, into two hostile parts. It was all in his own soul and blood: it was nothing outside himself' (p. 50). This points forward to, even prompts, a major change of approach in the second half of the 'Study', beginning when chapter 6 considers the poppy afresh – this time not as an individual whole vividly distinct from cabbages, but in terms of its internal dynamics.

Lawrence's way forward is to generate a set of terms for the polarized 'forces in the nature of Man'; and then to trace these historically, as one or the other force has been predominant in humanity at large over the last three thousand or so years. This picks up his previously mentioned concern with the individual's relation to the matrix of his time. But what justifies such a huge historical perspective or back projection? Above all, the procedure of Hardy himself, the 'great background' of whose characters is not only the Wessex landscape and the circumambient universe but also receding eras of morality, art and religion. Pagan, Hellenic, Hebraic, Mosaic, Pauline, Medieval, Renaissance, Puritan, 'the ache of modernism', 'the face of the future': Lawrence takes all these terms from Hardy, who took them from Pater and Mill and perhaps particularly from Arnold

whose chapter 'Hebraism and Hellenism' is central to his
Culture and Anarchy, and whose essay 'Pagan and Medieval
Religious Sentiment' profoundly influenced the rewriting of *The
Return of the Native*. But Lawrence claims a further justification, that Hardy fails to detect ways in which his characters
are 'products of our civilisation' because he unwittingly shares
those ways. Chapter 5 of the 'Study' launches an even more
daring and, if proven, damaging suggestion. This is that it is a
foregone conclusion, even before the gate goes up in a Hardy
novel, that the favourites will fall: they have been nobbled –
and by their owner. He has the *prédilection d'artiste* for the
aristocrat or distinct being, yet 'cannot help himself, but must
stand with the average against the exception' (p. 49), and to this
end 'he must select his individual with a definite weakness' (p.
49). And this, in Lawrence's diagnosis, is the most damaging
way in which Hardy himself remains embedded in that cultural
matrix which the third sequence of the 'Study' now aims to trace
historically.

IV

This historical part of the 'Study' can be read rewardingly in
several contexts. As art criticism it invites comparison with 'Introduction to These Paintings'; as religious history, with
Apocalypse. But my own present concern is purely with its
legitimacy and effectiveness in a study of Hardy. Even so, I am
conscious of drastic simplification as I pick a way through and
alert readers to its pitfalls. My aim here is not evaluation but
neutral-toned indication of the substance. But if the promise of
its ultimate application to Hardy, as it were the light at the end
of the tunnel, persuades anyone to read on through the
brightness and obscurity of chapters 7 and 8, several warnings
and encouragements will still be needed if he or she is to
persevere.

John Worthen would warn us off entirely: 'ideas fall into neat
shapes and patterns . . . he is moving around the coloured blocks
labelled Male and Female'.[36] The actual position is more complicated. Lawrence also works with the polarized terms
Law–Love, God the Father–God the Son, centrifugal–
centripetal, motion–rest; and these are not identical pairs but
overlapping alternatives.

Chapter 7, 'Of Being and Not-Being', analyses cross-currents of medieval art, more particularly of Italy, in a coherent way by means of a related set of pairs which derive from Judaism and Jesus. These excerpts give the outline:

> For centuries, the Jew knew God as David had perceived him, as Solomon had known him. It was the God of the body, the rudimentary God of physical laws and physical functions . . . It was a female conception, [whereas it would be] . . . a male conception to see God with a manifold Being, even though he be One God [, and to be] ever keenly aware of the multiplicity of things, and their diversity . . . Christ came with his contradiction [to Judaism]: that which is Not-Me, that is God . . . First I must lose Myself, then I find God. Ye must be born again . . . With Christ ended the Monism of the Jew.
>
> During the mediaeval times, the God had been Christ on the Cross, the Body Crucified . . .
>
> It is only when the Greek stimulus is received, with its addition of male influence . . . that mediaeval art became complete Renaissance Art, that there was the Union and fusion of the male and female spirits . . . this Joy reached its highest utterance perhaps in Botticelli, as in his 'Nativity of the Saviour' . . . (pp. 62–6)

This is convincingly substantiated at each stage, and in the analysis of Botticelli's painting Lawrence's terms really help both to convey the joy and explain its principles of organization. In any case those terms are readily accessible, indeed familiar and traditional: one recalls Pater's play with the centripetal and the centrifugal,[37] and more broadly Arnold's discussions of Jesus in such books as *God and the Bible* and *Literature and Dogma*.[38]

But Lawrence himself appears dissatisfied with this seventh chapter, for in the next he begins by going back over the same historical ground. This time he draws out a new stress on the Christian concept of the spirit, in a way which provides fresh momentum and analytic equipment when the chapter goes on from Italy to trace what art reveals of 'northern humanity' since the Renaissance. The spirit is 'The Light of the World' − these words of Jesus form the title of the eighth chapter − and in these terms Lawrence discusses Rembrandt and Turner. The latter exemplifies 'the striving for the Light, and the escape from the Flesh, from the Body, the Object' (p. 82), and 'such a picture as his "Norham Castle, Sunrise", where only the faintest shadow of life stains the light, is the last word that can be uttered, before the blazing and timeless silence' (p. 86).

V

'What he paints chiefly is *light as modified by objects*':[39] in this striking phrase, Hardy anticipated Lawrence's sense of the priorities in Turner's world. And he indicates a link between his own later art and that of late Turner: 'the much-decried, mad, late-Turner rendering is now necessary to create my interest. The exact truth as to material fact ceases to be of importance in art'.[40] Even earlier, 'I think the art lies in making these defects [of Nature] the basis of a hitherto unperceived beauty, by irradiating them with "the light that never was" on their surface, but is seen to be latent in them by the spiritual eye.'[41] This view informs *The Return of the Native*, and Lawrence's remark that Turner 'sought to make the light transfuse the body' could be applied to the 'luminous mist' in which Eustacia and Clym enjoy their first weeks of marriage, or the luminous autumnal day on which Thomasin helps Mrs Yeobright bring down apples from the loft and the sunlight falls 'so directly upon her brown hair and transparent tissues that it almost seemed to shine through her' (*RN* p. 131).

But despite these occasional anticipations of the art of *Tess of the d'Urbervilles*, the earlier novel more often uses dark and light as a representation of moral black and white in the 'little morality play' which, as Lawrence sees, is inset into the larger imaginative world of the book. *Tess* springs more to mind when we read Lawrence's pages on Turner: here again is a part of the 'Study' that points both forward and backward. But it is also characteristic of the work, its wayward, leapfrogging progress, that when Lawrence goes on from 'The Light of the World' to 'A nos Moutons' (chapter 9: 'but we were saying . . .' or 'back to the matter in hand' – a jocular recall of Hardy), he leaves entirely to the reader's own initiative the link between light, late Turner and *Tess of the d'Urbervilles*. He says nothing of that novel's luminous mists and twilights, of levitation and relief from the 'terrestrial and lumpy', when 'matter [is] but an adventitious intrusion'.[42] Commentary on these would have substantiated powerfully his claim, made immediately before the pages on *Tess*, that Hardy's 'feeling, . . . his sensuous understanding is . . . deeper than that perhaps of any other English novelist' (p. 93). But analysis of Hardy's uncertainty of allegiance in these scenes would also, I think, have substantiated his diagnosis of Hardy as a hapless product of post-Renaissance northern civilization, 'always divided within himself' (to adapt Lawrence; see pp. 105, 219) in respect of living in the flesh.

Jumping over all that, the critique of *Tess* reaches back to chapters 4 and 5 for the idea of the aristocrat, which has now been given a historical dimension. The novel makes this an appropriate approach but subjects it to many strains. At the outset Lawrence himself is both emphatic − Tess 'knows she is herself incontrovertibly' (p. 95); the central clause is repeated half-a-dozen times; the last word was used of the perfect individual woman in chapter 5, with the same emphatic effect at the end of a sentence) − and wavering: she is passive, but 'out of self-acceptance', which however 'amount[s] almost to self-indifference' (p. 95). If this problem is not resolved by the ensuing account of her relations with men, it is largely because the critique is so compressed, occupying only a quarter of the space given to *Jude the Obscure*. But, again characteristically of the 'Study', several pages in the section on *Jude*, about the ways in which we exploit, explore or enjoy being explored by the opposite sex, will implicitly amplify what has been said about Tess, Alec and Angel as well as being on Sue, Arabella and Jude.

Lawrence can do this largely because for him 'Jude is only Tess turned round about', while 'Arabella is Alec d'Urberville, Sue is Angel Clare. These represent the same pair of principles' (p. 101). From this bold beginning of the *Tess* critique stems the disquiet of two recent critics: Mary Jacobus and H. M. Daleski. Their parallel articles, 'Sue the Obscure'[43] and '*Tess of the d'Urbervilles*: Mastery and Abandon',[44] pay Lawrence the compliment of engaging closely, albeit dissentingly, with his accounts of the two later novels in something of the way that I attempted with *The Return of the Native*.

Having evaluated that earlier novel in relation to a generalized account of contemporary strands in Hardy's criticism, I want now to be specific and consider in some detail these two particular critics. On the other hand I will not enter into these novels themselves in detail, as I did with *The Return of the Native*, in order to appraise these critics' own readings of *Tess* and *Jude*. What I seek rather to do is to remove these articles as potential barriers to the reader's benefit from the 'Study' by showing how Jacobus and Daleski are inaccurate readers of its ninth chapter.

Indeed Daleski's main point rests on the inaccurate idea that Lawrence posits a 'simple' and 'fixed' opposition, between Alec and Angel, and fails to trace Tess's tragedy to 'her own failure to integrate flesh and spirit'.[45] For Lawrence's first paragraph on *Jude*, part of which I quoted just now, also says: 'instead of the heroine containing the two principles, male and female, at strife within her one being, it is Jude who contains them both' (p. 101). And Daleski's own stress on a vicious circle is anticipated in the 'Study': 'Tess, despising herself in the flesh, despising the deep Female she was, because Alec d'Urberville had betrayed her very sources, loved Angel Clare, who also despised and hated the flesh' (p. 98).

Lawrence's brevity perhaps explains Daleski's error; it also explains the somewhat distant tone of the 'Study''s pages on *Tess*. Lawrence moves too briskly here to descend to the heated welter of the scrimmage. His Angel Clare (who is also Daleski's − and, if we iron out some unsteadinesses of attitude and uncertainties of intention, also Hardy's) is a theoretical Pagan and an idealizing pursuer of the Female Principle who flinches from 'Woman in the Body' and 'the heated welter of the flesh' (p. 97). The historical explanation ('generations of ultra-Christian training' (p. 97)) is preferable to that part of the commentary on Clym which verged on invective ('how blind he was' and so on).[46] But it nonetheless confers an air of bloodless diagnosis, even of exculpation.

'Diagnosis' and 'diagram' are Mary Jacobus's words for Lawrence's account of *Jude*, which offers a 'blueprint' in lieu of the complexity of a novel that is 'more sympathetic, less diagnostic', especially towards Sue, than is Lawrence.[47] And one of her early paragraphs (very much in the manner of Daleski's second paragraph) makes the linked remarks that 'the Lawrentian view of Sue remains surprisingly current' and 'there can be no mistaking the depth of Hardy's sympathy for Jude, but has the novel been read too exclusively from his point of view?'[48]

It is an extension of this case that Jacobus 'can only find Lawrence's psychic interpretation appallingly inappropriate'.[49]

For Lawrence, 'it was not natural for her to have children' because it was unnatural for her to have sex, so that 'it is inevitable that the children die'; they are 'self-slain, these pledges of the physical life' (pp. 108, 120). For Jacobus, Sue's physicality, precarious though it is, suffices for her to achieve sexual happiness with Jude and its confirmation in children. Both happiness and children are then destroyed by the combined forces of nature and society: nature prompts sexual intercourse but also conception, society withholds first contraception, and then work and shelter for those who flout its marriage convention. Lawrence considers that this social motif, like the economic pressure on Tess to return to Alec, is a false trail which Hardy drags across his well-established psychosexual case in order to deflect attention from his inability to face following through its inherent cause-and-effect.[50]

As with any two conflicting readings, the task of adjudicating between Lawrence and Jacobus would involve considering several different kinds of evidence. The matter is relatively straightforward when the two critics use the same method and example to reach their divergent conclusions, as when Jacobus seeks to demonstrate a misreading in Lawrence's close commentary on the Agricultural Show (with Arabella jealous of Sue and Jude as they admire the roses) — a commentary important to his case that 'they never knew of happiness, actual, sure-footed happiness' (p. 118). Elsewhere, as when Jacobus claims that 'Hardy gives weight to ideas which the *Study of Thomas Hardy* entirely ignores', one has to gauge the weight which the novel actually succeeds in giving to the writer's intended themes, and estimate what element of bias in each critic's account derives from personal preoccupations and preferences. Doubtless, Lawrence's inherent impatience with social explanations counts as much in shaping his case as Jacobus's feminism in hers; although he has hardly been alone in seeing what he calls 'Hardy's bad art' (p. 101) in the scenes of social persecution and in the death of the children. And he reaches outside the novel, in the sense of making what Johnson called the appeal from criticism to nature, in asking the reader how often unmarried couples are challenged by their neighbours (p. 118). But Jacobus's procedure in these respects is far more questionable. It is not simply that she takes everything in the novel on trust as art (except for the ritual concession about Little Father Time, she like Daleski does not even allow the possibility that Hardy's art might falter, never mind be 'botched'). She goes further, reaching 'outside the novel' in a less legitimate way than Lawrence does, by quoting unquestioningly Hardy's remarks to Edmund Gosse that (for instance) Sue's sexuality was 'healthy as far as it goes, but unusually weak and fastidious', and 'that the twain were happy – between their times of sadness – was indubitable'. In this way her article might almost have provoked the caveat 'never trust the artist, trust the tale', that principle Lawrence evolves through the 'Study' which he went on to wield with deadly effect in *Studies in Classic American Literature.*

Be all that as it may, this dispute can be settled to a remarkable degree by the question of accuracy, not in each critic's description of the novel but in one critic's description of the other. For it is straightforwardly inaccurate for Jacobus to make the claim, on which the need for her counter-case turns, that Lawrence is either negligent of or purely hostile to Sue. One should not take out of proportion the opening defence of Arabella, parallel to that of Alec in *Tess*, which ends: 'At least let acknowledgement be made to her great female force of character. Her coarseness seems to me exaggerated to make the moralist's case good against her' (p. 106). On Jude, the 'Study' is suspicious of what Jacobus calls 'the depth of Hardy's sympathy', detecting an unclarity of thought towards Jude's pursuit of extraneous knowledge in which 'he persists with the tenacity of all perverseness', and stressing what Jude gained from Sue (as well as from Arabella) in 'clarifying his being' as much as his frustration at her hands. Sue is the salient figure on most pages of the commentary, the thread by which Lawrence makes his way through the novel; and the overwhelming impression is of mesmerized absorption and sympathetic horror.[51] He may begin with a hint of diagrammatic analysis ('She wanted no experience in the senses, she wished only to know . . . She was born with the vital female atrophied in her: she was almost male' (p. 108)). But he ends with the searingly figurative: the children vanish 'like hoar-frost from her', she is isolated, remote and rarefied as a star or a saint on a pinnacle, 'she must stamp [her mind] out of existence, as one stamps out fire', while Jude becomes 'frail as an ember' (pp. 119, 121). Here is a late paragraph which like many is locked into a forward-moving argument but also has in itself the paradoxical mixture of concentration and repetition of a verse in the Bible:

> And then Sue ceases to be: she strikes the line through her own existence, cancels herself. There exists no more Sue Fawley. She cancels herself . . . (p. 120)

These are twenty-two very tightly-woven as well as intense pages on *Jude*. But even a brief excerpt gives their feel:

> It is quite natural, that with all her mental alertness, she married Phillotson without ever considering the physical quality of marriage. Deep instinct made her avoid the consideration. And the duality of her nature made her extremely liable to self-destruction. The suppressed, atrophied female in her, like a potent fury, was always there, suggesting her to make the fatal mistake. She contained always the rarest, most deadly anarchy in her own being. (p. 109)

This is at once broad and specific in several ways. The polarity of male and female principles informs it, but the result is a kinetic view, on the dynamics, not a diagram. What equally informs it is the power and insight of both the Greek drama (the furies) and Shakespeare, perhaps particularly *Macbeth* (anarchy and civil war in the single state of man) which have constantly been brought into the 'Study''s imaginative terms of reference. The insight would also be broad enough to cover (for instance) Gwendolen Harleth or, as Robert Langbaum has also suggested,[52] Gudrun Brangwen. But it has a tight grip on the immediate case. And in 'deep instinct made her avoid the consideration' the deep insight is in league with basic horse-sense.

Lawrence begins that paragraph with the historical explanation, 'One of the supremest products of our civilisation is Sue'. He is borrowing and deepening what Hardy through Jude says of her: 'You are quite a product of civilisation' — retaining the point that this is so despite her idea of herself, but replacing the suggestion of social graces and conventions by that of 'centuries and centuries of weaning away from the body of life' (p. 115). But this is not offered as an anodyne; for Lawrence promptly adds that it is 'a product that well frightens us'. Yet when, two paragraphs on, he calls it 'a cruelly difficult position' he has his eye on her pain and Jude's equally. As for Jude, 'What man could receive this drainage, receiving nothing back again? He must either die, or revolt' (p. 110). But it is immediately after this that Lawrence dwells on what she did do for him in 'clarifying his being'. And before long the stress is that 'she was unhappy every moment of her life, poor Sue' (p. 114). At the end Lawrence, as Mary Jacobus concedes, 'voices the novel's central plea' by saying that 'Sue had a being, special and beautiful . . . why must Jude, owing to the conception he is brought up in, force her to act as if she were his "ordinary" abstraction, a woman' (p. 122). This is not so much 'one of those astonishing leaps of sympathy which occur in his own novels',[53] nor a change of position, as the continuation of a mobile mode of regard in the critique as a whole that is as powerful as what Jacobus earlier allows to be its 'imaginative intensity'.

Mary Jacobus begins by quoting Hardy's admission that 'the book is all contrasts', and warning that 'the bare bones of its design lie dangerously close to the surface, and the urgency of Hardy's commitment constantly threatens its imaginative autonomy'.[54] But, her article concludes, the novel 'imparts unique complexity and life to the static contrasts of the novel's original conception'.[55] It is a question whether this formulation is to be preferred to Lawrence's analogous notion of a novel's need to subvert its equally necessary theoretical base, and to Lawrence's divergent estimate of the success of *Jude* in this respect. But certainly those terms of Jacobus's praise for *Jude* could also be used to suggest both what makes Lawrence's pages on that climactic novel an apt climax to his 'Study' (only the brief peroration of chapter 10 follows), and also what vindicates his foregoing chapters as legitimate preparation.

'Botched and bungled'? Whether or not I have cleared the 'Study' itself of that charge, I hope to have put back into due proportion Lawrence's criticism of Hardy. Lawrence once said that we have to be unfair to our predecessors, in order to be free of their authority. But where is there a study of one great writer by another that is more sustained and absorbed − 'absorbed' in its imaginative intensity of involvement in Hardy and also in its evidence of Lawrence's absorption *of* Hardy, his images and textures? (Henry James's distinguished study of Hawthorne is in every sense a cooler affair.) Predominant is warm admiration for Hardy's strength which is 'very great and deep, deeper than that perhaps of any other English novelist' (p. 93).

2 'Full of philosophising and struggling to show things real': *Twilight in Italy*

MANY a doom-laden chapter on Lawrence's war years, or on his fiction after *Women in Love*, has built on letters like that of 23 May 1917, which says that

> Philosophy interests me most now − not novels or stories. I find people ultimately boring: and you can't have fiction without people. So fiction does not, at the bottom, interest me any more. I am weary of humanity and human things. One is happy in the thoughts only that transcend humanity. (To Middleton Murry: *Letters* 3, p. 127)

His preoccupation with transcendence must prompt recurrent comment in my present chapter. But whether or not you can have philosophy without humanity, you cannot have a study of Hardy without Hardy's fiction and therefore without what Lawrence calls 'Hardy's people', or a study of Italy without Italian people.

Not that the present chapter proposes to separate the creation of *Twilight in Italy* from the man who suffered. On the contrary: it makes three separate perusals of the letters to identify distinct aspects of the biographical context. But what is called for, by way of countering the collection of clippings which isolate Lawrence's most extreme declarations, is a recognition of his mobility in most individual letters as well as through a sequence.

A more varied sense of Lawrence's concurrent aims and concerns as *Twilight in Italy* took shape can be drawn from the letters he wrote to Cynthia Asquith through the second half of 1915, and even more particularly from a typical one of 5 September 1915 when the book as we know it was roughly half-complete (*Letters* 2, pp. 385–6). It announces the imminent publication of *The Rainbow*, and of 'England, My England' as 'the story of most men and women who are married today − of most men at the war, and wives at home'. He sends Frieda's

40

love: 'She hates me for the present. But I shall not go to the war.' He reports plans for a fortnightly paper, *The Signature*, in which 'I am going to do the preaching — sort of philosophy — the beliefs by which one can reconstruct the world'. For readers he seeks 'one or two people who care about the real living truth of things . . . not people who only trifle and don't care.' 'The sight of the people of London strikes me into a dumb fury', just as 'the persistent nothingness of the war makes me feel like a paralytic convulsed with rage.' All this is very much in the vein of that 1917 letter to Murry with its escape from people into philosophy. But the letter goes straight on: 'Meanwhile I am writing a book of sketches, or preparing a book of sketches, about the nations, Italian, German and English, full of philosophising and struggling to show things real.'

That same paragraph continues: 'My head feels like a hammer that keeps hammering on a nail. The only thing I know is, that the hammer is tougher than the nail, in the long run. It is not I who will break.' We might recall the well-known image in the later essay 'Morality and the Novel'.[1] Insofar as the remark refers to *Twilight in Italy*, does it suggest that Lawrence intended to use that book as he used 'The Crown', to nail things down 'in final form'? (If so, the book — or most of it — got up and walked away with the nail.) I think not: the remark could relate rather to the struggle to show things real. Real for all the philosophising. And real in the visible here-and-now world: for all its interest in the other, invisible, transcendent world *Twilight* resists the premise that that is the only real one and that 'nothing is but what is not'.[2]

I

'I am writing,' or rather, 'preparing a book of sketches': Lawrence corrects himself in that letter to Cynthia Asquith because *Twilight in Italy* was not done from scratch. He had felt he could 'prepare' — in effect simply assemble — the book pretty fast because the 'writing' was already in the bag, indeed much of it published in magazines a few years previously. Those earliest ventures in travel sketches were 'about the nations': four or five 'German Impressions', 'Christs in the Tirol', and three or more 'Italian Studies'.[3] By the time of that September letter, however, the job had already become more complicated. He evidently realized that the German pieces would not bear re-using, even if revised. This would mean writing five entirely new chapters (to make a total of ten). What thus emerged was not quite a book about the nations. It begins and ends with three transalpine journeys which bring out national contrasts. But the core is Italy (contrasted with the England from which the narrator comes and the America to which many of the Italians go). This core consists of the seven middle chapters under the running title 'On the Lago di Garda'.

Having set out those details, largely for the new reader (as I will not be giving each part of the book even or sequential attention), I now want to pick up the critical implications of another aspect of Lawrence's 'preparing' *Twilight in Italy*. 'Christs in the Tirol' (the basis of 'The Crucifix Across the Mountains') and the 'Italian Studies' ('The Spinner and the Monks', 'The Lemon Gardens' and 'The Theatre') clearly could not go in as they stood: in a phrase Lawrence used a year earlier when revising early stories for the *Prussian Officer* volume, those sketches needed 'forging . . . up' (*Letters* 2, p. 198). And the parallel between these two acts of revision is, I think, more instructive than has been acknowledged.

Here is a man killed in a pit accident:

> His wife looked at him. He seemed to be dreaming back, half awake. Life with its smoky burning gone from him, had left a purity and a candour like an adolescent's moulded upon his reverie. His intrinsic beauty was evident now . . . He had come from the discipleship of youth, through the Pentecost of adolescence, pledged to keep with honour his own individuality, to be steadily and unquenchably himself, electing his own masters and serving them till the wages were won. He betrayed himself in his search for amusement. Let Education teach us to amuse ourselves, necessity will train us to work. Once out of the pit, there was nothing to interest this man. He sought the public-house, where, by paying the price of his own integrity, he found amusement . . . In a wild and bloody passion she fought the recreant. Now this lay killed, the clean young knight was brought home to her. Elizabeth bowed her head upon the body and wept.

This is from 'Odour of Chrysanthemums' as the story appeared in *The English Review* in 1911 (p. 432). When Lawrence came to revise, he saw the wife's reaction (and the narrator's: they are complicit) to be sentimentally and complacently matronizing.

He must have felt death to be no moment of revelation for her, but a new version of that previous weary knowingness with which she had taken it for granted that her husband has slunk past the house and on to the pub. The narrator of the 1914 version is independent, and tempts the reader into sharing that knowingness so as to heighten the shock of its 'countermanding' in the drastically altered ending: 'Elizabeth felt countermanded. She saw him, how utterly inviolable he lay in himself . . . And now she saw, and turned silent in seeing. For she had been wrong. She had said he was something he was not; she had felt familiar with him.'[4]

Since the late J. C. F. Littlewood's article twenty years ago, it has been common to see the 'forging up' of this and other stories for the *Prussian Officer* volume as the most striking step in Lawrence's development as a fiction writer. In this we have taken our lead from Littlewood in seeing the final 'Odour of Chrysanthemums' not as a new story or an old story with a new interpretation, but as the drawing out of a significance embedded in the original tale: 'the author discovered the meaning that had always been waiting to be found in the story'.[5] For Elizabeth, death 'restored the truth': for the narrator, recovery of this meaning 'restores the experience'.[6] But we have still not countermanded the common view that when Lawrence forged up 'Italian Studies' for *Twilight*, he muddied pure experience with later preoccupations and alien theorizing. The implication is that the lapse in time, from both the original composition and the original autobiographical events, automatically defeats the struggle 'to show things real'.

Such a view has survived more easily because the early versions are safely out of sight, having never been reprinted. It is good to know that they will appear in the Cambridge Edition. Then readers will be able to compare Lawrence's second thoughts with passages like this from the original 'Spinner and the Monks':

> She was as indifferent to me as if she were the most sought after young woman of the Commune. Yet she must have been more than eighty . . . Nothing troubled her, and it was nothing she wanted . . . I was to her just a man, neither stranger nor gentleman . . . And she looked at me with her wonderful self-contented eyes . . . which remained candid and open to mine . . . I could not help wondering how many men had kissed her. She had scorned them all.[7]

This, the backbone of the sketch, is not 'pure experience' but a clutter of received ideas, of the old chestnuts about Italians being contented, carefree and living for the present, with the woman's sexual awareness and *hauteur* being unwithered by age. In place of Lawrence's much-celebrated revelation of strangeness in the familiar and wonder in the everyday, this reduces everything back to the commonplace, in a pejorative sense 'approximating the remote and familiarising the wonderful'.[8] As for the narrator, he is 'terribly afraid lest she should think me a fool', but only because of his poor Italian: her x-ray or sex-rayed eyes see past the foreigner to the male and as such he enjoys 'our tête-à-tête', for 'her eyes were quite as young as mine, and looked at one wonderfully. I know I was laughing to her'.[9] The Lawrence of 1915 must have felt this to be as flatteringly presumptuous as Mrs Bates's earlier-conceived reactions to her husband; as facile too, and probably implausible as a result – in short, less real.

This 'Italian Study' is also implausible because it does not add up. What I have just cited as the backbone (spineless though it is) might better be called one thread which sorts ill with others. What he had seen initially was, as already recorded in the 1913 version,

> under a caper-bush that hung like a dark cloud, almost the colour of blood-stain, on the grey wall above her, a little old woman, whose fingers were busy. Like the grey church, she made me feel as if I were not in existence. For if I had been a goat walking by the wall, and she a grey old stone, she would have taken as much notice of me . . . She was grey, and her apron, and her dress, and her kerchief, and her hands and her face were all sun-bleached or sun-stained, greyey, bluey, browny, like stones and half-coloured leaves, sunny in their colourlessness. In my black coat, I felt quite wrong.[10]

This thread comes to the fore again later in this 1913 'study', closely woven with the other: 'she scorned them still, old and weathered as she was . . . So she stood in the sunshine on the little plateau, erect and aloof, sun-coloured and sun-discoloured'.[11] The final reprise has: 'There she stood, belonging to the sunshine and the weather, taking no more notice of me than did the caper-bush hanging like a black blood-stain over her head'.[12] As with his story, Lawrence could find a less pat and less self-flattering understanding awaiting him in this strand of the original study, in the rhythm and syntax of such passages of elusive and slightly spell-bound strangeness as well as in their phrasing.[13] From this strand Lawrence could develop the elements which make his 1915 version distinctively haunting. One such element is that the incident was not like meeting a person, even less a woman; nor was it really a meeting. When Lawrence asks afresh what her look was like, he can follow a repetition of the original phrase 'she made me feel as if I were not in existence' by saying of her eyes that 'they had no looking in them' (pp. 22–3). Even when she tells some incomprehensible anecdote while 'looking at me wonderfully' (p. 25) (a carefully ambiguous last word, like the previous phrase quoted), it was nonetheless 'in her half-intimate, half-unconscious fashion, as if she were talking to her own world in me' (p. 26) − and in a manner that is indistinguishable from and as inanimate as her shuttle.[14] The effect on him is fear, not 'lest she should think me a fool' but 'lest she should deny me existence' (p. 26).

These eyes, which do nothing as reassuringly identifiable as holding him in derision, are 'clear, unconscious'. This suggestion refines the earlier idea of *unselfconscious*, that is self-assured, self-absorbed and thus contrasted with the Englishman's self-consciousness about his bad Italian and black coat. *Unconscious* connects her way of looking that is no looking with her unseparatedness from the substance of creation around her and from the sky and sun. 'It was this which gave the wonderful clear unconsciousness to her eyes. How could she be conscious of herself when all was herself?' (p. 25) − or be conscious, in our way, of someone or something not herself: 'that I had a world of my own, other than her own, was not conceived by her' (p. 24). I say 'in our way' because this is what Lawrence turns to for contrast with his passage 'So we conceive the stars': at times, at night, they come close and are part of our personal world, but more usually they illustrate our feeling that 'there is something which is unknown to me and which nevertheless exists . . . There is that which is not me' (p. 24). Why drag in the stars, ask Ursula-like critics? Simply (and briefly − it occupies only two crisp paragraphs) to apprehend the spinner by contrast: 'the old woman . . . did not know this'. There is nothing pigeonholingly formulaic. For the narrator, the spinner is an extreme example of something unknowably foreign to him which nevertheless exists; whereas in the 1913 version the piquant encounter entailed denying strangeness and assimilating the woman into the man's mental world, just as the woman assimilated the man in the 1911 'Odour of Chrysanthemums'.

II

It would be disingenuous to imply that Lawrence gets his bearings on the human phenomenon of the spinner in all conceptual innocence. If we read this chapter after the opening one, we will already have begun to see the book as a 'thought-adventure', as 'a work of the metaphysical imagination'.[15] Even a reader coming to this second chapter direct and in all innocence will become aware of several guiding and insistent terms. Its very title posits a type-contrast, its opening sentences another: 'The Holy Spirit is a Dove, or an Eagle. In the Old Testament it was an Eagle; in the New Testament it is a Dove' (p. 19).

But it is characteristic of the chapter, and indeed the book, that those two contrasts are not congruent, and the new readers will soon be discouraged if they worry too much at such bold Lawrentian marshalling-gestures. The chapter is content with an improvised if not opportunist correlation of *myself/not-myself*, *being/not-being*, *eagle/dove*, *light/dark*, *heaven/earth*. Nor should we hope to carry over into this chapter very much that Lawrence has striven to establish in the preceding study of crucifixes − not least because that establishing has been patchy and precarious and the second chapter is best taken as a fresh attempt on overlapping ground.

Transcendence, that recurring term and temptation in the war-time letters, is much worked with in 'The Crucifix Across the Mountains' and promptly reappears with 'The Spinner and the Monks'. The concept is powerfully present with the terrace of San Tommaso on which Lawrence finds the spinner, in that it is not so much at the top of the village as suspended above it from 'another world', 'like the lowest step of heaven, of Jacob's ladder' (p. 21). And the word itself is attached to the spinner whose eyes are 'clear as the sky, blue, empyrean, transcendent' (p. 23) − she belongs to the furthest, purest reach of 'the height'. But then again, and this is another way in which the 1915 revision finds its firm prompting in a strand of the original, she is like the solid substance of earth absorbing the light. The faintly whimsical 1913 idea, 'if . . . she [had been] a grey old stone', is strengthened to simile and then to fact: 'She was like a fragment of earth, she was a living stone of the terrace, sun-bleached' (p. 22). Sun-bleached and 'sun-stained': like a rock (or rather, *as* a rock) she absorbs what is called repeatedly 'sun-substance'. The sun stains and bleaches, colours and discolours, gives and takes; later we hear of rocks 'partaking of the sky' (p. 28). To reduce these beautifully suggestive expressions to dry terms: the initial idea of two opposed realms, with the spinner as transcendent, melts into one of reciprocity, of what Lawrence was shortly to call 'true correspondence'.[16]

Transcendence, with its extended family of terms, comes into play again when Lawrence leaves the high terrace and descends a steep little gorge to look for flowers. 'Looking up, out of the heavy shadow that lay in the cleft, I could see, right in the sky, grey rocks shining transcendent in the blue empyrean. "Are they so far up?" I thought. I did not dare to say, "Am I so far down?" ' (p. 27). We are put in mind of the descents into the Underworld of those Greek season-myths, Eurydice and Orpheus, Persephone and Pluto, which the chapter will end by recalling explicitly (p. 31); perhaps Pluto's torch is figured in the 'crocuses . . . with dark veins, pricking up keenly like . . . flames' (p. 27). But he then climbs back up to a realm of wholeness and reciprocation in which he now participates. Although this is called initially 'the upper world of glowing light', it is rather the embrace of light and substance with 'rocks partaking of the sky . . . no shadow, only clear sun-substance built up to the sky . . . pure sun-substance travelling on the surface of the sunmade world' (p. 28). In such a context, *transcendent* must now mean, not 'above and apart from the below or from me', but 'transcending any distinction between one realm and the other, whether heaven and earth, light and substance, me and not me'. This is the spirit in which Lawrence can now say, 'I sat in the warm stillness of the transcendent afternoon' (p. 28).[17]

'It was so still' that when Lawrence sees two monks pacing some way below 'I felt them talking' (p. 29). But *still* is now used of the monks, and with negative implications as well as with the double meaning often exploited by English writers.[18] 'And still the monks were pacing backwards and forwards, with a strange, neutral regularity' (p. 28): variations on this alternate with swift transitions from broad afternoon sun, to sunset when the snowy mountain range is 'like heaven breaking into blossom', until the frail moon grows stronger and it becomes deep night. The swiftness of these transitions conveys transitoriness; at each fleeting stage light and dark, heaven and earth stand in the most vivid counterpoise, and each stage is contrasted with the twilit merging of opposite realms in the monks. 'Neither the flare of day nor the completeness of night reached them, they paced the narrow path of the twilight' (p. 30). This is the first moment in the book that would have guided the eventual choice of title, although the term *twilight* will gather more significances, often 'socio-economic' rather than metaphysical.

The spinner has gone. 'She, all day-sunshine, would have none of the moon' (p. 31). This and other *reprises* seek to pull together the threads of the chapter's scheme. But what Lawrence elsewhere (*Letters* 2, p. 182) called a 'certain moral scheme' might be intrusive or hollow. This is why I have tried to show how the chapter's moments of transcendent unity and counterpoise are not metaphysico-cosmologico-ontological ideas but experiences – pictures not diagrams. And as experiences they come unwatched, valuable as instances of being blessed unawares or of catching the winged joy as it flies. The afternoon stillness in particular is not, I find, a passage given its due stress by commentators, compared with that which has the advantage of prominence in ending the chapter, and which draws attention to itself by its two paragraphs of heightened yearning: 'Where, then, is the meeting-point: where in mankind is the ecstasy of light and dark together . . . ?' (p. 31). I find this ending misguided in spirit, Lawrence trying to bind to himself a joy, and in any case redundant after the earlier passage of unforced discovery. Furthermore, nothing in the chapter has seemed to issue from a divided person with cause for such yearning. The narrator, the apprehender, is unlike both spinner and monks but blessedly so, blessed in perceiving their mutual unlikeness and his from them: to him all is not one and not all self but is 'so strange and varied' (p. 31) – yet is also strangely related and reciprocating, the affinities and exchanges beautiful and startling: 'moony' primroses (p. 30); 'the olive wood . . . was extinguished' (p. 29); 'a frail moon . . . like a thin, scalloped film of ice floated out on the slow current of the coming night' (p. 29); 'lovely buds like handfuls of snow' (p. 27); a woman like a stone with hands like butterflies, spinning 'like a little wind' (p. 22). This is a boldly simple cosmos of sun, moon and earth.

It will be clear by now that the kind of commentary I find most appropriate will press that 'Lawrence's peculiar gift of vivid evocation of the living world found full expression in this book', will insist on its being 'marvellously beautiful', and will single out 'The Spinner and the Monks' for 'so sensitive a touch' and 'such lovely writing' in 'its magical pages'. Such uninhibited epithets are the more welcome because most exegeses of the book make it sound like sawdust interspersed with mumbo-jumbo.

The enthusiastic words come from Richard Aldington.[19] Until it was replaced in print by Burgess's omnibus *D. H. Lawrence and Italy*, Aldington's introduction long served as a butt for seminar discussion. It was he, after all, who saw only something approaching mumbo-jumbo in the 1915 interpolations, 'passages written in a curious abstract, preaching sort of style which is rather forbidding, and strangely out of place in a book of poetic travel sketches.' Now that Burgess's introduction (which echoes that view)[20] is in the front line of fire, we can relax and recognize how Aldington was in some other respects right and helpful. If he was wrong that '*Twilight in Italy* was hardly a felicitous title for this beautiful book', he was not altogether wrong in his reason, that 'it has more of sunlight than of dusk in it.' Of course its title is apt, if only an afterthought (and quite possibly the publisher's at that).[21] And of course darkness gets due weight: Lawrence's revision makes it a positive attribute that although Italians are called 'Children of the Sun' they are really 'Children of the Shadow', with souls 'dark and nocturnal' (p. 20). In the church of San Tommaso darkness becomes a substance, not the absence of light. But equally, as I have pointed out, he repeatedly calls the light 'sun-substance'.[22] And it would be an utterly misguided and joyless account of the book which did not register such recurrent phrases, with their epithets as uninhibited as Aldington's, as 'the tremendous sunshine' and 'the marvellous clarity of sunshine' (pp. 21, 22), or such passages as this one which was carried over verbatim from 1913 to 1915:

> In the morning I often lie in bed and watch the sunrise. The lake lies dim and milky, the mountains are dark blue at the back, while over them the sky gushes and glistens with light. At a certain place on the mountain ridge the light burns gold, seems to fuse a little groove on the hill's rim. It fuses and fuses at this point, till of a sudden it comes, the intense, molten, living light. The mountains melt suddenly, the light steps down, there is a glitter, a spangle, a clutch of spangles, a great unbearable sun-track flashing across the milky lake, and the light falls on my face.
>
> (p. 49)

In that and other instances there is no shadow of a palpable metaphysical design. 'The Lemon Gardens', from which it comes, does as a whole rough out a design. The dark interior of the padrone's house prompts this: 'Again I had to think of the Italian soul, how it is dark, cleaving to the eternal night . . .' and soon this equation: 'The mind, that is the Light; the senses, they are the Darkness . . .' (pp. 34, 35). With this boldly abrupt transition comes the first of two passages of general thought which are far more extended and prominent if not obtrusive than any 'interpolation' in the revised 'Spinner and the Monks'. But first comes this:

> It was two o'clock, because the steamer going down the lake to Desenzano had bustled through the sunshine, and the rocking of the water still made lights that danced up and down upon the wall among the shadows by the piano . . . (p. 32)

and this:

> Outside, the sunshine runs like birds singing. (p. 34)

'Ever, he sought the Light': this is one truth about Lawrence in *Twilight in Italy*. When he used that phrase about Turner in the 'Study of Thomas Hardy' (see above, pp. 32–3), it was as a severely qualified tribute, identifying the 'striving for the Light' with 'the escape from the Flesh, from the Body, the Object'.[23] But the 'Study of Thomas Hardy' is as chameleon-like in its conceptualizing as *Twilight in Italy*, and a different valuation is conveyed by Lawrence's saying that Rembrandt's art 'is more than the "Hail, holy Light!" of Milton. It is the declaration that light is our medium of existence, that where the light falls upon our darkness, there we *are*: that I am but the point where light and darkness meet, and break upon one another.'[24] This (but for the equivocating *but*) is positive, and it describes well what

Lawrence felt as dawn fell on him by Lake Garda. At very least, 'Hail, holy Light!' is a constant cry of joy in *Twilight*.

III

'The dawns come white and translucent, the lake is a moonstone in the dark hills, then across the lake there stretches a vein of fire, then a whole, orange, flashing track over the whiteness' (p. 82). This comes from one of the most hauntingly 'strange and varied' passages in all Lawrence, the extended prologue to 'San Gaudenzio', which calls the lakeside flowers 'little living myths that I cannot understand' (p. 81). The changing flora and qualities of light mark the stealthy transformation of season into season. Between the 'chill fires' of autumn cyclamens and the primroses, violets and 'grey smoke of olive leaves' come Christmas roses – 'cold, lit up with the light from the snow' – and cypresses which 'poise like flames of forgotten darkness' (pp. 81–2). The cyclamen scent 'seems to belong to Greece' and the myths called up are again those of seasonal decline and renewal.[25]

One resonance of this extraordinarily rich passage is the sideglance at the seasons of man which is more telling because the description is not explicitly allegorical:

> day is leaping all clear and coloured from the earth, it is full Spring, full first rapture.
>   Does it pass away, or does it only lose its pristine quality? It deepens and intensifies, like experience. The days seem to be darker and richer, there is a sense of power in the strong air. (p. 83)[26]

This passage as a whole marks a transition in the book. The first three chapters of the long middle section have corresponded exactly to the running title: 'On the Lago di Garda'. And they belonged to winter. Spring comes, and draws Lawrence up into the unobstructed sunshine, to the farmhouse of San Gaudenzio high above the lake. This will be the setting for the remaining four chapters of the Garda sequence.

At first glance one might also expect a move to focus more distinctly on individual people. 'San Gaudenzio' is about a family and, after the crowded activity of 'The Dance', two chapters take their names from characters, 'Il Duro' and John. But Lawrence portrays these people in a mythic frame of reference.

He gives the farm family the fictional name Fiori, seeing them as the other flowers of the mountainside, living myths, isolated, arrested and staged for our contemplation (as are so many figures in *Twilight in Italy*).[27] The farm is high up a path on 'the steep, cliff-like side of the lake', beyond and above a chaos of rocks, on 'the bluff of a headland that hung over the lake', secluded by high walls and steep drops. It is a 'little Garden of Eden' (p. 83).

The myth of Adam and Eve is not, however, what Paolo and Maria Fiori enact. In seeing them as 'the opposite sides of the universe' Lawrence draws together – or rather, tries out in turn – several sets of opposites already planted in the book: 'the light and the dark' (the immediate gloss to the phrase just quoted, ending the same sentence); the self-containing but all-including vision and the eye for difference (and for inequality and injustice); the 'eternal look of motionlessness' and centripetal mobility; one might almost say the Will and the Anna (p. 84). As with that couple from *The Rainbow*, Lawrence turns for analogies to the non-human: to ox and eagle, pomegranate, agate and glass. Paolo's rare rages have 'the cruelty of a falling mass of snow, heavy, horrible' (p. 91). Maria and he are flint against steel. Here is the same stress on what is 'non-human, in humanity' that Lawrence had come to make in his fiction.[28]

One could call this mode of portrayal 'materialist', if Lawrence were not interested here in 'the fire' as 'the third thing', the marriage of flint and steel;[29] if he did not always have such an intensely un-materialist sense of natural objects and forces like ice and avalanches; and if the portrayal, however hard, bare and rocky a statement of elemental opposites, did not have room for the kind of circumstantial detail which *The Rainbow* also considers to be part of its business. I am thinking of, for instance, the Fiori children as diverse manifestations of their parents' natures. The novel is valued for its mutual reinforcement of the apocalyptic and the everyday, the awesome and the trivial: an example might be the minor, comic anticipation of the Cathedral clash (Will carried aloft by The Whole, Anna 'jeering at his soul' and drawn to the mocking gargoyles) in the early incident at church when she has a fit of the giggles at his loud, absorbed hymn-singing. *Twilight in Italy* has a rough equivalent in combining large formulations about Maria who 'in her soul

jeered at the Church and at religion' and Paolo's blind reverence
for representatives of the godhead with their respective reactions
to a particular local priest, drunk and disreputable. Anna does
more than jeer; she has divided feelings. So too has Maria, it is
suggested by at least one incident. It is she who sees the power
of money and wants for her children what it brings:

> When we were going to throw to the fowls a dry broken penny
> roll of white bread, Maria said, with anger and shame and resent-
> ment in her voice: 'Give it to Marco, he will eat it. It isn't too dry
> for him.' (p. 87)

My earlier phrase *circumstantial detail* is perhaps inappropriate
for such concentrated brevity, which is characteristic of *Twilight*.
In comparison, the middle chapters of *The Rainbow* may well
seem protracted and prolix.

Maria is herself, in one sense, a materialist. And Lawrence's
contrast of her with Paolo in this respect is a further, perhaps
more important ground for likening this chapter to the portrayal
of Will and Anna. Art, said the 'Study of Thomas Hardy',
'must give fair play all round',[30] and this has been claimed as
the over-riding realization gained in the 'Study' which governed
Lawrence's rewriting of *The Rainbow*.[31] In *Twilight in Italy* it
is Paolo whom 'we all loved', who is a peasant yet aristocratic,
noble; fine, statuesque, a figure from Mantegna. Lawrence goes
softly on the concomitant limitation, the 'eternal kind of sure-
ness' because 'he was so finished in his being', 'something con-
cluded and unalterable' and thereby 'inaccessible' (p. 84). But
the point emerges that inaccessible to him in turn, invisible and
inaudible, was much of life in Maria's sense, and in Lawrence's.
To Paolo, 'a priest must be a priest of God' even when he goes
about with a pair of pigs in a sack over his shoulder or sweats
and struggles to chop a fallen tree. At such scenes Paolo is
'unmoved and detached . . . his eyes fixed in the ageless stare',
while Lawrence sees the 'old ne'er-do-well in priests' black' as
if through Maria's eyes:

> Meanwhile the priest swung drunken blows at the tree, his thin
> buttocks bending in the green-black broadcloth, supported on
> thin shanks, and thin throat growing dull purple in the red-
> knotted kerchief. (pp. 90, 91)

The bread-roll incident also speaks of a closeness to Maria. It

reads like guilt roused by a flash of fatally-late understanding:
a criticism of the passage might if anything suggest that the rush
of empathy is too suspiciously strong, a case of the impulse to
sympathize forcing a claim to over-elaborate understanding (of
'anger and shame and resentment'). Concern for the children (as
well as some Gertrude Morel-like ambition for or through them)
figures in Maria throughout the chapter — for Marco it is 'a
fierce protective love, grounded on pain' (p. 86) — and she is not
seen strictly as a materialist or miser. 'The Dance' does end with
'her cupidity seemed like her very blossom' (p. 102), and the last
word rounds off the flower-Fiori image. But it is remarkable
how even that phrase lacks the air of being written with one
hand while the author's other is clutching his wallet: I refer to
the lack of personal concern or wariness in Lawrence's attitude
to Maria's moneymindedness, considering that his very
understanding of it must have come from his own extreme
carefulness about cash and considering that some of her cash
was currently coming from him. In this it is typical of the book
in that until the two last, very different, chapters, Lawrence
never pauses anxiously to check his change. So that the concern
about money which so pervades Lawrence's 'Introduction' to
Magnus's *Memoirs* (and, with a difference, *Sea and Sardinia*)
does not interfere when Lawrence has out with himself the question, Who was right? And his answer refuses a decision, throwing us back to the very terms of the difference between them:
'Paolo was mistaken in actual life, but Maria was ultimately
mistaken' (p. 90).

My point is that Lawrence is not blind to material considerations, even though he sees much more than them. More recent
surveys of Italy, for instance Luigi Barzini's *The Italians* or
Peter Nichols's *Italia, Italia*, suggest that he was as blind to
'actual life' as Paolo.[32] The matter can best be considered by
taking advantage of an extraordinary coincidence. It is startling
to find an obscure Italian peasant family, even more specifically
as it was within the same few months of 1913, as the central subject of *two* English books. The Lawrence's fellow-guest was a
Mrs Antonia Cyriax who went to the farm to paint — and to
elude her estranged husband. Several years later she published
her impressions as *Among Italian Peasants*, illustrated with
sixteen of her paintings.[33] Neither Lawrence nor Cyriax

acknowledges the other's presence, although Antonia Cyriax must be the other English woman in Lawrence's account of 'The Dance' (with Frieda, sailing under a flag of fictional convenience, being the first).

If one has in mind Lawrence's alleged indifference to material factors, reading these two books side by side prompts the comment that there was certainly a blindness in the other direction, or at least a here-and-now, bread-and-lira nearsightedness, in Cyriax. She was clearly one of the 'all' who Lawrence says loved the husband, although she is more comfortably familiar with her 'good old Bortolo' (as she calls him, the wife being Rosina). Her view harmonizes with Lawrence's but does not probe far:

> Rosina had the habit of treating Bortolo as if he was a fool. She was quicker than he was, and his slowness irritated her. He was a refined, thoughtful man, perhaps too lenient of others' failings to be quite just . . .
> Perhaps Bortolo was too easy-going and contented. His soul was wrapped up in the fields. He gloried in the growth and vigour of his plants; working early and late.
>
> (*Among Italian Peasants*, pp. 11–12)

Her sense of 'soul' goes no further than this. She writes much more about Rosina. She is far from merely critical of her, but when she does criticise it is with a resentment at the rate of transfer from her pocket to her landlady's which I said was absent from Lawrence. More broadly, *Among Italian Peasants* is all about self-preservation – about persisting and enduring. Peasant life consists of dirt, work, food and money.[34] The exceptions are a brief respite from the rule. At the local dance, which occupies one chapter as it also does in *Twilight in Italy*, 'forgotten were heavy loads and empty larders' (*Among Italian Peasants*, p. 23). The book appears to begin with religion, a procession from the church to bless the fields. But it is only in aid of self-preservation:

> At last I said: 'Whatever does it mean?'
> 'Signora', answered Rosina, 'we pray that the crops shall not be spoilt by the hail. In these parts we have great hailstorms which ruin the harvest . . . and then we starve.'
>
> (*Among Italian Peasants*, p. 3)

And it is ineffectual. Such a disaster happens, provoking in the peasants an outburst of anti-clerical rage and religious scepticism, and a further wave of emigration.[35]

We can now take the question of materialism outwards from 'San Gaudenzio' to other chapters, and right back to the first. In the second crucifix to draw close scrutiny, Lawrence sees a Christ in a red flannel cloak, 'dreaming, brooding, enduring, persisting'. A suggestion of Hamlet emerges with: 'there is a wistfulness about him, as if he knew that the whole of things was too much for him. There was no solution, either, in death', and becomes explicit with: 'It is a question of being − to be or not to be. To persist or not to persist, that is not the question; neither is it to endure or not to endure' (p. 8). This does not yet take us far with Hamlet, although it promptly launches the terms which the next two chapters will work with, thus permitting the deeper treatment of Hamlet in the fourth. But it underlines the effect of a change in an earlier passage, about the first crucifix with its peasant-Christ. This is how the 1912 essay 'Christs in the Tirol' saw it:

> In front of me hung a Bavarian peasant, a Christus . . . he hung doggedly on the cross, hating it. He reminded me of a peasant farmer, fighting slowly and meanly, but not giving in. His plain, rudimentary face stared stubbornly at the hills . . .
>
> (*Phoenix*, p. 82)

As for the actual peasants, that version stopped here:

> And, thinking of . . . how the man and his wife and his children worked on till dark, intent and silent, carrying the hay in their arms out of the streaming thunder-rain which soaked them through, I understood how the Christus was made.
>
> (*Phoenix*, p. 83)

In 1915 Lawrence made insignificant alterations to the phrasing of this, but entirely removed the final clause and went on with a more sustained and positive evocation of outdoor labour:

> The body bent forward towards the earth, closing round on itself; the arms clasped full of hay, clasped round the hay that presses soft and close to the breast of the body, that pricks heat into the arms and the skin of the breast . . . this is the peasant, this hot welter of physical sensation. And it is all intoxicating.
>
> (pp. 4–5)

'Positive', however, is not quite the right word, because such 'a blood heat, a blood sleep' becomes (as at the start of *The Rainbow*) a bondage, even a crucifixion. The passage then takes on a metaphysical dimension: directly beneath 'the upper radiance of snow', the realm of not-being into which all life passes away, the mountain peasant 'must needs live under the radiance of his own negation' (pp. 5–6). I cannot do full justice to this further dimension in the context of my present concern, which is to underline how little Lawrence's idea of labour is simply of physical endurance and material necessity.

As the book develops, it is as if Lawrence came to see that peasant as well as prince might ask Hamlet's question, or that one might ask of him Birkin's question to Gerald, 'What do you think is the aim and object of your life . . .?'[36] This means that, while emigration is as much a central thread and almost the organizing principle of his book as much as of Cyriax's, his explanation cannot be as straightfowardly economic as hers. Observing behaviour which suggests sexual wariness and power-struggles, he is suddenly prompted to say that 'this is why the men must go away to America. It is not the money' (p. 59). But the remark is not all that neat or self-contained; its elaboration leads to recessive layers of thought: 'It is the profound desire to rehabilitate themselves, to recover some dignity as men, as producers, as workers, as creators from the spirit, not only from the flesh' (p. 59). So the explanation *is* in a way materialist, although of course the book connects production, work, money and machines as products of 'the spirit', and fears the spirit too.

Twilight in Italy is never naive about economic forces. The sense of painful dilemma with which 'The Lemon Gardens' closes (pp. 52–4), somewhat like the close of the monastery episode in the 'Introduction' to Magnus's *Memoirs*,[37] comes from recognizing that the industrial future is horrifying but inevitable. After showing him round his semi-derelict estate, the elderly *padrone* purports to share Lawrence's response to the sun which ripens the lemons: Signor di Paoli 'lifted his withered hand to the sky, to the wonderful source of that blue day, and he smiled, in histrionic triumph.' But 'his triumph was only histrionic'. The *padrone*'s real attraction is to the future, to Italy's emulation of the industrial north. Despite Lawrence's horror at northern industrialism, he is realist enough to say that 'it is better to go forward into error than to stay fixed inextricably in the past'. And although the *padrone* praises the local lemons as worth two from elsewhere, Lawrence takes a paragraph to dismiss this as pure sentiment, and to do so in plain economic terms.

By what was perhaps verbal sleight of hand, my foregoing pages have used the word *materialism* to link two different questions: whether *Twilight* (and especially 'San Gaudenzio') insists on 'what is non-human in humanity' to the exclusion of what the 'Introduction' to Magnus's *Memoirs* will call 'sharp detail and definite event';[38] and whether Lawrence is blind to economic considerations. But my answers are bound together, in that Lawrence in both respects makes things real. This again disproves the maxim, quoted in my previous chapter, that Lawrence 'presumed [no] commission to write about the world as he found it' rather than to 'make all things new'.[39]

IV

Many a 'travel book', however it purports to be a travelogue or chronological journal with no design, finds itself falling into a plot; and that plot usually has the author as hero. The drift is that after many adventures and misunderstandings the traveller has come to understand and be understood − or even admired − by the locals, the point being underlined by contrasts with green newcomers. This is often clinched by the culture-shock of returning home. *Among Italian Peasants* is governed by this pattern.[40] Lawrence reflects just a hint of it with the shock of Switzerland, the encounter there with a fellow-countryman, and the final shock of returning to a changed or rapidly-changing Italy. But it is a negative virtue of *Twilight in Italy* that his role involves little self-congratulation.

Nor is it, however, a book of settled self-mockery.

In *Sea and Sardinia*, a young maid servant is sick. Her employers do not fuss over her: they are not unkind, just not upset:

> Not half as upset as we are—the q-b [the queen bee; 'the wife'] wanting to administer tea, and so on . . . It is just so.
> Their naturalness seems unnatural to us. Yet I am sure it is best. Sympathy would only complicate matters, and spoil that strange, remote virginal quality. The q-b says it is largely stupidity.
> (*Sea and Sardinia*, in *D. H. Lawrence in Italy*, p. 16)

Nobody gives Lawrence that kind of slap in the face in *Twilight*. (It puts me in mind of the heavy dinner-plate which Frieda is reported as breaking over his head as he unsuspectingly sang to himself while doing the washing-up.) Nor does he check himself in *Twilight*, as he does in the next paragraph: 'Nobody thinks of just throwing a pail of water. Why should he? It is all in the course of nature.—One begins to be a bit chary of this same "nature", in the south'. Nor does he, in this 'book about the nations', make gentle fun of his difficulties in distinguishing actual specimens of each, as does *Sea and Sardinia* in the passage which David Ellis quotes on pp. 99–100.

Twilight in Italy lacks the later book's prominent second character-commentator, 'the q-b'. Frieda's is here no speaking, never mind thinking, role, and so far as it is an occasional walk-on part it is a bit like the back end of a composite stage animal, being subsumed under the marital 'we'. If she is not there to check him, neither are human foils introduced to contrast with his imaginative searchingness, in the manner of the German student in *Etruscan Places* who does not believe in significance or symbolism, and the young artist in 'Introduction to These Paintings' who knows only about technique.[41] With any of the later travel books in mind, or the 'Introduction' to Magnus's *Memoirs*, we are scarcely prompted to attribute self-dramatization, still less self-mockery, to *Twilight*.[42]

In *Etruscan Places* Lawrence likes the guide to the tombs of Tarquinia because 'he knows a good deal, and has a quick, sensitive interest, absolutely unobtrusive' (p. 34). This sounds like Matthew Arnold's ideal critic who 'gets himself out of the way'. But if unobtrusive is the word for the narrator's role in most of *Twilight in Italy*, a lot depends nonetheless on the impression of personal discovery and debate. It becomes explicit in moments like the one already pointed out: 'So, then, that is where heaven and earth are divided' (p. 22). In the same chapter, being absorbed by, or in, the monks in the 1913 version is strengthened to being implicated: 'I listened to them, absorbed in their conversation' becomes 'I was one with them, a partaker' (p. 29). (The 'Italian Study' hardly does the same by ending with a jejune flirtation: 'as for the monks, I'm so glad I escaped being one myself – after all, it *would* be nice . . . '.) When Signor di Paoli's chagrin and melancholy leap into connection with his childlessness, 'I was startled. This, then . . .' (p. 44). The explanation which follows this discovery might at first seem to have an ex-cathedra certainty: 'This, then, is the secret of Italy's attraction for us, this phallic worship.' But an element of debate or dilemma in the narrator opens up with: 'We envy him . . . Yet at the same time we feel superior to him, as if he were a child and we adult' (a deft reapplication of the matter in hand); and although Lawrence goes on to claim that this sense of superiority involves self-deception, nonetheless here and elsewhere in the book phallic worship, which entails the childless being *annulled* and *obliterated*, is seen as a form of slavery. A rather different example of the narrator being in two minds, very characteristic of the manner of the final chapters, occurs with the English clerk Lawrence meets in Switzerland, who has crammed an exhausting hike through the Alps into his annual fortnight. Confronted with this dogged fellow-countryman, Lawrence's initial pity turns to angry contempt. But there is a further twist:

> The landlord came to talk to me. He was fat and comfortable and too respectful. But I had to tell him all the Englishman had done, in the way of a holiday, just to shame his own fat, ponderous, inn-keeper's luxuriousness that was too gross. Then all I got out of his enormous comfortableness was:
> 'Yes, that's a *very* long step to take.'   (pp. 151–2)

That is from 'The Return Journey', and for all its twists of feeling is part of the more straightforward way in which Lawrence is 'fearfully English'. (This phrase comes in a letter in 1912 reassuring David Garnett, who was coming out for a visit to Icking, that 'I look fearfully English, and so I guess do you, so there is no need for either of us to carry the Union Jack for recognition.'[43]) But the preceding chapter ends more puzzledly and puzzlingly, as he reports his subsequent feelings about a group of Italian immigrant workers he had got to know in Switzerland:

> The moment my memory touched them, my whole soul stopped and was null; I could not go on. Even now I cannot really consider them in thought. I shrink involuntarily away. I do not know why this is.   (p. 141)

This passage prompts me to take up a more complicated way in which Lawrence's own character, particularly his Englishness, enters the book — or, in this respect, lurks behind it. It is opportune here to make a second visit to the letters.

Those exiles had gone north: elsewhere in the book, Italians emigrate to America. On 26 October 1915 Lawrence wrote to Pinker: 'I send you the rest of the Italian Studies [i.e. what was to be published as *Twilight in Italy* – not the 1913 'Italian Studies']. I have sent the complete *MS.* to Duckworth. I am still thinking of going soon to America. I feel if I stay in Europe now I shall die' (*Letters* 2, p. 417). That feeling is expressed vividly and continuously through the letters of that time. My suggestion is that *Twilight in Italy* allowed Lawrence to explore his other feeling about exile, the one which he could hardly admit to in his letters or other direct personal expressions. In view of the strong element of self-protective defiance in those letters, it is reasonable to call *Twilight* the struggle to show his *real* feeling. It does come out once, however, in one letter, to Cynthia Asquith on 21 October, which responds to her brother's death in the war:

> I shall go away, soon, to America. Perhaps you will say it is cowardice: but how shall one submit to such ultimate wrong as this we commit, now, England – and the other nations. If thine eye offend thee, pluck it out. And I am English, and my Englishness is my very vision. But now I must go away, if my soul is sightless for ever. Let it then be blind, rather than commit that vast wickedness of acquiescence. (*Letters* 2, p. 414)

It is important to read in context that familiar middle sentence about his Englishness, which has often been quoted (by Leavis, for instance, as an epigraph to *D. H. Lawrence: Novelist*) as if it were proud and positive. The context, with the Lawrentian *buts* and *ands* locked in anguish, almost makes us read '*But* I am English . . .'; and, in the next sentence, '*even if* my soul is sightless for ever'. He must go despite the arresting thought that to go is to go blind. This is a quite different sense of his relation to England from that in most of the letters with their deliberate distancing devices, so that the echoes of the Matthew Gospel, Œdipus and, most powerfully, Macbeth convey a self-division and a necessary self-mutilation.[44]

Exile as a blinding: this is what *Twilight* explores. (I say 'explores' because the paradox 'tacitly expresses' may be baulked at, and 'covertly' is not my sense of it.) It is central to the 'double time-scheme' of the book that as the narrator gives his fascinated attention to a whole series of emigrants, Lawrence is writing of them in 1915 as past encounters but drawing on his preoccupation of the present. The unstated personal preoccupation is what prompts his fruitless questioning of Paolo about his impressions of America (there is a fruitful comparison here with Wordsworth's self-preoccupied interrogation of the leech-gatherer, and the latter's response). Paolo, he comes to realize, went to America with his soul sightless; or rather, 'in real truth' only his body went in a kind of sleep-walking from reality while 'his fate was riveted' at San Gaudenzio (p. 92). Accordingly he came back. But then Paolo, like Signor di Paoli, 'is too old. It remains for the young Italian to embrace his mistress, the machine' (p. 53). Yet young John (the subject of the next chapter) neither stays nor goes for good. Home is unreal or meaningless, abroad was pointless and largely painful. As he sets off again to America 'he seemed like a prisoner being conveyed from one form of life to another, or like a soul in trajectory' (p. 119). (My detection of a 1915 vibration of interest is not invalidated by this incident being firmly consigned to 1913 and being one of the few where the Lawrence and Frieda of that year are lightly sketched in: John repeats the obscenities of Americans 'so coarse and startling that we bit our lips, shocked almost to laughter'.) But the exiles in Switzerland 'would never go back' (p. 136).

I think Lawrence could not and cannot bear to think of them because they take to the extreme the contradictions inherent in exile. Plodding south through 'the utter cold materialism of Switzerland', a country 'utterly without flower or soul or transcendence' and hardly *real*,[45] he lights on six Italians 'creating a bonfire of life in the callousness of the inn' where he puts up (pp. 129, 130). They are animatedly rehearsing a play; after first treating him as an outsider they accept him and at least one seizes him as an Englishman, 'putting a sort of implicit faith in me, as representative of some further knowledge' (p. 139). He then flinches from this, and from their scorn for mountain peasants ('I thought of Paolo, and Il Duro, and the Signor Pietro, our padrone, and I resented these factory-hands for criticising them' (p. 132)). With that recall of earlier chapters, and with very many other recapitulations of theme, this chapter is devoting much of its energy to pulling the book together. But equally one might say that it is 'all so strange and varied'. Varied in the distinctions made between the individual emigrants here; strange and varied in the half-explanations ventured (they are anarchists, they are avoiding military service); strange in the double feelings of the narrator. He attributes to them 'the slight pain and contempt and fondness which every man feels towards his past, when he has struggled away from the past, from the conditions which made it' (p. 136). He himself refuses to be representative of England, or of the future which England represents to these exiles. But he sees in these exiles both the element of self-damage, and also the impossibility of cutting yourself off from your country and your past. That one's 'soul is sightless' if one goes away, even if one 'must go away': this is what the chapter sees but cannot bear to look at. The book's protagonist is, after all, an exile (the word need not convey unhappy or involuntary or permanent expatriation), Italy being seen through an exile's eyes. More keenly, it is written by a man in 1915 contemplating exile. Nowhere, it must be stressed, is this brought out explicitly: *Twilight in Italy* is rarely self-dramatizing in the sense we attach to *Sea and Sardinia* and the 'Introduction' to Magnus's *Memoirs*, but it is continuously self-exploratory.[46]

V

I now wish to pull together the strands of my present chapter by turning to the unity of *Twilight in Italy* itself.

That self-exploratory attention to exile provides a great measure of continuity. Unity, however, is a quality of the book for which it is wise to make only cautious claims. It 'just growed', and – as a third perusal of the letters will suggest – in response to commercial considerations as much as notions of organic unfolding.

Lawrence had a practical eye for home economics (getting some quick cash when things were tight) and hence for marketing techniques. The letters are aware that you may live in an inner world and write of the other world but you sell to agents and editors who inhabit this one. On 29 July 1915 he wrote to Ottoline Morrell about forming a select group with a vital purpose, and also wrote to his agent thus: 'I believe my sketches may easily prove good selling stuff, better than a novel' (*Letters* 2, pp. 372–3). On the day he wrote to Cynthia Asquith about a thunderstorm of a row with Russell leading to 'a sort of washed freshness in the sky, and the light beginning to shine for a new creation, I think' (*Letters* 2, p. 397: not quite what Russell thought!), he sent Pinker a first group of what were provisionally called 'Italian Sketches'. 'Shall I get them done for [Duckworth] quickly', he asks, so that they can catch the Christmas trade? He can push the whole thing up to 50,000 words by adding 'another or two other sketches, at choice'. However, 'the whole set would look nice as a serial'. A couple of sketches 'are just right for magazine publication as they stand – the 2nd and 3rd are too long' (*Letters* 2, p. 398). A couple of weeks later, on the same day that he wrote to Cynthia Asquith that 'the visible world is not true', he agreed terms with Pinker and suggested that 'perhaps a special format, with possible illustrations, might be rather jolly'; meanwhile 'I must get on and do more sketches now' (*Letters* 2, p. 405).

The practicalities of piecemeal composition with no pre-existing general theme (or a provisional one, 'the nations', which lost its primacy) counted as much in the book's shaping as the Lawrentian maxim that 'men live and see according to some gradually developing and gradually withering vision'.[47] The resulting effect is that several core-topics and sets of polarized terms gather to a greatness and then wither, or run into the sand, or give way to others. At other moments it is as if the author over-anxiously pulls tight the string around the bulging parcel; this, as well as unease about the abstractness of the former passage, is perhaps what made him attribute to a particular group of soldiers who form part of the audience in 'The Theatre' the tigerish soldierliness defined in 'The Lemon Gardens'. Such picking up of earlier motifs is especially frequent in the two concluding chapters.

But the parcel does not spill apart. 'Being and not-being' builds up steadily until it becomes central to the description of Hamlet in 'The Theatre', yet it still figures in 'San Gaudenzio', and it informs the subject of emigration which becomes the primary focus of all subsequent chapters. Equally, this latter subject was already hinted at in the end of 'The Lemon Gardens' and first emerges strongly in 'The Theatre', from which I have already quoted: 'And this is why the men must go away to America.'

The foregoing comments also show that 'The Theatre' is the centrepiece, not simply in coming near the middle of the book and being the longest chapter, but as the major junction of its themes. It therefore deserves dwelling on at the end of my commentary.

If 'The Theatre' bestows an element of unity on the book, its intrinsic quality has to do with its own, intrinsic, unity. Of the four opening chapters which were all revised from earlier articles, this is the one whose additions least strike us as extraneous interpolations. By contrast 'The Lemon Gardens', switching abruptly from narrative to two long added passages of general thought, presents problems of integration – and, more acutely with the first addition, the variations on Blake's 'Tiger', problems of conceptual coherence and concrete applicability.[48]

The matching of 1913 and 1915 elements in 'The Theatre' is both more intricate and more smooth-edged. It is no longer meaningful to talk of general thought as distinct from narrative; there is a continuum between the account of a series of visits to the lakeside theatre, the analysis of *Hamlet*, and the outline for a Psychic History of Europe. Not that it is possible to play down the adventurousness of thought here, nor is it desirable. In the words of Johnson that we invoked at the outset of this book, Lawrence's mind here is 'active, ambitious and adventurous, always investigating, always aspiring'.[49] But we should also recall that in the 'Study of Thomas Hardy' one of the stressed pairs of necessary opposites is 'the aspiration and the resistant'. And the distinctive cogency and integrity of 'The Theatre' comes from its having so many varied but related resistants, forming the ground with which even 'its highest flights' are in unbroken communication. The grounds for its speculations are: several dramatic masterpieces (the *Oresteia*, *Hamlet*, *Ghosts*), performances of the last two and, to come down several pegs, of a d'Annunzio play; the travelling actors and actresses in these; and the reactions and interval behaviour of the local audience. In the phrase from that letter sent to Catherine Carswell soon after revising 'The Theatre', all these are 'things real'.

The term *resistant* may be seized on as only too apt by those who resist Lawrence and suspect him of distorting the plays: did he not override their resistance, making them too compliant in marshalling his thought the way that it was going? But his interpretation of *Hamlet*, particularly of the protagonist as self-disgusted and disgusting, has become much less startling in the context of recent criticism, and when read in the context not of Bradley eleven years earlier but of T. S. Eliot only four years later, with Wilson Knight following hard upon. Moreover

Ernest Jones and Gilbert Murray had recently brought to bear Freudian analysis, anthropology, and comparative literature and mythology. In a later phrase of Lawrence's, the play was now seen as coming from the speaking for 'the race, as it were'.[50] It is because Lawrence takes account of these extended contextual horizons undreamt of in Bradley's psychology that, however one disputes his interpretation in detail, it can hardly be said that Lawrence fails to give Shakespeare's play its due weight. It is for him 'the statement of the most significant philosophic position of the Renaissance' and is its most significant and powerful statement too (p. 68). No question of Shakespeare haplessly revealing this position, as Eliot argues: that is reserved for the peasant actor who displays but does not understand the feelings or the 'maudlin compromise' of the modern Italian.

Finally, what was that 'position' which *Hamlet* expressed? The play is very important to Lawrence because (to re-apply my earlier word for the 'Theatre' chapter itself) it marks a crossroads in European history: the point where personal, political and religious history most firmly interconnect; and a point of no return, the irreversible new prevalence of 'the convulsed reaction of the mind from the flesh, of the spirit from the self, the reaction from the great aristocratic to the great democratic principle' (p. 69). It testifies to the book's own ample measure of interconnectedness, of cumulative thought, that those terms have little weight as they stand in a quotation thus isolated as if it were a formula. But even this passage points to the orientation of *Twilight in Italy*. It may hanker intermittently after transcendence, worlds elsewhere, flesh thawing and resolving itself into a dew, but its prevailing current is identical with the famous end of Lawrence's *Apocalypse*: 'the magnificent here and now of life in the flesh is ours . . . in the flesh, and part of the living, incarnate cosmos'.[51]

3 Poetry and science in the psychology books

IN January 1920 Lawrence promised to send the American publisher, Benjamin Huebsch, 'six little essays on Freudian Unconscious'.[1] In May 1921 these appeared as *Psychoanalysis and the Unconscious*, published not by Huebsch but by Thomas Seltzer. Eighteen months later Seltzer also published Lawrence's *Fantasia of the Unconscious* (referred to as *Fantasia* in what follows, for convenience). Both these 'psychology books', as they are often called, were offered to American readers in the first instance. This was the period when Lawrence was saying, 'I feel it is my business now to secure an American public'; or, more firmly, 'But I want to plant my stuff *first* in America, and let England take second chance every time'.[2] *Psychoanalysis and the Unconscious* appeared in England in July 1923 and *Fantasia* in September of the same year.

It is only mildly surprising to find Lawrence writing about psychology. In June 1920 he was busy extending several essays which he had originally hoped to have published in *The Times Educational Supplement* into a short book (known as 'Education of the People', but never published in Lawrence's lifetime). Six months before, he had been correcting the proofs of a text book for young schoolchildren called *Movements in European History*. All this of course in addition to his more familiar preoccupation with novels, stories, poems and even plays. But the books on education and history are rather different in character from his work on psychology and the unconscious. He had begun the education essays after having been graded fit for some kind of non-military service at the medical inspection in Derby, described in such painful detail in the 'Nightmare' chapter of *Kangaroo*. If he was going to have to find a job, he presumably felt that it might as well be in an area where he could show he had some expertise. His history book was begun at a time when he was more or less destitute, or even more destitute than usual. But there was no need for any motive from outside

67

to prompt him to work on the idea of the unconscious. That was a consuming interest, as the essays on American writers which he was writing during the later war years show. Much revised, these essays were eventually to appear in 1923 as *Studies in Classic American Literature*. But in September 1919 Lawrence had already announced to Huebsch that they were finished.

> I have finished the *Classic American* essays − end up with an essay on Whitman. The essay on Whitman you may find it politic not to publish − if so leave it out altogether − don't alter it. The rest is unexceptionable. − These essays are the result of five years of persistent work. They contain a whole Weltanschauung − new, if old − even a new science of psychology − pure science. I don't want to give them to a publisher here − not yet. − I don't really want people to read them − till they are in cold print. I don't mind if you don't publish them − or if you keep them back. − I only know the psycho-analysts here − one of them − has gone to Vienna, partly to graft some of the ideas on to Freud and the Freudian theory of the unconscious − is at this moment busy doing it. I *know* they are trying to get the theory of primal consciousness out of these essays, to solidify their windy theory of the unconscious. Then they'll pop out with it, as a discovery of their own.[3]

It is strange that Lawrence should speak here of neither wanting to give his essays to an English publisher nor having them read when several had already appeared in the 'cold print' of the *English Review*.[4] From this distance in time, it may seem stranger still that he could have imagined the Freudians should want to steal from him. His letter may well contain an element of sales promotion but, even allowing for that, what it demonstrates above all is how seriously Lawrence took his ideas on the unconscious. He was not overly discouraged when his detailed and systematic development of them in *Psychoanalysis and the Unconscious* was so badly received in America. In a part of the 'Foreword' to *Fantasia* which never appeared, he replied jauntily to his critics and in an 'Epilogue' which was published he warned his American readers not to think that 'the show is over', adding, 'I've got another volume up my sleeve'.[5] 'Mountsier loathes me because I will develop my *Unconscious* ideas', he wrote to Seltzer in July 1921, 'But I have written the second book, and know it good. In about three years time I'll write the third book, and then − fertig'; and sending Seltzer his amended typescript of *Fantasia* on 22 October of the same year, he said, 'I think, if any book of mine is going to make your fortune, this *Fantasia* will be the one'.[6]

It might be thought that Lawrence was the kind of writer for whom the latest work is always the best; but that isn't so. Although he became absorbed in his books on history and education, they never seemed to have been quite free in his mind from an initial element of constraint: the need to make money, or to establish his credentials in the educational field. Between finishing *Psychoanalysis and the Unconscious* and writing *Fantasia* he dashed off *Sea and Sardinia*, about which he speaks very casually in his letters. In comparison with these and other works, the psychology books mattered to him a great deal and he expected a great deal from them. On the whole, his expectations were disappointed at the time and it could hardly be said they have been justified since. Middleton Murry declared his enthusiasm for *Fantasia*[7] but after him, and with the one notable and distinguished exception I discuss later, the critics have tended to be wary. They have been happy enough to pillage both psychology books for resounding summaries of Lawrence's 'beliefs' but, considering how much has now been written on him, they have provided comparatively little appraisal of their character or worth and not much discussion of their relation to his other writings.

It is indicative of this relative lack of interest that, even by those who pay attention to them, the two psychology books are so often lumped together: taken as the sum-total of Lawrence's views on the psyche and quoted from indiscriminately. But although in his 'Foreword' Lawrence accurately describes *Fantasia* as a 'continuation from *Psychoanalysis and the Unconscious*' (p. 11), it is a very different book. The most obviously striking differences are in scale. In *Psychoanalysis and the Unconscious*, Lawrence is concerned to substitute for what he thinks of as Freud's 'windy theory of the unconscious' his own conception of a 'primal consciousness' biologically grounded in four 'body centres': the solar and cardiac plexuses in the front, 'sympathetic' part of the body and the lumbar and thoracic ganglia in the hard, 'voluntary' back. It is from these four great nerve centres (whose existence, he insists, can be verified in any medical or scientific text book), and from their interaction with equivalent or complementary nerve centres in the mother, that the life of the child − conscious or unconscious − develops. In establishing this 'biological psyche', as he was to call it in *Fantasia*, Lawrence is also concerned to prove that the 'incest craving' which he rightly saw as central to Freud's thinking about child development is not a spontaneous impulse from the body centres but a feeling with its origin in the brain and one more proof, therefore, of that tendency to brain-dominance which was for him the chief curse of modern life. Both the nature of the primal consciousness and the case against Freud are sketched with great economy (in the Penguin edition, *Psychoanalysis and the Unconscious* is only forty-nine pages long) so that Lawrence has room only for hints about the education of children or relations between adults. Nor does he have space to do more than suggest how his insistence on the psyche as 'biological' bears on those questions of the relation of mind to matter which preoccupied Lawrence as much as they do the Ursula of *The Rainbow* when, waiting for Skrebensky, she asks herself what will or purpose holds together the forces in the unicellular organism she is observing through a microscope in a laboratory of her university.[8]

When he comes to *Fantasia*, Lawrence adds four more body centres (in the neck and loins) to the original four of *Psychoanalysis and the Unconscious* and in a chapter called 'The Five Senses' tries to substantiate in some detail his claim in the earlier book that 'the unconscious brings forth not only consciousness, but tissue and organs also' (p. 242). But in a text which is nearly four times as long as its predecessor, he also develops the hints and suggestions of *Psychoanalysis and the Unconscious* into a comprehensive world view. It is in *Fantasia*, therefore, rather than in the early American studies, that one really finds the 'Weltanschauung' Lawrence writes about to Huebsch. His sense of the need for steady, even development of the body centres and of the dangers of any too early solicitation of ideas from a child's brain − not for him a 'centre' at all − leads to questions of upbringing and parental care, and then to detailed proposals for a reform of the state education system, very similar to those he makes in 'Education of the People', but more radical. His concern not only to expand and reinforce his case against the Freudian interpretation of incest-craving but also to combat the view (which he supposes to be Freud's) that 'a sexual motive is to be attributed to all human activity' (p. 17), causes him to propose as even greater than the sexual impulse the 'essentially religious or creative motive' (p. 18). But since this motive for Lawrence is above all masculine – the 'desire of the human male to build a world' (p. 18) – he is prompted to thought about the power-relations between men and an elaboration of his feelings about the vital importance of leadership. Taking him to questions of education and political organization in one direction, in another Lawrence's body centres lure him even further afield. As a young man, his more orthodox religious faith had withered away in an intellectual climate which for him was probably associated most closely with the names of Darwin, Spencer and Huxley. In *Fantasia*, he returns to the issues which had troubled him then, and tries to demonstrate why a belief in his body centres as the sites of consciousness does not inevitably imply any concession to scientific materialism. Hence – if by a distinctly roundabout route – a chapter in his book entitled 'Cosmological'. Apologizing for it in his 'Foreword', to what he imagines as 'the remnants of a remainder' of readers who have refused to be warned off by his preceding remarks, he writes, 'I wish to say that the whole thing hangs inevitably together' (p. 11). *Fantasia* is Lawrence's attempt to show why a true conception of the primal consciousness does make everything hang together. It is not such an eccentric production when one recalls how far from the initial starting-point Freud's enquiries eventually led.[9]

In addition to being different in scale, *Fantasia* has on occasions a very different tone from anything to be heard in *Psychoanalysis and the Unconscious*. Characteristic of these is the opening of the 'cosmological' chapter I have just mentioned.

> Well, dear reader, Chapter XII was short, and I hope you found it sweet.
> But remember, this is an essay on Child Consciousness, not a tract on Salvation. It isn't my fault that I am led at moments into exhortation.
> Well, then, what about it? One fact now seems very clear – at any rate to me. We've got to pause. We haven't got to gird our loins with a new frenzy and our larynxes with a new Glory Song. Not a bit of it. Before you dash off to put salt on the tail of a new religion or of a new Leader of Men, dear reader, sit down

quietly and pull yourself together. Say to yourself: 'Come now, what is it all about?' And you'll realize, dear reader, that you're all in a fluster, inwardly. Then say to yourself: 'Why am I in such a fluster?' And you'll see you've no reason at all to be so: except that it's rather exciting to be in a fluster, and it may seem rather stale eggs to be in no fluster at all about anything. And yet, dear little reader, once you consider it quietly, it's *so* much better to get up and say to the waters of one's own troubled spirit: Peace, be still . . .! And they will be still . . . perhaps. (p. 148)

There is a limit to how much of this the most well-disposed readers (big or little) can take. Even if they were in a position to realize that by abandoning the book at this point they would be depriving themselves of very good things, common pride — of the kind Lawrence himself strongly approved — might well lead them to sacrifice ulterior gain for the satisfaction of immediate resentment. A certain percentage of the copies of *Fantasia* must always have crashed against the wall at this point.

Patronizing yet defensive, this occasional tone of Lawrence's suggests unease about his readership: a radical uncertainty about who could be expected to listen. Elsewhere in *Fantasia*, a similar suspicion of the reader, whether disguised in condescension as it is here or expressing itself more straightforwardly, can be associated with the unfavourable reception of *Psychoanalysis and the Unconscious* in America. On the first page of the 'Foreword' to *Fantasia* as it now exists, for example, Lawrence warns 'the generality of readers' that 'this present book will seem . . . only a rather more revolting mass of wordy nonsense than the last' and he suggests to the 'generality of critics' that they 'throw it in the waste paper basket without more ado' (p. 11). These hostile preliminaries become more understandable when one discovers that they were once not preliminary at all but the continuation of 'An Answer to some Critics' (Lawrence's initial sub-title for his 'Foreword'), the first, major part of which Seltzer declined to publish. In September 1921 he had sent Lawrence a score of reviews of *Psychoanalysis and the Unconscious*, to which the original opening of *Fantasia* is a relatively detailed response. Their general manner — it is from one of the reviews that Lawrence takes the phrase 'a revolting mass of wordy nonsense' — helps to explain the defiant tone of the passages which were initially about two-thirds the way through the 'Foreword', but with which it now begins.

Yet not all the peculiarities of tone which distinguish *Fantasia* from *Psychoanalysis and the Unconscious* can be accounted for so specifically. After all, this type of direct address to the reader can also be found in the second half of *Mr Noon*, where it is similarly uneasy and unsuccessful. Lawrence appears to have abandoned *Mr Noon* about six months before plunging into *Fantasia* but, after completing its major part, he had written *Sea and Sardinia* and about a month after dispatching *Fantasia* off to Seltzer he wrote *The Captain's Doll*. These two triumphs of tone (as of so many other things) are a discouragement against dramatizing 1921 as an *especially* critical period in the history of Lawrence's feelings about his audience. He had been obliged to be anxious about it from at least the time of the banning of *The Rainbow*. The form of direct address found in parts of *Mr Noon* and *Fantasia* was only one of several strategies he evolved for dealing with the anxiety and is perhaps best regarded in the light of a failed experiment by a writer most of whose experiments came off. At the beginning of 1922 Lawrence wrote the 'Introduction' to Magnus's *Memoirs*, and at the end of the year the revised versions of *Studies in Classic American Literature*, two works as successfully achieved, in their very different ways, as *Sea and Sardinia* and *The Captain's Doll*. The variety of form in his work would not be the striking phenomenon it is without an accompanying variety of manner.

As Evelyn Hinz has pointed out in one of the best of the relatively few accounts of the psychology books, *Fantasia* differs from *Psychoanalysis and the Unconscious* not only in scope and tone but also in what might be called method.[10] There is some indication of this difference in its title, which Lawrence at one time intended to be 'Harlequinade of the Unconscious'.[11] Neither 'Harlequinade' nor 'Fantasia' means that he isn't being serious or doesn't want to be taken seriously; but they do suggest that he feels he has nothing to lose from a more free-and-easy manner or that the anti-rationalist elements in his stance make such a manner more appropriate. To imagine that mind could have evolved from matter, he says at one point, would be to take the cart, rub it all over with grease, spray it with white wine, spin the right wheel round at five hundred revolutions to the minute, etc., and then really expect to see it groan and writhe until the horse lay panting between the shafts. Half-comic extended similes of this kind are quite common in *Fantasia*, where Lawrence is also inclined to shift the focus to himself in the act of writing.

> Oh, damn the miserable baby with its complicated ping-pong table of an unconscious. I'm sure, dear reader, you'd rather have to listen to the brat howling in its crib than to me expounding its plexuses. As for 'mixing those babies up', I'd mix him up like a shot if I'd anything to mix him with. Unfortunately he's my own anatomical specimen of a pickled rabbit, so there's nothing to be done with the bits.
>
> But he gets on my nerves. I come out solemnly with a pencil and an exercise book, and take my seat in all gravity at the foot of a large fir-tree, and wait for thoughts to come, gnawing like a squirrel on a nut. But the nut's hollow. (p. 42)

This is the beginning of chapter 4 ('Trees and Babies and Papas and Mamas'). The reference to 'mixing those babies up' – a phrase from a review of *Psychoanalysis and the Unconscious* in the *Pittsburgh Dispatch*, some of which Lawrence quotes in the unpublished section of his 'Foreword'[12] – identifies it as having been added to a typescript of *Fantasia* in October 1921. Examination of this typescript – now in the Harry Ransom Humanities Research Center in Austin – shows that this is also the case with the next few pages. Handwritten and linked to the original, typed opening of chapter 4 with 'Excuse my digression, gentle reader. At first I left it out, thinking we might not see wood for trees', these pages offer to describe Lawrence's feelings as he sits in the Black Forest near Ebersteinburg and tries to write. The trees, he explains, appear to force themselves on his awareness. 'It almost seems I can hear the slow powerful sap drumming in their trunks.' He says he now understands why the Roman armies should have been intimidated by the Black Forest, and why 'the old Aryan worshipped the tree'. This, he concludes, will be one of the places his soul will haunt when he is dead, 'Among the trees here near Ebersteinburg, where I have been alone and written this book'. Lawrence finished the first version of *Fantasia* in Ebersteinburg in June or July but he didn't get it back from his typist until September (and it was not of course until September that he saw the review to which he begins his hand-written addition by referring). All this makes it as reasonably certain as these things can be that when Lawrence was correcting his typescript and wrote the phrase 'here in

Ebersteinburg', he was several hundred miles away in Taormina.[13] As *Sea and Sardinia* so triumphantly demonstrates, no English writer is better than Lawrence at simulating the here and now, and fostering the illusion that there is no gap between what is described and the act of description. But it is rare to be made aware as forcibly as one is in this instance that simulation is precisely what is involved. The circumstances support the idea of a certain degree of deliberateness or calculation in Lawrence's efforts to alter his method in *Fantasia* since the new opening of chapter 4 is not really 'digression', as he must have been aware, but an effective way of pursuing the argument by non-ratiocinative means. Whenever Lawrence describes the world around him he writes very well − this is the period of *Birds, Beasts and Flowers*.[14] The opening of chapter 4 exemplifies his belief in the importance of an instinctive, non-cerebral relation with the outside world and simultaneously invests him with an authority for propounding it. There is no such variety of method in *Psychoanalysis and the Unconscious*. In *Fantasia*, it corresponds to a much greater use of the first person singular and has the effect of making the reader more aware of Lawrence as an individual and a writer. Evelyn Hinz makes the good point that the relatively more sober, expository manner of the first psychology book is evident in the use of the 'we' of conventional intellectual debate more or less throughout.[15]

Her case for the nature of the difference between the two books strikes me as considerably over-stated nevertheless. It is, she claims, the difference 'between an empirical and a poetic methodology, between an analytic and an archetypal approach to the unconscious'. Whereas *Psychoanalysis and the Unconscious* was designed as 'a scientific answer' to Freud, *Fantasia* needs to be approached as a 'work of art'.[16] Since Dr Hinz says in a note that she belongs to a group called the Massachusetts Archetypalists who tentatively define 'archetypal' as 'the conscious use of mythical patterns and symbols as the ritualistic means of abrogating historical time and its attendant evils . . .',[17] that word may perhaps be left on one side as raising questions which would not in this context be immediately relevant. Without it, the oppositions she proposes are all too clear and familiar. They are between science, empiricism and analysis on the one hand, and poetry and art on the other. A convenient way of showing that they do not adequately define the principal differences between the two psychology books is to follow the development in *Fantasia* of the two chief anti-'scientific' pronouncements of *Psychoanalysis and the Unconscious*: the two declarations in which Lawrence most obviously and explicitly turns his back on the science of his day.

In the first his claim is that matter not only came second but depends for its continued existence on living beings, rather than vice-versa. This is asserted almost incidentally in *Psychoanalysis and the Unconscious* as Lawrence is discussing the 'active quick, the nuclear centre' of the foetus. 'From this centre the whole individual arises, and upon this centre the whole universe, by implication, impinges. For the fixed and stable universe of law and matter, even the whole cosmos, would wear out and disintegrate if it did not rest and find renewal in the quick centre of creative life in individual creatures' (pp. 218–9). The reader can pass this by with no more than the lift of an eyebrow, but in *Fantasia* what was previously unobtrusive and relatively incidental has become very prominent. In his 'Foreword' Lawrence insists on his belief that, 'Instead of life being drawn from the sun, it is the emanation from life itself, that is, from all the living plants and creatures which nourish the sun', and attributes it to the 'early Greek philosophers'. In chapter 13 he develops his whole new cosmology, partly inspired by these philosophers and by his reading in theosophy and anthropology. If the idea that 'life' somehow emerged from matter is a prime example of putting the cart before the horse, then it seems to follow for Lawrence that in the workings of the universe life must be far more instrumental than science allows.

> It is life we have to live by, not machines and ideals. And life means nothing else, even, but the spontaneous living soul which is our central reality. The spontaneous, living, individual soul, this is the clue, and the only clue. All the rest is derived.
> How it is contrived that the individual soul in the living sways the very sun in its centrality, I do not know. But it is so. It is the peculiar dynamic polarity of the living soul in every weed or bug or beast, each one separately and individually polarized with the great returning pole of the sun, that maintains the sun alive. For I take it that the sun is the great sympathetic centre of our inanimate universe. I take it that the sun breathes in the effluence of all that fades and dies. Across space fly the innumerable vibrations which are the basis of all matter. They fly, breathed out

from the dying and the dead, from all that which is passing away, even in the living. These vibrations, these elements, pass away across space, and are breathed back again. The sun itself is invisible as the soul. The sun itself is the soul of the inanimate universe, the aggregate clue to the substantial death, if we may call it so. The sun is the great active pole of the sympathetic death-activity. To the sun fly the vibrations or the molecules in the great sympathy-mode of death, and in the sun they are renewed, they turn again as the great gift back again from the sympathetic death-centre towards life, towards living. But it is not even the dead which *really* sustain the sun. It is the dynamic relation between the solar plexus of individuals and the sun's core, a perfect circuit. The sun is materially composed of all the effluence of the dead. But the *quick* of the sun is polarized with the living, the sun's quick is polarized in dynamic relation with the quick of life in all living things, that is, with the solar plexus in mankind. A direct dynamic connection between my solar plexus and the sun.   (pp. 152–3)

Between writing *Psychoanalysis and the Unconscious* and its successor, Lawrence became interested in Einstein. Relativity Theory pleased him because it appeared to put the universe back into what he calls in *Fantasia* 'the mental melting pot' (p. 149) and entitle everyone – or so he seems to feel here – to a stir. His account on this occasion begins with 'soul', although it ends in the familiar region of the solar plexus. In his first psychology book, he had contemplated using 'soul' for the unconscious in general: for the 'unanalysable, undefinable, unconceivable . . . unique nature of every individual creature', but had rejected the word as 'vitiated by the idealistic use' ('nowadays it means only that which a man conceives himself to be') (p. 215). His own use of it in *Fantasia* is occasionally idealistic in a different sense as when, shortly before the passage I quote, he says that, 'The dead souls likewise decompose – or else they don't decompose. But if they do decompose, then it is not into any elements of Matter and physical energy. They decompose into some psychic reality, and into some potential will. They re-enter into the living psyche of living individuals' (pp. 151–2). By making his psyche 'bio-logical', Lawrence had largely been able to skirt around many of the more familiar problems of mind versus body. His use of soul here plunges him back into them. At another point, he also uses it as part of a new set of terms – 'Mind, and conservative psyche, and the incalculable soul, these three are a trinity of powers in every human being' – the effect of whose sudden appearance is confusing, especially as the three powers in question are then said to be somehow transcended by what Lawrence calls the Holy Ghost – 'the individual in his pure singleness, in his totality of consciousness' (p. 133).

So it is not only that Lawrence develops his idea of the biological psyche in *Fantasia*, he also complicates it by introducing incompatible elements. But the immediate point at issue doesn't call for exploration of the complications here. In the passage I quote, his manner is self-avowedly speculative ('How it is contrived that the individual soul in the living sways the very sun in its centrality, I do not know'), and he is clearly very much aware that what he is imagining could not be verified in the text books – as he firmly believed his body centres could. For all that, it would hardly be right to say that, in comparison with *Psychoanalysis and the Unconscious*, one can detect in this passage the shift from an empirical to a poetic methodology, from science to art. The reader who threw *Fantasia* against the wall at the beginning of chapter 13 will ask why poetry or art should take the blame. The more moderate response involves noting just how keen Lawrence is to imagine cosmological activity as a quasi-scientific process. This is clear enough in his account of death. 'To the sun fly the vibrations or the molecules in the great sympathy-mode of death, and in the sun they are renewed, they turn again as the great gift back again from the sympathetic death-centre towards life, towards living.' It is important that in Lawrence's mind there is nothing at all fanciful or abstract about his 'vibrations'. Previously in *Fantasia* he has said that there is a 'definite vital flow' between an individual and any external object, 'as definite and concrete as the electric current whose polarized circuit sets our tram-cars running and our lamps shining, or our Marconi wires vibrating'. Even his dog or canary, he claimed, had a polarized connection with him. 'Nay, the very cells in the ash tree I loved as a child had a dynamic vibratory connection with the nuclei in my own centres of primary consciousness' (pp. 131–2). This way of conceiving the world is still evident in Lawrence's speculations about the death process. What they echo most distinctly are those descriptions in the biology text books of his day designed to demonstrate the operation in Nature of the laws involving the conservation of energy and the indestructibility of matter. The decomposing matter of the dead or dying makes its way to the sun where by some process analogous to (say) photosynthesis it is converted into elements or powers which are life-supporting. In addition to noting that this conception implies mutual dependence rather than the priority of life over matter, one can perhaps best indicate its essential spirit by saying that it is far more reminiscent of Hartley than of Blake.

'Perhaps' will seem too tentative but it is hard to dispense with without looking more closely at Evelyn Hinz's terms and asking, in the first instance, what exactly she might mean by a 'poetic methodology'. A moment ago her use of 'archetypal' appeared irrelevant but it comes into play again now if one assumes that, in one popular view, a 'poet' will help to develop our feelings about matters very imperfectly understood by making up stories. That is to say that his 'method' will involve the deliberate use of myth and allegory. There is no such use in the passage I quote, despite the ways in which the views it expresses might be associated with those myths which, according to the anthropologists Lawrence knew, led the Aztecs to practise human sacrifice in order to keep the sun alive. Like many of the early Greeks he had read about in Burnet, Lawrence appears to be trying to give to his speculations what − in the prevailing state of knowledge − could be construed as a scientific probability, even though the basis of those speculations is so resolutely unscientific.[18] In poets like Donne, scientific concepts are sometimes present for their rhetorical or metaphorical value only. Here Lawrence's evident if paradoxical intention is to say that, although he doesn't know how the universe operates and can't accept the explanations of orthodox science, it is likely that it does so in some such alternatively scientific way as this.

If 'poetic' calls for some definition, so of course does 'scientific'. The difficulties both words present are suggested by I. A. Richards's decision in 1970 to change the title of his short book, *Science and Poetry* − first published in 1926 − to the less euphonious but more circumspect *Poetries and Sciences*. It was in this book that Richards presented Lawrence (along with Yeats) as the type of anti-scientific poet. He referred in doing so to *Fantasia* (the 'elaborate prose exposition . . . of the positions which so many of the poems advocate'), and more specifically to the contention in it that the sun's energy is recruited from life on earth.[19] Like Kenneth Burke in his reply to several of the main positions in *Science and Poetry* – the section in *Permanence and Change* (1935) called 'In Qualified Defence of Lawrence' – Richards offers very little detail. Both he and Burke treat *Fantasia* like a dubious acquaintance it would be compromising to reveal one knew at all well. The impression they offer of Lawrence's attitude to science is the same as that in Huxley's introduction to his 1932 edition of the letters. For Lawrence, Huxley says, all scientists were liars, and he recalls one long and violent argument on evolution, in the reality of which (he adds), 'Lawrence always passionately disbelieved'. ' "But look at the evidence, Lawrence," I insisted, "look at all the evidence". His answer was characteristic. "But I don't care about evidence. Evidence doesn't mean anything to me. I don't feel it *here*." And he pressed his two hands on his solar plexus. I abandoned the argument and thereafter never, if I could avoid it, mentioned the hated name of science in his presence.'[20] For years this exchange summed up everything that most people – including, apparently, Richards and Burke – had to say about Lawrence's feelings towards science.

No doubt there were occasions when Lawrence was as bigoted as Huxley – whose interest in evolution could fairly be described as vested – suggests; and certainly there are passages in his works which can be quoted in support of Huxley's idea of him. In the 'Foreword' to *Fantasia* itself, where Lawrence echoes the Theosophists' notion of a body of esoteric knowledge invested in an ante-diluvian priesthood, to be found all over the then-existing world, he states categorically, 'I do not believe in evolution, but in the strangeness and rainbow-change of ever renewed civilisations' (p. 14). Yet this is after he has referred to the view, seriously entertained not only by Theosophists but also by many reputable naturalists and geologists at the end of the nineteenth century, that there had been during the glacial period a great land-mass and therefore, perhaps, a great civilization – the Atlantis of Plato and other Ancient writers – which was destroyed when the ice-caps melted.[21] The 'evolution' in which he declares his disbelief can therefore be taken as the concept of a relatively uninterrupted development of present-day man from lower forms, with the accompanying assumption that the development in question had been steadily progressive. 'But as for me', he says a little later in his 'Foreword', in a remark which conveys his scepticism in a memorably witty and economical way, 'I have some respect for my ancestors, and believe they had more up their sleeve than just the marvel of the unborn me' (p. 15).

If this seems to some like special pleading, it can at least be shown that there is no automatic hardening of Lawrence's attitude to these matters in his later years and that in a text which very much belongs to them – 'Introduction to These Paintings' – his treatment of science is not at all what the exchange with Huxley would lead one to expect. There is a difference, he begins by saying, between the 'alert science' which teaches that – under certain circumstances – water produces two volumes of hydrogen and one of oxygen, and telling schoolchildren that water *is* H_2O. He goes on to complain of the tendency in modern scientific books on astronomy to cite figures for the number of miles between stars, for example, which are too absurdly huge for the human mind to grasp – 'it is just occult'. Finally, he comes to the question of evolution.

> The mind can assert anything, and pretend it has proved it. My beliefs I test on my body, on my intuitional consciousness, and when I get a response there, then I accept. The same is true of great scientific 'laws', like the law of evolution. After years of acceptance of the laws of evolution – rather desultory or 'humble' acceptance – now I realize that my vital imagination makes great reservations. I find I can't, with the best will in the world, believe that the species have 'evolved' from one common life-form. I just can't feel it, I have to violate my intuitive and instinctive awareness of something else, to make myself believe it. But since I know that my intuitions and instincts may still be held back by prejudice, I seek in the world for someone to make me intuitively and instinctively feel the truth of the 'law' – and I don't find anybody. I find scientists, just like artists, asserting things they are *mentally* sure of, in fact cocksure, but about which they are much too egoistic and ranting to be *intuitively, instinctively* sure. When I find a man, or a woman, intuitively and instinctively sure of anything, I am all respect.[22]

There is a lot more in this passage than the uncompromising 'I don't feel it *here*'. It corrects, in the first place, Huxley's very obviously mistaken assumption that Lawrence had always 'passionately disbelieved' in evolution. (No one who read the 'Study of Thomas Hardy' or indeed *The Rainbow* could accept that.) But it also shows that his hostility could be a matter of 'great reservations' rather than total rejection, and that it concentrated on one particular logical inference of evolutionary theory: the now-discredited idea that all the species must 'have "evolved" from one common life-form'. Even in dealing with that idea, it seems to me likely that in this case Lawrence is less the opponent of 'alert science' than of its more popular interpretations: of the notion in popular Darwinism that there is no overwhelming difficulty in conceiving a genealogical tree which has at the top 'primeval soup' (although as in all questions involving first causes, the starting-point is in fact arbitrary) and at the bottom – or near it – Rostropovich and Red Rum. It is the problem of making any such tree real to the human imagination which concerns him.

It would be wrong to imply that Lawrence was incapable of sheer anti-scientific *prejudice*, especially when discussing how he presents his belief that the sun recruits its energy from the earth. But his attitude to science is a complex matter. In the thirteenth chapter of *Fantasia* he says that he won't be told that 'the sun is a ball of blazing gas which spins round and fizzes. No, thank you'. Yet the reason he gives for this refusal is that 'There is nothing in the world that is true except empiric discoveries which work in actual appliances' (p. 151). His 'science' is very much that of the nineteenth-century positivist working in the laboratory. Which is to say – with all due respect to that mythical figure – that it is perhaps not science at all, since all true scientific enquiry is likely at some point to involve abstraction, and to make suggestions which either contradict our everyday experience of the world or cannot be verified by it. The development which Lawrence gives to his first anti-scientific proposition in *Fantasia* is only 'scientific' within the terms of reference Evelyn Hinz provides. What it shows above all is how strong his instinct was to imagine how things might work *in practice.*

If the Hinz case for a radical difference in method between the two psychology books is at least damaged by the way the first proposition is developed, the fate of the second in *Fantasia* destroys it completely. That case is not of course helped by the fact that both Lawrence's major anti-scientific contentions already appear in *Psychoanalysis and the Unconscious*, especially as the second — an insistence on the causeless nature of all new life — is expressed in that book with an uncompromising bluntness. 'We deny that the nature of any new creature derives from the nature of its parents. The nature of the infant does *not* follow from the natures of its parents.' Lawrence attributes the belief that it does to science's faith in cause-and-effect. But, 'cause-and-effect will not explain even the individuality of a single dandelion . . . On the contrary, individuality appears in defiance of all scientific law, in defiance even of reason' (pp. 213–14). That he then goes on to say that the acceptance of this 'first new item of knowledge' would provide the basis for a new science of the unconscious, more complete in knowledge, encourages Hinz to characterize *Psychoanalysis and the Unconscious* as a 'scientific exposition . . . a scientific piece designed to expose psychoanalysis as a pseudo-science'. Whether it is or not, Lawrence is much closer to genuine 'scientific exposition' when he treats the issue of new life in *Fantasia* than he had been in its predecessor. That is, his account of a new being and its progenitors in the later book has become qualified and more carefully reasoned. In all of us, he claims, the 'parent nuclei' are continually present — 'well heads of vivid life itself' giving 'direct connection, blood connection we call it, with the rest of the family'. But this, he then says, pulling himself up, is a preliminary rather than intrinsic truth. 'The intrinsic truth of every individual is the new unit of unique individuality which emanates from the parent nuclei.' He dwells for a paragraph on what is underived, utterly unprecedented and unique in a new soul, but continues with the qualification that 'only at his maximum does an individual surpass all his derivative elements, and become purely himself. And most people never get there . . . very few people surpass their parents nowadays and attain any individuality beyond them' (pp. 30–1). This is a far cry from the blunt denial that 'the nature of the infant does *not* follow from the nature of its parents'. Whatever one thinks of it — and advances in genetics since Lawrence's time are bound to make both his treatments of this question seem inadequate — it is not the exchange of an empirical for a poetic methodology.

It is important not to lump the two psychology books

together: they do have a different character. *Psychoanalysis and the Unconscious* is a deliberately limited endeavour – 'We merely wish intelligibly to open the way' (p. 235) – in which, on the whole, Lawrence does try to meet Freud on his own 'scientific' ground. In *Fantasia*, he gives himself a much freer hand and extends his scope enormously, pursuing the implications of his idea of the unconscious into politics, educational policy and cosmology. By continuing to take the psyche as his starting-point, returning to the question of incest, and challenging in his penultimate chapter the Freudian interpretation of dreams, the link with the earlier book is nevertheless maintained. In matters other than scope, *Fantasia* is much less of a departure than it tends at first to seem. It is, for example, by no means consistently uneasy and provocative in tone. For most of the time, Lawrence can be found earnestly expounding his views, just as he had done – more briefly – in *Psychoanalysis and the Unconscious*. The switches to his situation – supposed or real – at the time of writing are infrequent. Like its predecessor, *Fantasia* is recognizably the work of a literary artist but it also shows, as *Psychoanalysis and the Unconscious* did, that hostility to the apparent conclusions and implications of late nineteenth-century science can co-exist with a surprisingly high degree of sympathy – much of it perhaps instinctive – with the methods, tone and spirit of that science in its more popular manifestations. The two books need to be distinguished carefully; but that is no argument against the well-established habit of printing them together. It will be a great help towards their better understanding however if, when they next appear, the perverse decision of whoever was responsible for the Penguin edition is rescinded, and the two texts are presented in chronological order.

More important than distinguishing *Fantasia* from *Psychoanalysis and the Unconscious* is why any one should bother with either. This is not a difficult question for a reader who comes to them already interested in Lawrence. Both books are full of valuable indications of the development of Lawrence's thought and feeling – about his parents, for example, or the marriage relation – and both can be relevant to the more obscure moments in the novels. In much of Lawrence's fiction before 1921, there are episodes where the moon figures prominently, but not always in a way or to an effect which is easily understood. Two of the most striking are in *The Rainbow* when, with a full moon shining, Ursula is transformed into a harpy and 'destroys' Skrebensky. It helps in thinking about these occasions to know what role Lawrence assigns to the moon when he describes the cosmos in *Fantasia*: 'The moon is the centre of our terrestrial individuality . . . She it is who burns white with the intense friction of her withdrawal into separation, that cold, proud white fire of furious, almost malignant apartness, the struggle into fierce, frictional separation . . .' (p. 162).

But this is not all Lawrence has to say about the moon in *Fantasia*. She is also, he insists, 'the mother of darkness . . . the clue to the active darkness' and the power under whose spell 'night-consummation takes place' (pp. 179, 185). His account of the moon's place and role has complications which very much lessen the temptation to search through *Fantasia*, or either of the psychology books, for this or that *definitely* interpretative key. Their relation to the fiction is complex, rather more so in fact than is suggested by that deservedly famous paragraph from the 'Foreword' to *Fantasia* which so many critics choose to quote.

> One last weary little word. This pseudo-philosophy of mine – 'pollyanalytics', as one of my respected critics might say – is deduced from the novels and poems, not the reverse. The novels and poems come unwatched out of one's pen. And then the absolute need which one has for some sort of satisfactory mental attitude towards oneself and things in general makes one try to abstract some definite conclusions from one's experiences as a writer and as a man. The novels and poems are pure passionate experience. These 'pollyanalytics' are inferences made afterwards, from the experience. (p. 15)

The 'respected critics' Lawrence refers to here are once again the American reviewers of *Psychoanalysis and the Unconscious* from one of whom he not only might but does derive the term 'pollyanalytics'.[23] His paragraph has been eagerly seized on because it expresses so neatly a cardinal feature of his aesthetic: the familiar, Romantic idea that 'creative' writing cannot be premeditated and that the conscious self of its author is often no more than a channel or conduit. Implied in the paragraph also is the superiority of 'pure passionate experience' to the 'inferences made afterwards'. It would be wrong to endorse this hierarchy without then pointing out, as only a few of those who quote the paragraph have done, that it is half-contradicted by the way Lawrence continues. 'And finally', he says, immediately after the paragraph above, 'it seems to me that even art is utterly dependent on philosophy; or if you prefer it, on a metaphysic . . . Our vision, our belief, our metaphysic', he complains, 'is wearing woefully thin and the art is wearing absolutely threadbare' (pp. 15–16). The art which comes unwatched out of a man's pen will not be much good, it seems, unless it has *behind* it the kind of philosophy or metaphysic which Lawrence is struggling to define in the psychology books. No wonder then that they should point forwards as well as back: not only provide an aid, of however fragile and easily misused a kind, in the reading of *The Rainbow*, but also establish or develop attitudes (about woman's role, for example, or leadership) that one then finds dramatized in a novel such as *Kangaroo*. All Lawrence's discursive works are not merely rationalizations after the event but part of his continuous development as a writer.

Much of what happens to Lawrence's thoughts about women and leaders in *Kangaroo* is a reminder of the novel-form's advantages. In *Fantasia*, several of the passages which deal with the true role of women are indefensible. This is not because there could be no case for insisting on the differences between the sexes or the satisfaction the traditional roles have brought, or might still bring, to both women and men. (Such a case is in fact made by F. R. Leavis in his impressively subtle account of *The Captain's Doll*.)[24] But in describing how a woman should minister to her husband after he returns from initiating action in the world, contributing to the 'great unison of manhood in some passionate *purpose*' (p. 109), Lawrence is inclined to betray motives for his position which, uncomfortably regressive, undermine it in the reader's mind.

> If you want to see the real desirable wife-spirit, look at a mother with her boy of eighteen. How she serves him, how she stimulates him, how her true female self is his, is wife-submissive to him as never, never it could be to a husband. This is the quiescent,

flowering love of a mature woman. It is the very flower of woman's love: sexually asking nothing, asking nothing of the beloved, save that he shall be himself, and that for his living he shall accept the gift of her love. This is the perfect flower of married love, which a husband should put in his cap as he goes forward into the future in his supreme activity.   (pp. 126–7)

In *Kangaroo*, the most directly autobiographical of Lawrence's novels published during his lifetime, Richard Lovat Somers is the advocate of a marriage relation in which the female partner limits herself to ministering to an enterprising husband. But his wife Harriet's bright aggressivity, the strength of her personality and her exceptional resistance to the danger of giving respect where respect isn't due, are all created so vividly that the reader feels Somers has no prospect of ever finding her 'wife-submissive'. As in the case of Birkin, the 'Lawrentian views' have a different feel when one is made dramatically aware of the situation of the person who holds them. Harriet has a shrewd eye for an unworthy motive – she would have made short work of the passage above, detecting immediately the element of weak nostalgia focused in 'sexually asking nothing' – and a devastating line in cruel mockery: 'Him, a lord and master! Why, he was not really lord of his own bread and butter: next year they might both be starving. And he was not even master of himself, with his ungovernable furies and his uncritical intimacies with people.'[25] She expresses the reader's scepticism about Somers's opinions with such destructive effectiveness that one might begin to feel there is something in them after all. That is to say that at least the novel shows how the future of a marriage which has reached an *impasse*, and which involves two such determined and combative people, might well depend on one or other of them yielding precedence.

The effect of exposing Somers's views on marriage to criticism by Harriet is that the reader is inclined to consider them more sympathetically, or with more understanding, than when views and pronouncements which are very similar are offered to him *ex cathedra*. But there is a rather different and more complicated result when several of Lawrence's own thoughts about leadership are dramatized in *Kangaroo*. *Fantasia* is not the only discursive text in which he insists on the need for leaders, but there cannot be many other places in his work where he so explicitly offers himself as an answer to that need. Has President Wilson, or Karl Marx, or Bernard Shaw ever felt 'one hot blood-pulse of love for the working man', he asks; and he goes on, 'I would like [the working man] to give me back the responsibility for general affairs, a responsibility which he can't acquit, and which saps his life. I would like him to give me back the responsibility for the future. I would like him to give me back responsibility for thought, for direction. I wish we could take hope and belief together. I would undertake my share of the responsibility, if he gave me his belief' (p. 115). Whatever Lawrence's own qualifications for leadership, it seems to be a help in judging thoughts on that subject when one can imagine the person who propounds them himself accepting to be led. In a rigorously hierarchical society there will be very many different levels at which leadership is required, and the willingness to assume responsibility is therefore likely to be more of a positive attribute if it is accompanied by the recognition that there must be occasions when responsibility will be assumed by others on one's own behalf. After all, the chances of being the only person in such a society who has no one to answer to are slim; and as Lawrence says in *Apocalypse*, 'Give homage and allegiance to a hero, and you become yourself heroic', but 'deny power in a greater man, and you have no power yourself'.[26] The main action of *Kangaroo* shows Somers, who advocates leadership in terms very like those Lawrence has used elsewhere, struggling but then failing to accept someone else as his leader. The premise is that he has written essays which make him seem an invaluable potential ally to both the Australian Left, represented by Willie Struthers, and its Right, in the person of Ben Cooley (whose nickname gives the title to the novel). But as Somers tries hard to decide which of them he should follow, or whether the promptings of his deepest self will ever allow him to follow either, the drama suggests thoughts about Lawrence's whole 'philosophy', as well as his views on leadership. In the psychology books, where this philosophy is expressed directly, he dwells frequently on the duty every individual has to be delicately responsive to the impulses originating in the 'pristine unconscious' – the first four body centres. In *Kangaroo*, Somers is presented as a man who lives in general obedience to these impulses with the inevitable result that he often seems to others inconsistent or indecisive. Genuinely attracted to Ben Cooley's organization, he shows a degree of interest which is partly responsible for his being both elaborately wooed and then made privy to its masonic-like secrets. It is not surprising then that when Somers decides that he can't after all bring himself to join the organization, some of its members should feel themselves betrayed. In the chapter in which one of them expresses this feeling forcefully ('Jack Slaps Back'), Somers's own unease at the situation is also apparent.

> 'You take no risks,' said Jack quietly. Another home-thrust.
> 'Why − I would take risks − if only I felt it was any good.'
> 'What does it matter about its being any good? You can't tell what good a thing will be or won't be. All you can do is to take a bet on it.'
> 'You see it isn't my nature to bet.'
> 'Not a sporting nature, you mean?'
> 'No, not a sporting nature.'
> 'Like a woman − you like to feel safe all round,' said Jack, slowly raising his dark eyes to Somers in a faint smile of contempt and malevolence. And Richard had to acknowledge to himself that he was cutting a poor figure: nosing in, like a Mr Nosy Parker, then drawing back quickly if he saw two sparks fly.[27]

What emerges from the drama of *Kangaroo* is that Somers is willing enough to lead, but temperamentally disinclined to be led. When it is a question of what he calls 'the joy of obedience and the sacred responsibility of authority', his imagination is only really fired by the latter. More significantly, one is made aware in the novel of the obvious difficulty of reconciling commitment to those collective male endeavours Lawrence is so keen on, with a man's loyalty to his own 'dark gods': those urgings which come from his innermost being but not only from there (the way they come being evidence to the individual of some power which is beyond him).

Kangaroo may not make Lawrence's thoughts on leadership appear more attractive or convincing, but at least their unconvincingness is shown, acted out. This is not exactly basing one's art on a metaphysic, but seeing whether one has indeed a metaphysic to base one's art on. Readers of the long, 'political' segments of *The Plumed Serpent* will tend to regret, and on the whole rightly, that Lawrence cannot have considered the results of his enquiry in *Kangaroo* conclusive. But the enquiry itself −

the testing in a dramatic context of *Fantasia*'s political proposals – is of sufficient interest to make it seem a matter for regret that the educational programme he outlines in that book was not also woven into a subsequent drama. Lawrence's own involvement in the educational system of his day gives peculiar force and authority to his characterization of its barbarity and helps to explain why the changes he proposes should be so radical. But it would have been an encouragement to take the letter of those changes more seriously – the seriousness of their spirit being compelling enough – if there had been some later, imaginative realization of family life in a society where parents were to be held responsible for their children's education up to the age of ten; or more exploration of the likely nature of those 'directors' who (Lawrence suggests) would have the final responsibility for deciding whether, after ten, a boy should go to a workshop of skilled labour, of technical industry or of art. A regret that there is neither seems natural, but one of its possible effects is to suggest that the psychology books are chiefly ancillary – repositories of suggestions worked out more satisfactorily elsewhere, when the question which has eventually to be asked is what they are worth in themselves; or, since that form of words risks sounding brutal or naive, how or whether they can be recommended to someone not already familiar with Lawrence's life and work.

There are many arresting and memorable passages in both psychology books. It is possible that Lawrence never properly read any Freud but learnt about him in discussion with unusually well-informed friends.[28] If he was not, therefore, qualified to write a serious critique of Freud himself, he can be impressively shrewd when it comes to the facile assumptions of popular Freudianism. His alternative explanation of 'incest-craving' as mind-generated bears comparison with Jung's and allows him to demonstrate how extraordinarily intuitive he was about the feelings of very young children. Since the evidence he relies on includes Renaissance paintings of the Madonna and child, it also shows the perceptiveness of his art criticism. When he describes the various ways in which mothers can distort the emotional development of their children, Lawrence is at his best and only marginally less so in his account of the effect of the distortions on married life. The account which can be gathered from these books of 'how we live now' is powerful enough to make the most nervously discontented readers discover protected enclaves of smugness in themselves. But Lawrence's finest writing cannot be confined to a list of topics. It comes at almost any time and on almost any subject as his thought moves back and forth from small intricate questions, which require close reasoning, to the larger, more speculative issues.

The commonsensical approach to the psychology books involves taking the rough with the smooth; of acknowledging that much in them is absurd, eccentric or illogical in order to secure a hearing for fine moments of the kind to which I refer. For only a small number of commentators would this attitude depress either book below its real value, but it is an awkward fact that the dissident group would certainly have included the most distinguished and influential of Lawrence's English critics. In his two books on Lawrence, F. R. Leavis has most to say about *Psychoanalysis and the Unconscious* (perhaps because *Fantasia* had already been praised by Middleton Murry and, to a much lesser extent, by T. S. Eliot). 'Serene and lucid', 'closely argued', of 'wonderful lucidity and complete convincingness' are some of the phrases he uses to describe it in *D. H. Lawrence: Novelist*; and in the later *Thought, Words and Creativity*, the first psychology book is called a 'sustained piece of cogent exposition' and praised for its 'clear expository efficiency'. Leavis clearly recognizes *Fantasia* as a different kind of endeavour, but his reference in *D. H. Lawrence: Novelist* to 'the poise of lucid and assured intelligence' which *both* books demonstrate indicates that the distinctions he would want to make are not invidious.[29]

The cautionary effect of these remarks is reinforced by a feature of the psychology books which Leavis rightly emphasizes. One of the strengths for which they could be recommended to readers unfamiliar with Lawrence lies in their treatment of the dangers of automatic living. *Kangaroo* may demonstrate that to be true to the promptings of the deepest self can have awkward consequences for others, but these may be finally less dangerous for a community than a situation in which many of its members are living according to ideas of themselves which have become sclerotic. More than most writers, Lawrence is sensitive to how human beings develop notions about their own needs or aims which, although quickly made irrelevant or inappropriate by 'events' – psychological or otherwise – nevertheless become fixed and preclude further change or development. These notions, which Lawrence calls both ideas and ideals, are characterized by him as machine-principles, so that he is then able to draw a parallel between the 'idealism' of particular men or women and the mechanization of modern industrial society (as in the first sentence of the quotation on p. 76). It is not only individuals but society as a whole which in his view has become unresponsive to both its surroundings and needs, and essentially mechanical, therefore, in operation. 'Instead of living from the spontaneous centres', he complains in *Fantasia*, 'we live from the head' (p. 83). Living 'from the head' is a major theme in many of Lawrence's books. The phrase is given a special resonance in these two by the attempt to make it more than metaphorical and, specifically, by the relatively minor importance Lawrence attributes to the brain in his biological psyche. For him the brain is only 'the terminal instrument of the dynamic consciousness', printing off ideas 'like a telegraph instrument' (p. 247). This insistence leads Lawrence to make claims for his biological psyche which one commentator has accurately characterized as 'anatomical nonsense'.[30] His nerve or body centres do not have the autonomous power of creating consciousness he would like them to have and he ignores the inconvenient fact that, far from the brain waiting passively to receive ideas, there is nothing which could be called an idea without it. 'Idea', of course, is a word with a traditionally broad meaning in discussions of the mind. By making it equivalent to 'ideal', Lawrence is able to confine the brain exclusively to its higher functions and thus find new ways of insisting on the difference between what in common speech is called the 'merely cerebral' and the dependence of all genuine thought on experience: our above all physical involvement in the world. This is a distinction which, at the beginning of his career, had come unwatched out of his pen with the portrait of Mr Massy in 'The Daughters of the Vicar'. For all its scientific inaccuracies, the biological psyche allows Lawrence to reaffirm it very effectively but in a different mode, proving the aptness of John Wisdom's reference to the psychology books as 'physiological mythology for psychological description'.[31]

'Knowledge', Lawrence writes in *Psychoanalysis and the Unconscious*, 'is always a matter of whole experience, what St Paul calls knowing in full and never a matter of mental conception merely' (p. 215). His complaints against the brain, in both that book and its successor, add to the cautionary effect of Leavis's remarks because, to criticize the texts in which they are embodied for their occasional absurdities, inaccuracies or illogicalities is to expose oneself to a charge of missing the point. Leavis himself sets against Lawrence's notions of true thinking 'the commonsense, the whole cultural ethos in which one has been brought up' and that 'routine conception of sound thought as controlled by *la clarté* and *la logique*' (in context, the French words have overtones which are heavily pejorative).[32] He finds himself forced to admit nevertheless that the psychology books are 'discursive expositions (as I must call them)', even though 'Lawrentian and unique'.[33] But that they were written by Lawrence does not seem to me to make inapplicable certain standards associated with their particular discursive mode or prevent readers from asking questions about logical sequence and accuracy of information. It is of course evident that there are whole areas of life where logic's writ should not inevitably run and where psychological health can depend on evading the tyranny of apparently consecutive ideas. Rationalism, especially the late nineteenth-century scientific rationalism with which Lawrence was familiar, is quite clearly not the only avenue to truth. It is nevertheless an enemy hard to meet on its own discursive ground without involving oneself in the paradox of opposition by rational means, and having the effectiveness of that opposition judged by criteria which those means imply. The truth of this is startlingly demonstrated by Leavis's choosing the terms for his praise of *Psychoanalysis and the Unconscious* from the very 'routine conception of sound thought' he disparages; and it is, perhaps, Lawrence's understanding of it which helps to explain why, in the two years or so after the publication of *Fantasia*, he should have written a number of short pieces in praise of the novel-form, pointing out (for example) that in a novel there are no absolutes and 'Everything is true in its own time, place, circumstance and untrue outside of its own place, time, circumstance'.[34] For Lawrence in the mood in which he wrote these pieces, art-speech *is* the only speech.

But if the difference between art-speech and discursive exposition is difficult to eliminate entirely, it isn't only in Lawrence's novels that the former can be effective. In *Sea and Sardinia* a triumphant exercise in humorous self-dramatization persuades readers to entertain views which – had they been presented as general or absolute and not the consequence of a particular individual's immediate situation, experience or temperament – might well have interested them far less. In the first chapter of *Mornings in Mexico*, a perfectly-achieved lightness of touch suggests that it is possible to take 'evolution' too much for granted (as Lawrence says he himself had once done). His method in this chapter is self-avowedly 'poetic' in the sense in which I must speculate Evelyn Hinz uses that word. 'Myself', he writes, conveniently defining his terms, 'I don't believe in evolution, like a long string hooked on to a First Cause and being slowly twisted in unbroken continuity through the ages. *I prefer to believe* in what the Aztecs called Suns: that is, Worlds successively created and destroyed'. And he goes on, '*This pleases my fancy better* than the long and weary twisting of the rope of Time and Evolution, hitched on to the revolving hook of a First Cause'.[35] The words I have italicized announce very clearly Lawrence's deliberate preference here for myth over science; and the account that follows them of how worlds are successively created and destroyed in Aztec mythology is in no way the kind of effort to imagine a scientific process which it might well have been in the psychology books. It is far from being frivolous for all that. By making his readers so vividly aware of his dog Corasmin, the parrots in the trees which surround the veranda where he says he is writing, and his Mexican servant Rosalino, Lawrence is able to bring home to them how fundamentally different these 'life-forms' are from each other and himself. The implication is that there are differences here which too mechanical or simplistic a belief in the evolutionary string or rope would tend to obscure. In his remarks on water as H_2O in 'Introduction to These Paintings', Lawrence shows himself aware that a scientific description of our surroundings does not necessarily weaken or restrict our sensuous involvement in them. But one can imagine that if, as part of that precocious mental training he denounces so passionately in *Fantasia*, schoolchildren were repeatedly and insistently told that all life has a common ancestor, the 'knowledge' might well dull their sense of what is various, different and 'other' in the world. It is a point the author of *Birds, Beasts and Flowers* was peculiarly equipped to make. He does so in *Mornings in Mexico* with a perfectly-judged lightness of tone which leaves his readers free to draw their own conclusions.

By comparison with the tone of *Mornings in Mexico*, Lawrence's search for an appropriate voice in *Fantasia* is often a failure, and so too is his limited degree of self-dramatization in that book when compared with *Sea and Sardinia*. His travel writing is consistently successful whereas the psychology books, in which he commits himself to presenting a case and arguing discursively, are a challenge to write about precisely because they call for such a constant effort of discrimination. Chapter 5 of *Fantasia* for example ('The Five Senses') is by no means the most satisfactory. 'The growth and the life of the teeth', Lawrence claims, 'depend almost entirely on the lumbar ganglion'. But in the modern world we have succeeded in suppressing 'the avid, negroid, sensual will' and converted ourselves into 'ideal creatures'. The consequence is that, 'We are sympathy-rotten, and spirit-rotten, and idea-rotten. We have forfeited our flashing sensual power. And we have false teeth in our mouths' (p. 61). The reasons for the poor state of the nation's teeth (dramatically improved in recent times, apparently, by the addition of fluoride to toothpaste and water) are surely more complex than this. And so are the reasons for the shape of our noses which, Lawrence says, depends 'on the direct control of the deepest centres of consciousness'. Thus, 'a short snub nose goes with an over-sympathetic nature, not proud enough; while a long nose derives from the centre of upper will, the thoracic ganglion' . . . etc. (p. 63). It may be (though I very much doubt it) that the nose is as Lawrence says 'one of the greatest indicators of character'. But if it is, the indications must be harder to interpret than he assumes.

Passages like these on teeth and noses make one wonder which other great novelist was capable of such rubbish; or how the man who wrote them could, only a few months later, have written *The Captain's Doll*, with all its refined humour, sophistication and delicacy of feeling. Yet as chapter 5 continues, and Lawrence moves from teeth and noses to the eyes, there is a distinct change of atmosphere.

> When I go forth from my own eyes, in delight to dwell upon the
> world which is beyond me, outside me, then I go forth from wide
> open windows, through which shows the full and living lambent
> darkness of my present inward self. I go forth, and I leave the
> lovely open darkness of my sentient self revealed; when I go forth
> in the wonder of vision to dwell upon the beloved, or upon the
> wonder of the world, I go from the centre of the glad breast,
> through the eyes, and who will may look into the full soft
> darkness of me, rich with my undiscovered presence. But if I am
> displeased, then hard and cold my self stands in my eyes, and
> refuses any communication, any sympathy, but merely stares out-
> wards. It is the motion of cold objectivity from the thoracic
> ganglion. Or, from the same centre of will, cold but intense my
> eyes may watch with curiosity, as a cat watches a fly. It may be
> into my curiosity will creep an element of warm gladness in the
> wonder which I am beholding outside myself. Or it may be that
> my curiosity will be purely and simply the cold, almost cruel
> curiosity of the upper will, directed from the ganglion of the
> shoulders: such as is the acute attention of an experimental scien-
> tist. (p. 64)

This is not vintage Lawrence. 'Living lambent darkness' followed by 'lovely open darkness' and 'full soft darkness' make for
an effect which, in this context, is inappropriately insistent. But
the writing here is nevertheless absorbing in ways which the
passages on teeth and noses definitely are not. It shows how
acutely Lawrence had observed different kinds of seeing and
how his biological psyche helps him to retain the differences he
had noted. Every writer interprets the world according to some
psychological code, yet in most cases this code is both implicit
and in tune with common understandings. There are both advantages and disadvantages for Lawrence in having elaborated
his own system. When he discusses noses, it leads him into
absurdity and results in the translation of a few stale com-
monplaces of folk wisdom into what is at that point his own
even less satisfactory idiom. But here the system, by providing
him with an explanation for certain differences, allows him to
retain them for the reader and make distinctions which might
otherwise have gone unnoticed.

It is important to mark the superiority of the remarks on vision to what precedes them, and a disservice to Lawrence to do
otherwise if only because blanket judgments are much more likely to work against than for him. There are remarkable things in
Fantasia and *Psychoanalysis and the Unconscious*, and both the

psychology books can be recommended for what they are in themselves, as well as for what they reveal about Lawrence and his work. But one ought to be restrained from claiming too much for them, especially as regards lucidity and coherence, by Lawrence's own reply to Earl Brewster's request for further details. 'When I urged him to write at greater length on his philosophical and psychological conceptions, he would shake his head and say: "I would contradict myself on every page".'[36] Thus the third book on the unconscious which Lawrence had promised Seltzer was never completed. It is reasonable to be very glad that Lawrence chose to write about this subject and not be sorry that he stopped − or rather, not be sorry that he eventually found it a subject whose ramifications were better dealt with in other, less obviously discursive literary forms.

4 Here and now in Sardinia: the art of Lawrence's travel writing

T HE general manner of Mabel Dodge Luhan's reminiscences does not inspire confidence in her powers of either observation or analysis. Yet there is one incident she recalls which
rings reasonably true because it corresponds with so much that
can be inferred from Lawrence's writings, and from his travel
books especially. She and her husband Tony Luhan were accompanying Lawrence into Arizona in order to see that Hopi snake
dance he was to write about rather dismissively at first and then
to describe with great skill and appreciation in the essay which
now appears in *Mornings in Mexico*. Stopping in Albuquerque
for lunch, they went into a 'large and luxurious dining room'
where, according to Mrs Luhan, Lawrence suddenly became extremely conscious of Tony, who was of course an Indian from
the Taos pueblo. (It is not too long ago that one could find the
sign 'No Indians served here' in certain parts of the Southwest.)

> Lorenzo tightened up and flashed a quick, half-impatient, half-
> protective glance at him. [Tony] had seated himself with unper-
> turbed majesty and was calmly unfolding a large napkin and
> tucking the end of it into his shirt-front. Lorenzo threw looks of
> hatred up at the head waiter, who was a large, efficient woman
> with a manner aloof, and at the pleasant waitress standing with
> the menu in her hand. His glances were confined for the first
> moments to our own small circumference, though he imagined a
> roomful of hostile critics surrounded us. His malaise made him
> snappy with us all. He began to ridicule American food and to
> nod his head violently to emphasize the words. His foreign flavor
> became apparent, advertised as it was by his manner, so that by
> the time his timidity allowed him to gaze a little farther than our
> neighborhood, he found smiles on travelling men, half concealed
> behind large fin-shaped hands, heads leaning together, eyebrows
> rising and falling. As is frequently the case, he had provoked the
> real event which at first his imagination had summoned up to give
> an opportunity for his prejudices to exercise themselves.

98

There was a hostile atmosphere in the room, directed, however, not at Tony, but at him.[1]

Here is a picture of the Lawrence who − as the sports writers say − 'gets his retaliation in first'. If it carries conviction, it is because the embarrassment he appears to feel on behalf of Tony Luhan is identifiable as a derivative of that self-consciousness he so frequently stigmatizes as the curse of modern living. It is the recognition of self-consciousness in the Englishman who, in the last section of *Twilight in Italy*, hides his face in his bowl of milk and shakes his red ears in painful confusion, merely because Lawrence has addressed him in German, which immediately establishes an uncomfortable bond of fellow-feeling between them. And although Howard Mills has mentioned other factors, it is the total absence of self-consciousness in the old woman whom Lawrence discovers spinning in the second section of that book − her complete inability to imagine what it would be like to be someone else and, therefore, how she might seem to others − which helps to make her appear to him such a challenging figure.[2] Lawrence's own sensitivity to what others would make of him is clear enough in an episode from *Sea and Sardinia* which suggests that, in her observation of his behaviour in the Albuquerque restaurant, Mabel Luhan was not merely imagining Lawrence imagining things.

> You would look in vain this morning for the swarthy feline southerner of romance. It might, as far as features are concerned, be an early morning crowd waiting for the train on a north London suburb station. As far as features go. For some are fair and some colourless and none racially typical. The only one that is absolutely like a race caricature is a tall stout elderly fellow with spectacles and a short nose and a bristling moustache, and he is the German of the comic papers of twenty years ago. But he is pure Sicilian.
>
> They are mostly young fellows going up the line to Messina to their jobs: not artisans, lower middle class. And externally, so like any other clerks and shopmen, only rather more shabby, much less *socially* self-conscious. They are lively, they throw their arms round one another's necks, they all but kiss. One poor chap has had earache, so a black kerchief is tied round his face, and his black hat is perched above, and a comic sight he looks. No one seems to think so, however. Yet they view my arrival with a knapsack on my back with cold disapproval, as unseemly as if I had arrived riding on a pig. I ought to be in a carriage,

and the knapsack ought to be a new suitcase. I know it, but am inflexible.

That is how they are. Each one thinks he is as handsome as Adonis, and as 'fetching' as Don Juan. Extraordinary! At the same time, all flesh is grass, and if a few trouser-buttons are missing or if a black hat perches above a thick black muffler and a long excruciated face, it is all in the course of nature. They seize the black-edged one by the arm, and in profound commiseration: 'Do you suffer? Are you suffering?' they ask.[3]

This comes at the beginning of *Sea and Sardinia* when Lawrence and Frieda have made their way to the local station and are waiting for the train to Messina. Typical of the book in the sharpness and rapidity of its humorous notation, the passage shows a Lawrence who strikes the first blow by taking in the human landscape at a glance but who almost simultaneously feels that he is being observed critically. The discomfort of this feeling then prompts him to retaliate by emphasizing further what is ridiculous in his apparent critics. It is a question of the observer observed; and the passage is prophetic, in its general movement, of the rendering of many of the narrator's contacts with other human beings throughout *Sea and Sardinia*. The knapsack mentioned here, for example, continues to figure in the book like some kind of physical deformity, drawing attention to the narrator and making him feel that he is always disappointing other people's expectations of how he ought to travel. His inflexibility − he says later, in a similar context, that he is 'case-hardened' (p. 19) − is at the opposite pole from the natural insouciance Lawrence so admired. Involving as it does rigid defiance and the determination to overcome difficulties, it is not a good augury for the forthcoming trip. In fact, what *Sea and Sardinia* shows is that to be continually imagining the experience of others will make the whole business of travel (tipping is a prime example) a torment which needs to be mitigated, as in the passage above, by broad retaliatory humour.

Self-consciousness is a complicated business, as Lawrence knew. The 'enormously large' but handsome woman in his carriage on the train to Palermo is described by him as having 'that queenly stupid beauty of a classic Hera' and 'a remote self-consciousness' (p. 14). The twelve-year-old dressed as a French marquis of the eighteenth century whom he sees going to a fancy-dress ball in Cagliari is 'perhaps so perfect in his

self-consciousness that it becomes an elegant "aplomb" in him'
(p. 56). More complicated still is the behaviour of the commercial traveller who ruins Lawrence's sea-journey back home to
Sicily. His performance at the ship's 'black upright piano' is
largely, it is made clear, for the benefit of Frieda, or the 'q-b'
(queen bee) as Lawrence calls his wife throughout *Sea and
Sardinia*. 'And the q-b sat bright-eyed and excited, admiring
that a man could perform so unself-consciously self-conscious,
and give himself away with such generous wiggles' (p. 197).

In these three figures, self-consciousness does not imply
vulnerability as it clearly does for the red-eared Englishman and
for Lawrence himself. But in the case of Lawrence at least,
weakness is only an obverse side of impressive strengths. It is
only because he is able to imagine another person's point of view
so readily that the drama of their appearance can become in a
flash the drama of his own, viewed through foreign and probably hostile eyes. If his curiosity and receptiveness make him
vulnerable to seeing himself from the outside and as only one,
perhaps discordant, feature in a general social context, they are
also what help to make his travel writing so full of interest. Had
the old spinning woman recorded her meeting with Lawrence, it
is highly unlikely that the result would have been in any way informative. The quality she possesses is admired by Lawrence in
all of his travel writing. The workmen who pile into the train
on the way to Sorgono, for example, provide one of several
occasions in *Sea and Sardinia* for distinguishing modern self-
consciousness from a different and older way of apprehending
the outside world. 'But there is a gulf between oneself and them.
They have no inkling of our crucifixion, our universal consciousness. Each of them is pivoted and limited to himself, as the
animals are . . . their life is centripetal, pivoted inside itself, and
does not run out towards others and mankind' (pp. 90–1). It is
because Lawrence's own life ran out towards others and
mankind that *Sea and Sardinia* exists, and the unusual degree to
which it did so, the extent to which he exemplifies what he
characterizes in *Twilight in Italy* as Hamlet's decision 'not to
be',[4] is inseparable from the liveliness of all his travel books.

Lively they may be, but a doubt which is instinctive with some
readers is whether they are 'trustworthy'. In Mabel Luhan's
anecdote, the feelings which Lawrence attributes to the

other people in the restaurant do not at first exist, and it is very much open to a reader of *Sea and Sardinia* to think that the 'young fellows going up the line to Messina' would not have been sufficiently interested in Lawrence's arrival at the station to be coldly disapproving. 'We were still going third class', he writes at the beginning of 'To Sorgono', 'rather to the disgust of the railway officials at Mandas' (p. 86). Perhaps this says less about Mandas railway officials than Lawrence's own self-consciously elaborated idea of what was expected of him. In some of his dealings with the outside world there may well be a tendency in Lawrence (as there is in most people) to project on to others criticisms which have their origin in his own uncertainties.

It is important to see this tendency in perspective since, grossly exaggerated, it can lend support to the view which is now prevalent – something of a minor critical orthodoxy – that Lawrence's travel writings are immeasurably less trips to foreign parts than journeys through his own mind. Because there are works of his in which landscape undoubtedly has a major symbolic significance – 'The Princess' is an obvious example – there is an inclination to forget that even in those, or rather just as much in those as elsewhere in his writing, the landscape concerned is always specifically and concretely evoked. As this truth is lost sight of, and as procedures for dealing with the fiction are extended to the travel books, the picture emerges of a Lawrence so preoccupied with his own problems or neuroses that he could never see what was (as it were) 'there'. Just as he imagined that people were hostile to him when they weren't (or might not have been), so – the prevalent view goes – he projected to the point of obvious distortion on both the human and natural landscape around him, his own fear of female power or his desire for a world of ideal male comradeship. Some of the essential spirit of this view, which is more often an underlying and unargued assumption than an explicit proposition, is suggested by Jeffrey Meyers's conveniently blunt claim, in *D. H. Lawrence and the Experience of Italy*, that Lawrence 'saw the natural world with his imagination rather than his eye'.[5]

In ways I shall describe later, *Sea and Sardinia* especially, but the other three travel books also, are so written that a reader is allowed and perhaps even invited to speculate that some of the people Lawrence met on his journeys did not respond to him as he thinks they did. There are areas in them all where Lawrence's interpretations are either in abeyance or open to dispute and reading him properly becomes a matter of taking up the interpretative challenge. But since the material to be interpreted belongs exclusively to him and there is usually no other source of information, these areas can exist only because, in an overwhelming number of cases, the methods Lawrence has for setting the scene and ensuring his reader's involvement carry so much conviction. The point can be illustrated from page after page of his travel writing. Here are Lawrence and Frieda being led to their room in the inn at Sorgono.

> Was there a bedroom?
> Yes.
> And he led the way down the passage, just as dirty as the road outside, up the hollow, wooden stairs also just as clean as the passage, along a hollow, drum-rearing[6] dirty corridor, and into a bedroom. Well, it contained a large bed, thin and flat with a grey-white counterpane, like a large, poor, marble-slabbed tomb in the room's sordid emptiness; one dilapidated chair on which stood the miserablest weed of a candle I have ever seen: a broken wash-saucer in a wire ring: and for the rest, an expanse of wooden floor as dirty-grey-black as it could be, and an expanse of wall charted with the bloody deaths of mosquitoes. The window was about two feet above the level of a sort of stable yard outside, with a fowl-house just by the sash. There, at the window flew lousy feathers and dirty straw, the ground was thick with chicken-droppings. An ass and two oxen comfortably chewed hay in an open shed just across, and plump in the middle of the yard lay a bristly black pig taking the last of the sun. Smells of course were varied.
>   (pp. 95–6)

To compare a 'grey-white counterpane' to a tombstone requires imagination. But if imagination and the eye are always to be opposed then Wordsworth and Coleridge, as well as a good number of philosophers and psychologists, will have lived in vain. Of course the details here are specially selected (there is no other way of seeing), and in accord with a predominant feeling of disgust; but given their particularity – the 'broken wash-saucer in a wire ring' – and the abundance of this kind of writing elsewhere in *Sea and Sardinia*, why should one be tempted to say that this hotel bedroom was not as Lawrence saw it? Although other people would not have seen it exactly as he did (it is the unexamined false premise of much of the commentary on Lawrence's travel writing that the outside world exists as a norm from which a highly-strung individual like himself deviates), his account has an energy which would make one want to describe that obvious truth as their misfortune.

But it is above all Nature, rather than hotel rooms, which Lawrence is accused of not being able to see straight. Most short accounts of *Sea and Sardinia* lay heavy emphasis on the opening description of Mount Etna as 'white' and 'witch-like', a maleficent female power depriving men of their souls (pp. 1–2). They then tend to move relatively quickly to the final episode when Lawrence is once more back in Sicily and, at a marionette show for men and boys, watches the wicked witch – 'this white, submerged idea of woman which rules from the depths of the unconscious' – set alight by the Paladins of France (p. 204). Commentary on these two moments in the book is inclined to obscure the fact that, between them, Lawrence took a trip to Sardinia. 'But in *Sea and Sardinia*', writes Billy T. Tracy Jnr, 'Lawrence is really writing about the state of his own soul'.[7] Yet for one passage like the opening description of Etna, there are dozens such as this.

> The landscape really begins to change. The hillsides tilt sharper and sharper. A man is ploughing with two small red cattle on a craggy, tree-hanging slope as sharp as a roof-side. He stoops at the small wooden plough, jerks the ploughlines. The oxen lift their noses to heaven, with a strange and beseeching snakelike movement, and taking two tiny steps with their frail feet, move slantingly across the slope-face, between the rocks and tree-roots. Little, frail, jerky steps the bullocks take, and again they put their horns back and lift their muzzles snakily to heaven, as the man pulls the line. And he skids his wooden plough round another scoop of earth. It is marvellous how they hang upon that steep, craggy slope. An English labourer's eyes would bolt out of his head at the sight.   (p. 88)

This is a glimpse of the Sardinian countryside from the train window on the way to Sorgono. Its delicacy and precision, the sharpness of its visual detail, are far more characteristic of *Sea and Sardinia* than the book's opening. Between that opening and the passage above there is of course a whole range of descriptive writing. How Lawrence renders landscape depends on his mood and aims at the time, but as Howard Mills's quotations from *Twilight in Italy* show, these are almost never such that the landscape itself becomes immaterial. Lawrence was rarely so preoccupied with such matters as the evils of the female will, or any of his other anxieties and concerns, to become unresponsive to the outside world. In *Sea and Sardinia*, it is the unusual degree to which that world ('reality' as it tends to be called) impinged upon him, the extent to which he appears to have been obliged by temperament to remain preternaturally alert and observant, which sustains the dramatic tension. Lawrence goes to Sardinia, as he went to most new places, hoping to discover a society more in accord with his ideal than any he had yet known. Certain aspects of the countryside and the bearing of several Sardinians in their native costumes, raise his hopes; but these are partly disappointed after closer contact with Sardinian life (at the Sorgono inn, for example), or when he realizes that all the small towns he and Frieda pass through on their way from Cagliari to Terranova would be far too dull for them to live in. There is a continual conflict in him between high expectations of life: an optimism amounting almost to naivety, and an equally instinctive fidelity to what he knows and sees. This is so typical of Lawrence in all his writing that it is strange he should have been portrayed so often recently as not engaged in any significant *rapport* with foreign countries in his travel writing, but largely pursuing through them his own obsessions. It is true that this view puts him more on the common level (if not below it) whereas to note that, in addition to an eye for detail inseparable from his powers of expression, Lawrence must have had an extraordinary visual *memory* is a reminder of that amalgam of gifts of nature or fortune which makes for absolute distinctions between great writers and everyone else.

Memory, what tends to be known in casual exchange as 'total recall', is startlingly evident when in *Sea and Sardinia* Lawrence and Frieda visit the Cagliari market. It is hard to believe that the remarkable description this visit gives rise to, of all the various fruit and vegetables on sale, with all their different colours, shapes and textures, was written without detailed notes; but the evidence is very strong against Lawrence having been a note-taker in anything like the Zola mould.[8] Mabel Luhan finds a good word for the effect on a reader of descriptions like this, and of *Sea and Sardinia* in general, in a passage from her memoir where she also raises an interesting critical issue.

> It was after reading *Sea and Sardinia* that I wrote to him to come to Taos. This is one of the most actual of travel books, I think, for in it, in that queer way of his, he gives the feel and touch and smell of places so that their reality and their essence are open to one, and one can step right into them. Perhaps it is because, when he is writing, the experience is more actual to him than when it occurred. He is in the place again, reliving in retrospect more vividly than he was able to do at the time it happened. Lawrence couldn't live, with pleasure, in the real moment. He lived afterwards. . .[9]

Most of Lawrence's other friends and acquaintances record that one of his most attractive characteristics was precisely his ability to live with pleasure in the real moment. But that biographical puzzle apart, what may here be lurking behind Mrs Luhan's claim is a misunderstanding about the nature of experience. Living with pleasure in the moment is one thing but *realizing* what has happpened to us is another and largely retrospective process. Lawrence was back in Taormina after his ten days in Sardinia by 14 January 1921 and he was correcting the typescript of the account of his travels (his 'Diary of a Trip to Sardinia' as he initially called it)[10] by the middle of March. This is characteristically rapid composition but the rapidity does not preclude a certain degree of recollection in tranquillity and the time for the significant detail of his recent experience, and therefore its meaning, to emerge. That kind of meaning – the truth of an episode for the person concerned – can never be entirely fixed, so that it would be foolish to claim for Lawrence's first account of the Hopi snake dance, for example – the short, dismissive and bad-tempered letter which appeared in *Laughing Horse* as 'Just back from the Snake-Dance – Tired Out' – any greater authenticity or fidelity to experience than one finds in the relevant chapter of *Mornings in Mexico*. The knowledge that both descriptions of the snake-dance were written close together may make this mistake unlikely,[11] but it is a common assumption that in re-writing for *Twilight in Italy* the 'Italian Studies' which had initially appeared in the *English Review* over two years before, Lawrence *of course* lost sight of the original episodes: that they became for him, as Delavenay puts it, '*un lointain et inaccessible mirage*'.[12] In *Twilight in Italy*, Lawrence certainly does re-interpret many of his Italian experiences according to all he had felt and understood since they occurred and were first recorded, but that does not necessarily transform them into fantasies. The new descriptive details one tends to find in the episodes are much less likely to be fabrications than features which were registered at the time and emerge into the conscious mind as the experience is recalled.

With a use of 'actual' that appears to owe more to French than English, Mabel Luhan attributes the extraordinary 'nowness' of *Sea and Sardinia* to experience having been more vivid to Lawrence in retrospect than at the time. But if one includes in vividness notions of inclusiveness and penetration, the 'reality and essence' she mentions, then she is wrong to imply that what was true of Lawrence is not also more or less true of everybody else, or that its being more so would somehow be a deficiency rather than a strength. We are only made aware of the strength of Lawrence's capacity for 're-living' the past, of course, because he happpens to have been a great writer. By reminding herself that *Sea and Sardinia* came into being after Lawrence's return from his journey, Mabel Luhan appears to be recognizing this fact; yet it may well have been the skill that he devotes in that book to disguising the idea that it is the past he is dealing with – to maintaining the illusion of writing on the spot, in the here and now – which betrayed her into finding his behaviour on any given expedition they took together disappointing. Benefiting from retrospection without acknowledging it, and offering as immediate response what must in fact have had the time – like a photograph in developing fluid – to reach full definition, Lawrence's descriptions of his time in Sardinia have a richness which might well have made anything he said to Mrs Luhan in New Mexico appear insipid, even if he had been the kind of irritating travelling companion prone to running commentary.

It is hard to focus on Lawrence's literary skill when so much of it is directed to making one forget it exists. To maintain what appears to be a minute adherence to chronology, so that the reader has the impression of following Lawrence in his travels step by step and hour by hour, may seem a simple matter, but it requires on his part great virtuosity in the handling of a whole variety of linguistic or syntactical devices many of which, the historic present (for example) or telegraphese, are notoriously treacherous. Writing at even the most simple level of technicality about Lawrence's prose can seem like a betrayal, perhaps because he himself inveighs so powerfully against 'all the critical twiddle-twaddle about style and form'.[13] But style and form there is in *Sea and Sardinia* nevertheless, and crucial to it is the decision, which one can qualify as artistic without implying that it must have been consciously deliberated, largely to dispense with the hindsight available to a man who sits at home and can see his recent journey in perspective. Individual accounts benefit from a retrospection Lawrence's art works to disguise, but there is *between* them a remarkable absence of what might be called infiltration. He apppears to describe each one, re-live it (to use Mabel Luhan's term), in almost complete innocence of what came next. His minute chronology is not merely a chronology of event but also one of mood and feeling.

No generalization about a literary text is ever entirely true, and there is at least one moment in *Sea and Sardinia* when Lawrence explicitly recognizes how any one single mood can be compromised by its successors. The workmen in the train on the way to Sorgono, whose life is centripetal, not running towards others and mankind, have long stocking-caps which they can adjust into all kinds of marvellously expressive shapes. But after Lawrence has been exposed to the squalor of the Sorgono inn, and has discovered that one of the alleys he and Frieda take in an effort to escape into the countryside is used by the villagers as a public lavatory, he is overcome with rage.

> I cursed the degenerate aborigines, the dirty-breasted host who *dared* to keep such an inn, the sordid villagers who had the baseness to squat their beastly human nastiness in the upland valley. All my praise of the long stocking-cap – you remember? – vanished from my mouth. (pp. 99–100)

The rarity of the appeal to remember and therefore compare emphasizes how much more frequently this task is left to readers and how they consequently find themselves very actively involved in the book, and with that freedom I mentioned to challenge Lawrence's interpretations of various categories of events.

Both these results of Lawrence's artistic method can be illustrated by reference to the episode involving the piano-playing commercial traveller. This figure, who so completely spoils for Lawrence the sea trip from Naples to Palermo at the end of *Sea and Sardinia*, is made to correspond in its scheme to the ship's carpenter who takes the edge off any enjoyment Lawrence might have had at the beginning when sailing from Palermo to Cagliari. Both these unwelcome travelling companions make their appeal primarily to Frieda (the carpenter by exciting her sympathy for his sufferings in the war and the commercial traveller through his unself-consciously self-conscious showing-off). When they talk to Lawrence himself it is usually as if he were personally responsible for all the British government's recent policies and above all for what they regard as the criminal injustice of the current lira/sterling exchange rate. But in the opening of the book, the ship's carpenter is partly subsumed in a general context of humour: that comedy of exasperation which, for all its debt to Dickens, is distinctively Lawrentian and centres here on the perverse ability of the ship's cooks to produce – in a vessel 'already heaving its heart out' – a peculiarly formidable menu: 'thick, oily, cabbage soup, very full, swilkering over the sides', 'a massive yellow omelette, like some log of bilious wood', etc. (pp. 31–2). The waiters who serve this feast seem to Lawrence like a buzzing swarm of malevolent blow-flies ready to claim the food as their own once the passengers, whom they appear to outnumber, have been defeated by it. This boisterous method of dealing with the unavoidable disappointments and discomforts of travelling makes the ship's carpenter a minor irritation only. On the trip home Lawrence is less resilient and less able to protect himself from irritation with comic exaggeration.

Yet the mood in which the return trip begins is promisingly buoyant. Travelling is always a matter of minor triumphs and disasters and Lawrence very much enjoys one of the former when, having arrived at Naples via Terranova and Civita Vecchia, and decided to risk walking down from the Naples station to the docks, rather than wait to be carried there by the train, he struggles through a crowd of men to 'a hole in a blank wall' and secures the last two first-class tickets for the ship to Palermo (p. 190). This makes him all the more appreciative of the palatial deck-cabins, single but adjoining, which are assigned to him and Frieda, and all the more grateful for the calm and comfort of the ship's luxurious state room. Everything goes well therefore, until the Lawrences are joined at dinner by the commercial traveller, with his smattering of European languages. As the final stages of the meal are reached, the conversation works round from recent political events to the seemingly inevitable topic of the foreign exchange. Partly because of the whisky he has been drinking, Lawrence feels that he cannot listen once again to the usual complaints and explodes into angry remonstrance about the miseries for an Englishman of travelling in Italy. There are seven people at the table and all of them feel uncomfortable, not least of course Lawrence himself. His discomfort is only increased once the commercial traveller has discovered the ship's piano. However much Frieda may admire the resulting performance, Lawrence is disgusted by it. 'I had had enough. Rising, I bowed and marched off. The q-b came after me. Good-night, said I, at the head of the corridor. She turned in, and I went round the ship, to look at the dark night of the sea' (p. 197).

Typical of Lawrence's travel writing in its immediacy, or actuality as Mabel Luhan would say, this episode has to be in the forefront of a reader's mind when Lawrence describes how on the following morning his feelings had turned violently against the ship. 'For I hated her now. I hated her swankiness, she seemed made for commercial travellers with cash. . . . I hated the waiters and the cheap elegance, the common *de luxe*. I disliked the people who all turned their worst, cash-greasy sides outwards on this ship. Vulgar, vulgar post-war commercialism and dog-fish money-stink. I longed to get off.' And when he is able to disembark, 'Glad, glad I was to get off that ship: I don't know why, for she was clean and comfortable and the attendants were perfectly civil'. The explanation for his relief comes in the following sentence, 'Glad, glad I was not to share the deck with any more commercial travellers' (p. 198), but it is not one which Lawrence himself explicitly offers. He limits himself to vivid descriptions of how he felt at the time, leaving the reader to remember how glad, glad Lawrence was to board the ship initially, after his triumph at the ticket office, and to suspect therefore that, but for an unfortunate meeting with one individual, the evils of 'vulgar, post-war commercialism' would not have bulked so large.

This is an obvious conclusion to draw, but less obvious is the link, which Lawrence does not even hint at, between this episode and his visit to the marionette show on the evening of disembarkation. Lawrence's irritation with the commercial traveller arises partly because he makes his appeal to Frieda, and because Frieda responds. The consequence is that tension between the Lawrences subtly conveyed at the episode's conclusion. When he is watching the marionette show, he is able to forget temporarily the vulnerabilities implicit in any form of association with the opposite sex and delight in what appears to be an uncomplicated world of male companionship. His enjoyment at the theatre follows hard on the heels of his meeting with the commercial traveller, but for Lawrence, as the narrator of his travels, it does no more than that. For the reader, on the other hand, it is tempting to conclude that the pleasure of the second episode must have been very considerably enhanced by the irritations of the first: that if Lawrence enjoys the marionette show so much it is partly because he had so recently experienced discomfort in his relationship with Frieda.

Lawrence does very little to forestall or anticipate responses of this kind, so that reading him is at the opposite extreme from reading a work such as Rousseau's *Confessions*. His chosen method means presenting episodes in virtual independence of each other. The result is that there is no lessening in the drama of following him in his travels – the reader never knows what event or mood will come next – and involvement in the text becomes, if not greater than it might otherwise have been (Rousseau's anxious manoeuvrings excite yet more responses rather than dampening down those which were already there), at least peculiarly free and unimpeded. The natural instinct to analyse Lawrence's motives – explain his behaviour – is unhindered by any obvious or persistent efforts at self-discovery on the author's part. The Lawrence of the text is not shadowed by another Lawrence who has drawn the lesson from his experiences and may therefore be suspected of making sure that he illustrates it in his account of them. The consequence is a highly distinctive atmosphere of openendedness, and a variety of frank self-exposure not at all Rousseauesque.

To bring in the *Confessions* at this point will seem arbitrary or tendentious, since in them travel writing is at the service of autobiography; whereas in the books by Lawrence that I am discussing autobiographical detail is only a necessary part of his method for describing his travels. But it is a question of contrast, and Rousseau is an appropriate name to mention because he is the founding-father of a modern tradition in the search for self-knowledge of which Lawrence appears to have thought less and less the older he grew. There are at least four reflections on this topic in *Last Poems*, and in the course of one of them Lawrence writes,

> And still through knowledge and will, he can break away
> man can break way, and fall from the hands of God
> into himself alone, down the godless plunge of the abyss,
> a god-lost creature turning upon himself
> in the long, long fall, revolving upon himself
> in the endless writhe of the last, the last self-knowledge
> which he can never reach till he touch the bottom of the abyss
> which he can never touch, for the abyss is bottomless.[14]

If Lawrence can be so confident that the search for self-knowledge is endless − a bottomless abyss − it is because 150 years separate him from Rousseau, and there had been so many exploration parties in the intervening period. Whatever suspicions he had entertained about its fruitlessness may very well have been confirmed, in any case, by those hours of discussion with his Freudian friends. (The Freudian theory of the unconscious makes complete self-analysis a conceptual impossibility.) For an endeavour he suspected more and more, he was inclined to substitute a sophisticated ingenuousness and a determination to protect as far as he could that core of naivety which he felt was essential to manhood.[15] This may help to explain why he should have opted to 're-live' his days in Sardinia so relatively free from analytic hindsight. Whether it does or not − the motives of a writer so determinedly 'instinctive' as Lawrence, and so apparently free from conscious artistic calculation, must always be difficult to define with any certainty − the consequences are highly individual. His own figure is always in the foreground − the converse of the more or less anonymous cicerones in the conventional Guides. But although he expresses his feelings continually, the organization of those expressions is in no way self-consciously cumulative, and any responsibility there might be for deducing from them a coherent idea of what Billy T.

Tracy Jnr calls Lawrence's 'soul' is chiefly left to the reader.

The kinds of reader-involvement which derive from fidelity to a strict chronology of mood are more evident in *Sea and Sardinia* than in Lawrence's other three travel books because in none of those is there an equivalently sustained and concentrated experience of being on the move. *Twilight in Italy* contains episodes from two different periods of Lawrence's time in Europe. Although eventually printed out of order, the first four pieces in *Mornings in Mexico* were initially intended to describe four consecutive days in December 1924; but the following three relate to Lawrence's experiences in the American Southwest some time before.[16] Whereas *Sea and Sardinia* has the unity and momentum consequent on describing in detail an excursion which took only ten days, and which necessarily involved the Lawrences in almost continual movement, the other two books cover many months of their life. The work which is closest to *Sea and Sardinia* in organization is *Etruscan Places*, since all its six chapters relate to visits Lawrence made to Etruscan sites with Earl Brewster between 6 and 11 April 1927. But that book, published posthumously, had been intended by Lawrence as part of a much larger enterprise and, perhaps in consequence, is relatively loose in organization. There are links between the individual visits, but they are more casual and less circumstantial than in *Sea and Sardinia*. What also distinguishes *Etruscan Places* from the earlier work is Lawrence's mood, which is less volatile, largely because his response to Etruscan art is almost uniformly favourable. *Sea and Sardinia* represents a hectic and on the whole unsuccessful search; but in *Etruscan Places* Lawrence gives the impression, not of having himself found a better life, but at least of having seen irrefutable evidence that such a life once existed.

For all these differences, there are moments in *Etruscan Places*, just as there are in the books on Italy and the two Mexicos, when the reader is able to compare one of Lawrence's moods with another and thereby confirm the truth of his dictum that everything (and especially, perhaps, a judgment or opinion) is 'true in its own place, time, circumstance' and likely to be less true when time, place and circumstances change. And in all three, individual sections or chapters frequently exhibit that same strict adherence to chronology, and all the other features which helped to make *Sea and Sardinia* seem so actual to Mabel Luhan. The second chapter of *Mornings in Mexico*, for example, describes a 'Walk to Huayapa' with so artful a succession of well-chosen detail that life in Mexico begins to feel like second nature for the reader. The account is typical in that Huayapa itself proves disappointing: the chief concern of the Lawrences, once they are in the village, being the struggle to find at least one inhabitant from whom they will be able to buy a few of the oranges that appear to grow in abundance in the village gardens. This focus on his battle against local recalcitrance, and on his efforts to rescue a Sunday excursion from complete bathos, allows Lawrence to convey with effective indirection several of the wilder incongruities of a country where Western habits, politics and religion have been superimposed on Indian culture. Whatever one learns about Mexico is incidental to Lawrence's hour-to-hour confrontation with alien habits. As an introduction to the country, this chapter and its three companions are nevertheless worth more than equivalent passages of description in *The Plumed Serpent*, even though most of what is valuable in that novel belongs to travel literature. They are worth more because the reader is enlightened so effortlessly, whereas whatever understanding of Mexico he derives from *The Plumed Serpent* is at the cost of ploughing through a political intrigue which is at best improbable and at its worst highly self-indulgent. Lawrence wrote the first four chapters of *Mornings in Mexico* as a relaxation from the effort of completing *The Plumed Serpent*. They seem to have come very easily to him, like all his 'journalism', and perhaps for that reason have been regarded as necessarily slight (the idea for a volume of 'American' pieces came from a publisher rather than from Lawrence himself).[17] His novel, on the other hand, he laboured over considerably, and at one time thought it 'My most important novel so far'.[18] Long as it is, it now seems to me to weigh less in the scale of literary value than the 180-odd pages in Ross Parmenter's generously-spaced edition of *Mornings in Mexico*. (If one learns nothing else from Lawrence's literary criticism, it is to trust a text rather than the author's own estimation of it.)

A more striking example of an excursion whose chief interest turns out to be incidental to its initial aim is the chapter on Vulci in *Etruscan Places*. The party which eventually found itself in Huayapa had not headed there with any great or specific hopes, but in setting out for Vulci Lawrence and Earl Brewster might reasonably have expected to see something at least vaguely equivalent to the imposing city of the dead at Cerveteri or the painted tombs of Tarquinia. They manage to get to the beautiful Ponte dell'Abbadia in the area where Vulci was once supposed to be, but in the neighbouring tombs there is, to Lawrence's eye at least, very little more than rubble to see. Since their discovery in 1828, the tombs have been so systematically rifled that nothing appears to have been left. Compared therefore with what he and Brewster have already seen, and are next to see in the museum at Volterra, the excursion to Vulci is a non-event. Yet as in the 'Walk to Huayapa', Lawrence is able to make a description of frustration and comparative failure extraordinarily absorbing and informative. The information concerned cannot in the nature of the case bear the same relation to the main theme of *Etruscan Places* as the Huayapa chapter can to *Mornings in Mexico*, because the signs of former Etruscan life in the Vulci region are so vestigial. But through an account of the kinds of struggle any traveller is liable to have with it, contemporary Italian life in the little known or visited Maremma (the marshy coastal plain some hundred kilometres north of Rome) is made vividly present and memorable. Starting out from Montalto di Castro, Lawrence and Brewster have to wait until the baker has finished his deliveries before they can use his horse for the small carriage they have hired. Their driver, Luigi, is the baker's assistant, but as a boy was brought up as a herdsman in the Maremma, and is pleased now to escape back into his own, malaria-infested home ground. He is an excellent guide to the countryside but shy and unenterprising when it comes to finding someone who can show them where the tombs are, or to buying the candles they will need when they visit them. The 'short but strong *maremmano* of about forty' they eventually recruit at Lawrence's insistence proves competent, but accompanying them also into the tombs, uninvited, is 'a little black-eyed fellow on a bicycle'. Together with him, and the *maremmano*'s thirteen-year-old boy, Lawrence's party soon find themselves crawling through gloomy passages opening out into chambers which provide a natural home for bats.

> Sometimes we had to wriggle into the tombs on our bellies, over

the mounds of rubble, going down into holes like rats, while the bats flew blindly in our faces. Once inside, we clambered in the faint darkness over huge pieces of rock and broken stone, from dark chamber to chamber, four or five or even more chambers to a tomb, all cut out of the rock and made to look like houses, with the sloping roof-tilts and the central roof-beam. From these roofs hung clusters of pale brown furry bats, in bunches, like bunches of huge furry hops. One could hardly believe they were alive, till I saw the squat little fellow of the bicycle holding his candle up to one of the bunches, singeing the bats' hair, burning the torpid creatures, so the skinny wings began to flutter, and half-stupified, half-dead bats fell from the clusters of the roof, then groped on the wing and began to fly low, staggering towards the outlet. The dark little fellow took pleasure in burning them. But I stopped him at it, and he was afraid, and left them alone.[19]

All these details, and others like them, conveyed with the directness and economy illustrated here (with the deceptive air, that is, of someone so absorbed by the sequence of events that questions of style become irrelevant), make the disappointing outcome of the trip to Vulci immaterial to the reader. It becomes immaterial to Lawrence also as, on the way back to Montalto di Castro, he warms to his young guide and imagines how − if he could only be convinced that the local inhabitants were right to minimize the threat of malaria (a disease he believed he had almost died of in Mexico) − he would enjoy taking some abandoned house in the area and go hunting with Luigi, 'even out of season, for there was no one to catch you'.

Like a good deal in *Etruscan Places*, this prospect has a dream-like quality. By the time of his excursion with Brewster, Lawrence had lost some of his trust in the likelihood of his own world ever providing a life which he could regard as satisfactory. His expectations had been disappointed so often that he no longer entertained them quite so confidently. Only a few months before his Etruscan tour, he had written in a review of H.M. Tomlinson's *Gifts of Fortune*, 'We travel, perhaps, with a secret and absurd hope of setting forth on the Hesperides, or running our boat up a little creek and landing in the Garden of Eden', and he added, 'This hope is always defeated. There is no Garden of Eden and the Hesperides never were.'[20] Several years previously, in a remarkably acute and economical account of Melville's travel writing, he had said, 'Poor Melville! He was determined Paradise existed. So he was always in Purgatory. He was born for Purgatory. Some souls are purgatorial by destiny.'[21] The form of the last phrase here is equivalent to Lawrence's use of 'we' in the review of Tomlinson. But if he himself was also 'purgatorial by destiny', his experiences taught him to lessen the discomfort by not investing in his schemes for a better life quite the same absolute faith they had had behind them in his youth. To go hunting with Luigi is not a serious proposal for the future, but an idea he is conscious of entertaining for the immediate pleasure it gives him. Paradise, he had learnt, was not to be found in this twentieth-century world, although this did not mean that ways of living had not once existed infinitely preferable to any which he himself had been able to discover, or organize with friends in his numerous schemes for an ideal microcosmic community. That the Hesperides never were was no proof for Lawrence that, before the Western world became dominated by Greek and Christian thought, the Etruscans had not evolved a society in which relations between the sexes were harmonious, the social structure hierarchical without being oppressive, body and spirit undivided, and death the natural complement of life. His belief in such a society and his evocation of it for the reader chiefly depend on a large number of perceptive accounts of Etruscan paintings and artefacts — similar in method to those which allow him to define various forms of Christianity through descriptions of crucifixes in the first chapter of *Twilight in Italy*, or to see behind a number of famous paintings a Cézanne heroically struggling, for the sake of civilization as a whole, to see the object as it really is. Whether or not these accounts of Etruscan art are only useful as a model of how life ought to be, or do in fact approximate to some possible historical reality, is an interesting question to explore, but not one that bears very directly on their value. Because of them *Etruscan Places* seems different from Lawrence's other travel books where the societies being considered still have their living representatives; but although the preponderance of art criticism makes it in one sense the companion of the roughly contemporary 'Introduction to These Paintings', in another, the descriptions of how Lawrence found his way to the various Etruscan sites and whom he met there (the fourth chapter includes a classic account of his encounter with a very young German 'expert') place it firmly with *Twilight in*

Italy, *Sea and Sardinia* and *Mornings in Mexico*. The similarity appears particularly strong of course when one concentrates on the Vulci chapter (to come back to that), since there it turns out that the paintings, or at least artefacts, which Lawrence sets out to see no longer exist.

Lawrence's ability to make his day in the Maremma appear so meaningful was praised by the wife of the man who accompanied him there when she wrote in her memoirs that he had a way of 'transmuting' the dull stuff of life into cloth of gold.[22] It is doubtful whether Lawrence ever found the stuff of life dull. An obviously related but more apposite remark was made by a woman friend from his earlier days. 'It was', Jessie Chambers wrote, 'his power to transmute the common experiences of life into significance that I always felt was Lawrence's greatest gift'.[23] Familiar as these words are, they are not perhaps as obvious or as completely satisfactory as they tend at first to seem. They fail to explain, for instance, quite why the description of Mrs Morel spitting on her iron to test its heat (the illustration of Lawrence's power Jessie Chambers offers) should be significant; and through the notion of transmutation they retain, however faintly, Achsah Brewster's suggestion of the magician's art. But there is no reason to believe that Lawrence's representation of the world is in any necessary contradiction with what it is 'really like'. If the travel books present him as a man who invested his own vitality so completely in every moment, and who was at the same time so unusually receptive to what it had to offer ('creator and receiver both', in Wordsworth's phrase) that no experience could ever be common or insignificant to him, the results argue just as powerfully for our having become unresponsive to surroundings as for his 'transmutation' of them. Whether or not these results are a reflection of Lawrence's own immediate involvement in living (as I think they partly are) makes the difference between whether they are an example of how to live or how to think about life (Mabel Luhan's 're-living'). The issue probably comes down to the insuperable difficulty of deciding in quite what different proportions they are both. Jessie Chambers is one of the many witnesses who could be cited against Mabel Luhan's claim that Lawrence 'couldn't live, with pleasure, in the real moment'; but in her famous remark about significance she is of course con-

fining her attention to literary effect. It used to be a convenient
way of damning Lawrence with faint praise to say that his ability
to produce this effect tailed off after *Sons and Lovers* (or after
Sons and Lovers, Part One). All his succeeding works refute this
charge, but perhaps his travel books do so most obviously and
effectively. It is true that after *Sons and Lovers*, and with the
outbreak of the war, Lawrence became increasingly concerned
with large social, political and religious issues. It is true also that
neither the death of his mother nor his marriage put an end to
his acute personal difficulties. (Criticism in the 1950s so
understated the ambivalence of his sexual nature that it is hardly
surprising to find it receiving undue, reductive and pseudo-
Freudian emphasis in much recent work.) But as the travel
books show, none of these concerns and difficulties prevented
him from continuing to demonstrate an appreciation of those
day-to-day realities which, quantitatively speaking, have the
strongest claim to be called life and were certainly respected by
Lawrence under that name. There is a letter in which he complains that he is alienated from members of his family in ways
they fail to realize and is no longer their Bert.[24] Yet in
November 1928 Lawrence wrote to Jessie's younger brother,
David Chambers, urging him to say if there was anything he
could do for him, 'Because whatever else I am, I am somewhere
still the same Bert who rushed with such joy to the Haggs.'[25]
The Vulci chapter in *Etruscan Places* proves that in his feeling
for the world Lawrence did very much remain the same person
Jessie Chambers's remark recalls. Without that feeling, he might
well have become the immensely gifted but slightly pathetic
'case' of so much of the latest writing about him; or the inspired
seer who, in Rebecca West's influential view, took the material
universe and made allegations about it which 'were only true of
the universe within his own soul'.[26]

5 'My best single piece of writing': 'Introduction to *Memoirs of the Foreign Legion* by M.M.'

T o bring works of art back to life: that is 'the great, the perennial, task of criticism'.[1] Lawrence's 'Introduction to *Memoirs of the Foreign Legion* by M.M.' is certainly worth resuscitating if we go by its author, who 'considered this the best single piece of writing, *as writing*, that he had ever done'.[2] Clearly, too, it has long been dead and buried in itself as a piece of writing, as distinct from its outside context of biographical sources and aftermath of controversy. To win the readers it deserves I propose to remove it entirely from the lurid arena of that 'minor but rancorous spectacle' which has preoccupied the previous, sparse commentary.[3]

Is this a proposal to forget about fact and read the piece as we read fiction? I can best start to answer this by meeting the initial need to introduce the piece to new readers: for I feel obliged to offer two complementary descriptions answering to its dual status. First, in terms of the external world of historical fact, it is the middle one of three texts by three acquaintances. A man called Maurice Magnus wrote a book called 'Dregs', which Lawrence arranged to be published as *Memoirs of the Foreign Legion*. Lawrence, who knew Magnus on and off before the latter's suicide in 1920, wrote his piece in 1922 to be published with Magnus's book by way of an introduction to it – although he writes more about the man than the book. This prompted Norman Douglas to write the third piece, a pamphlet called *A Plea for Better Manners*, which protests that Lawrence had no right to take on the publication of Magnus's book and got Magnus's character all wrong.[4] A long controversy ensued. And it is to this status, in that context, that Lawrence himself appears to consign his piece by claiming that it was 'the exact truth'.[5]

However, the very different terms of Lawrence's other claim with which I started, for the piece '*as writing*', invite us to withdraw it from the outside context and attempt an internal description on more intrinsic criteria. We can draw encouragement for this from the very piece which set the controversy rolling: insofar as it operates as criticism, the main part of Douglas's rejoinder lies not in any *ad hominem* attack on Lawrence's motives, or on his factual accuracy, but precisely in a discussion of the quality of Lawrence's piece 'as writing'.

But as what *kind* of writing? This will be the main matter of the present chapter. Does Lawrence keep good faith with his subject and with the contract he offers the readers?[6] Here Douglas's discussion is useful even though I diverge from his findings. For him the 'Introduction' adopts a bastard form that compromises complete biographical truth: by 'the novelist's touch' which selects colourful but distorting detail; by a format of judicial inquest which licences character-assassination; and by autobiographical intrusions. By meeting these particular charges *en route* I hope to show Lawrence's piece rather as paradigmatic of the way a generically hybrid work may thrive honestly and healthily in an extensive area of overlap between memoir, autobiography and fiction − or at least, some of the forms of narrative we find in fiction.

Accordingly I offer this second description, truer to the feel of the text and more likely to alert the new reader to its pleasures. The narrative concerns two main characters: M, to use the text's own abbreviation, and a first-person participant who shares the author's name but whom we can call L. Their relationship is traced over a year or so, and through four episodes in vividly-described settings: L meets M in Florence; visits him at the monastery of Monte Cassino; half-helps him when M, on the run from the police, visits L in Sicily; and watches his escape to Malta. A letter from an eye-witness gives L the outcome of this episode: M cornered and killing himself. This prompts the narrator to turn over the rights and wrongs of that suicide and to question his own responsibility. In all of this, the reader will find many of those imaginative resources which we are accustomed to enjoy in fiction, here at the service of thought about such matters as religion, friendship, the ethics and touchiness of borrowing and lending, and the way we use or perhaps exploit others to reach or confirm our life-choices.

This is not to pass off the whole piece *as* fiction (say as a novella – it is about that length), as one extreme of current critical theory might invite one to do.[7] That cannot be done: partly because it goes on from where my summary ended to anchor itself to Magnus's book and to a Magnus who existed outside Lawrence's piece; and partly because fiction can play off first-person characters against first-person narrators, and also against the authorial presence, in ways that do not occur here and possibly cannot occur in memoirs. The aim is rather to show how far we get in the piece by approaching it quite straightforwardly, as a form of narrative. Not, however, as a straightforward narrative, for the most striking aspect of this kind of 'writing, as writing' is the extreme intricacy of its patterns and strategies.

My own strategy will be to begin by linking these comments at some length to two sample episodes, chosen because they are the most vividly contrasted: it happens that they are consecutive, and further are the first two. It will then be convenient to discuss other aspects and episodes, especially the encounter in Sicily, in the framework of a direct comparison with Douglas's piece.

I

The opening paragraphs, giving L's arrival in Florence, press on us the kind of circumstantial detail by which a teller of stories, true or tall, seeks to assure us that what follows will be 'the exact truth'. Or, to posit a different context, they lay claims to that clarity and consistency of memory which a cross-questioner seeks to undermine in order to discredit a witness's larger reliability: they field without fumbling such questions as 'Was it daylight, dusk, or dark? Was the Arno swollen or low? Exactly how much money were you carrying?' Already, however, the writing has a further intention, catching up the facts in an imaginative evocation of a dark, wet, wintry evening in a 'strange' Florence 'grim and dark and rather awful'. Strange, that is, in contrast with the remembered Italy of springs and summers and of an era before 'that fatal year 1914'; thus the place and time evoked belong to the speaker's inner life and memory (p. 303).

War, as central to the end of Lawrence's 'Introduction' as it is to Magnus's *Memoirs* on which that end concentrates, forms at the start a strong background. Money – or lack of it – is already, and will everywhere be, foreground. The war has caused the money worries. 'But,' (the reader will hear more of these frequent 'turns' of *but* and *yet*) 'after the desperate weariness of the war, one could not bother' (p. 303). This last sentence of the first paragraph is closely echoed twice in the next few pages, which dramatize that swing of attitudes. To borrow terms from the opening of Lawrence's 'Study of Thomas Hardy', which treated the same subject in the early days of the war, the systole of self-preservation gives way to the diastole of taking no thought for the morrow.

The first half-page or so, then, balances a systole of factuality against a diastole evoking the spirit of time and place and the inner state of one character-narrator, L – a character who in himself experiences a balanced heart-beat of moods. Several changes appear to occur in what follows:

> I had unconsciously seen the two men approaching, D tall and portly, the other man rather short and strutting. They were both buttoned up in their overcoats, and both had rather curly little hats. But D was decidedly shabby and a gentleman, with his wicked red face and tufted eyebrows. The other man was almost smart, all in grey, and he looked at first sight like an actor-manager, common. There was a touch of down-on-his-luck about him too. He looked at me, buttoned up in my old thick overcoat, and with my beard bushy and raggy because of my horror at entering a strange barber's shop, and he greeted me in a rather fastidious voice, and a little patronizingly. I forgot to say I was carrying a small hand-bag. But I realized at once that I ought, in this little grey-sparrow man's eyes – he stuck his front out tubbily, like a bird, and his legs seemed to perch behind him, as a bird's do – I ought to be in a cab. But I wasn't. He eyed me in that shrewd and rather impertinent way of the world of actor-managers: cosmopolitan, knocking shabbily round the world.
>
> He looked like a man of about forty, spruce and youngish in his deportment, very pink-faced, and very clean, very natty, very alert, like a sparrow painted to resemble a tom-tit. He was just the kind of man I had never met: little smart man of the shabby world, very much on the spot, don't you know. (pp. 303–4)

One change is beyond question: a whole-hearted swing to all the novelistic resources of description, seizing on idiosyncrasies of feature, clothing, build and stance ('deportment'). On the face of it, there is another change, the centre of attention moving away from the first person, the balance tilting from the autobiographical to the biographical aspect of memoir. But the description of M (and equally of D) is conveyed as the conditioned response of L, the participating character, and the intricate interest of my quotation and all that follows arises from the complexity of that response.

This complexity consists firstly of a tension between the two impulses summed up in the last sentence of that passage: the urge to master this man, to pin him down, label him as a 'little smart man of the shabby world, very much on the spot, don't you know', is just held at bay in the passage as a whole by the recognition that 'he was just the kind of man I had never met'. If L is − to reach for a phrase from Samuel Johnson − 'in the highest degree curious and attentive' here,[8] his curiosity is a matter of being fascinated and puzzled by this curious phenomenon which, despite the impulse to be knowing, he cannot quite fit into an established human type. In fact it is in terms of birds rather than humans that L gets his bearings; which has the advantage of covering many of M's features with a playfulness that removes any nasty edge from the belittling; it even takes the cutting edge off 'common' if we think of its more neutrally descriptive use in 'common sparrow'. This impression of knowingness and dismissal held in check continues through the Florence pages, not least in the one describing M in his hotel *boudoir*, of which this is the gist: 'He was like a little pontiff in a blue kimono-shaped dressing-gown . . . So he minced about, in demi-toilette . . . A very elegant little prayer-book lay by his bed − and a life of St Benedict. For M was a Roman Catholic convert. All he had was expensive and finicking . . . I wondered over him and his niceties and little pomposities. He was a new bird to me' (p. 307). This is a classic of 'writing, as writing', Douglas concedes: 'I commend this short paragraph to those simpletons who say that friend Lawrence cannot write' (*Experiments*, p. 231). But the readers I hope to win would also be simpletons, would be missing the dynamics of the piece, if they shared Douglas's view that such a passage was an exception of 'pure' description to his rule about Lawrence's prevailing vices of the judge's eye and the novelist's touch. Certainly the 'Introduction' here, as throughout, resists the interpretative short-cuts *effeminate*, *homosexual*, and *mother's boy*: by contrast, my own shorthand *boudoir* pushed too far; it is not L but

D who dismissively uses those formulae (' "fussing about like a woman . . . I *can't stand* these fussy——'' And D went off into improprieties' (p. 308)). On the other hand one little word recurs here (it continues to pop up throughout the 'Introduction') which checks the stream of L's fresh and fluid thought: the word *little*. To put it mildly, the effect is that of James's 'good little Thomas Hardy' writ large. However we balance these two elements, this is an instance of judgment kept at bay rather than in abeyance; so that it differs not in kind but only in degree from the would-be summary that follows it: 'For he wasn't at all just the common person he looked. He was queer and sensitive as a woman with D, and patient and fastidious. And yet he *was* common, his very accent was common, and D despised him' (p. 307). In this dramatization of the struggle to summarize, *for* ushers in the systole of generous qualification, *and yet* the diastole of an impatient urge to slam the case shut. (The metaphor leaves us short of a third term for what follows *and yet*. For – in ways there is no space to develop here – the fact that 'D despised him', even while exploiting his patient and devoted attention, far from speeding the slamming dismissal, opens up in L a field of fellow-feeling for M.)

'And M rather despised me', L goes straight on: which points back to the second kind of complexity in their initial encounter. From the start L suspects M of despising L's own 'style'; so that, beside the tension in L between puzzlement and the desire to master, there is his eagerness to master M before M masters him. This has obvious affinities with the exchange of looks and the 'pre-emptive strike' which David Ellis describes in the railway-platform scene in *Sea and Sardinia* (see above, pp. 99–100). The present scene is like a mirror-picture. L 'see[s] the two men approaching', but to a remarkable extent the narrative concentrates on portraying L detachedly, recording how those other two would see *him* approaching and size him up as an equally odd bird. As L looks at M in particular, the main thing he sees is M looking back at him: 'he looked at me . . . eyed me in that shrewd and rather impertinent way . . .'. The feeling of each character meeting his match is intensified when L sees that, if he thinks M a bit shabby and down-on-his-luck, M is weighing him up as even more so. As indeed, L feels, he is: as he eyes M and follows M's eyes back to himself, he spends much space owning up to his scruffy coat and bag, his beard bushy and raggy, and his not being in a taxi as he ought. The whole Florence episode is full of L's self-consciousness. If he is touchy about his beard, it is like that because of his worse 'horror of entering a strange barber's shop'; at the hotel he is too shy to ring the bell and ask for a better room. ('Not ring it!' rings out D's voice. 'Well you're a man, you are!' (p. 305).) For all this we can apply to L the word *sensitive* which punctuates his appraisal of M, where it veers between the positive sense of 'alert and considerate' and what is implied by another recurring word, *touchy*, which links up with the equally frequent terms *testy* and *irritable*. Dwelling on such mirror effects does not in itself settle the question of the value of reliability of this or similar memoirs: in some instances a hyper-awareness of self and of others' awareness of oneself may appear as the necessary condition of being 'someone on whom nothing is lost'; in others we may diagnose distorting or tunnel or solipsistic vision.[9] But it does bring out that the 'Introduction''s merging of biography and autobiography, which Douglas thinks unwitting, is a deliberate form of intricacy.

Equally deliberate, we have seen, is the flexible relation of the factual and imaginative modes: and with particular success at the very beginning. To enforce this by contrast it is worth ending comment on the first episode with a passage which, apparently at the furthest reaches of dramatized narrative, reaches back nervously for reassurance to the sanctions of fact and so falls between two stools. It comes up with the particular reason why L suspects M despises him – 'because I did not spend money'.

> I had no money to spend, since I knew I must live and my wife must live.
>
> 'Oh,' said M. 'Why, that's the very time to spend money, when you've got none. If you've got none, why try to save it? That's been my philosophy all my life; when you've got no money, you may just as well spend it. If you've got a good deal, that's the time to look after it.' Then he laughed his queer little laugh, rather squeaky. These were his exact words.
>
> 'Precisely,' said D. 'Spend when you've nothing to spend, my boy. Spend *hard* then.'
>
> 'No,' said I. 'If I can help it, I will never let myself be penniless while I live. I mistrust the world too much.'
>
> 'But if you're going to live in fear of the world,' said M, 'what's the good of living at all? Might as well die.'
>
> I think I give his words almost verbatim.   (pp. 307–8)

At first L refrains from any impulse to score, letting himself sound dour and dogged. It hurts to give the witty and attractive lines to others: one thinks in contrast what a warm glow it must have given to write the conversation about money in *Aaron's Rod*, with the cautious (although rich!) Sir William perplexed by but admiring the fine blend of carelessness and courage in Aaron's 'my trust is in the eye of God, and him who passes by.'[10] But then come two false notes. After many pages of uninhibitedly presented dialogue complete with elaborate stage directions, lacking any such protestations of accuracy, why should Lawrence (for we feel it is the author interrupting his reporter-participant) now anxiously reassure us that 'these were his exact words', 'his words almost verbatim'? The reason lies, I suggest, in the particular words of M which those protestations directly follow and seek to validate: 'that's been my philosophy all my life', and 'if you're going to live in fear of the world . . . [you] might as well die.' Lawrence may well have felt that, if taken as essential rather than literal truth, this would be bad art, in that M's character-revelation was all too neatly 'essential' and the writing on the wall for M daubed too crudely and too early.[11] Another way of putting this is that the passage breaks a vital abstinence that controls the 'Introduction' as a whole, which takes each incident as it registers in L without the interference of authorial omniscience, or at least hindsight, about either M's past ('all my life') or his life (and death − you 'might as well die') subsequent to a given episode. This is not to argue the superiority of Lawrence's method over, for example, that of Johnson's *Life of Savage*, the texture of which is hindsight comment and underlinings of the ominous. It is simply that we catch Lawrence here in a moment of inconsistency and in a mode of indicating character which is premature and crude; so that analogies might be the anxious attribution of ultra-typical remarks and actions to the Crawfords the moment they step into *Mansfield Park*, or the Leiversers into *Sons and Lovers*. In this way the self-revelations attributed to M join forces with those touches of epitomizing which are already in danger of closing in on him, one of which occurs in this same passage: 'he laughed *his* queer *little* laugh' (my italics). Such touches, over-repeated, would amount to what Douglas attacked as 'the leitmotif method' of characterization.[12]

I have dwelt on that momentary falter to show that, even when Lawrence reaches back for the sanctions of 'exact truth', it is 'as writing' that we judge the piece and it is probably a perceived weakness in that respect which causes Lawrence so to reach out. The moment also heightens by contrast the way that our pleasure in the whole piece has to do with its strong resistance of an equally strong impulse to jump to a conclusion – to make a short circuit in response to M and take short cuts to judgment.

II

'So the little outsider was gone, and I was rather glad. I don't think he liked me. Yet . . .' (p. 310). These words, at M's departure from Florence, mark a transition between the first two episodes. They epitomize features of the former: the strand of patronizing *leitmotif* counterpoised by the final conjunction, and the frankness about motive (with a tacit *because* between the first and second sentences). In all this the snippet can equally herald the next episode, but should also signal drastic changes. After being glad to be rid of M in Florence, L confessedly went to Monte Cassino to see not M but the monastery. As would-be-monk-to-be and guest with distinguished family connections, M issues the invitation, provides the entrée and poses as guide; but L increasingly looks past M and in so doing claims to see through him. The monastery, which he claims to get 'more inside' than does M, is for L the big experience in terms of which he sees M as decidedly little and really an outsider.

L is in part content to counter M's lyricism at 'the peace, the beauty, the eternity of it' with his own cooler if approving eye: 'one felt one was at college with one's college mates' (pp. 315, 314). However a gentle check issues from the monastery itself, in the reply L registers when M enthuses 'You're going to let me be a monk and be one of you, aren't you, Don Bernardo?'

> 'We will see,' smiled Don Bernardo. 'When you have begun your studies.' (p. 315)

And in the midst of these first-evening preliminaries the gap between L and M opens wide as L, free of M, from his room sees

> outside the net curtain a balcony looking down on the garden, a narrow strip beneath the walls, and beyond, the clustered

> buildings of the farm, and the oak woods and arable fields of the
> hill summit: and beyond again, the gulf where the world's valley
> was, and all the mountains that stand in Italy on the plains as if
> God had just put them down ready made. The sun had already
> sunk, the snow on the mountains was full of a rosy glow, the
> valleys were full of shadow. One heard, far below, the trains
> shunting, the world clinking in the cold air.   (p. 314)

Magnus's casual eye is thus replaced by that Lawrentian mode
of perception which, in a previous chapter, I illustrated from
Twilight in Italy and particularly from 'The Spinner and the
Monks'.

This is the first of three passages in which L's eye travels
beyond M, to the *outside*, the *below* and the *beyond*; passages
so striking that one is not surprised to have found one or other
extracted from context and anthologized to show Lawrence's
feel for 'The Spirit of Place'. But their full force only comes out
when taken in the context of the whole episode. Their position-
ing is almost symmetrical: they come at the start, middle and end
of L's visit, on the evening, morning and afternoon of three consecutive days. They are separated by returns of the focus to M
and to more everyday impressions of the monastery (and of the
monk's impressions of M!); returns which, however, are in turn
punctuated by brief *reprises* in which L looks out, around and
down. But 'symmetry' implies stasis, whereas the three passages
show a progressive increase in length and also in intensity and
complexity. If the narrative is moving to oust M as understanding so little (see p. 325) it is by offering to show L seeing and
feeling more and more.

Lack of space demands that I give only the structure and key
elements of the second passage (pp. 318–9). But those I can
prompt to read this in full will see that its structure and direction
are misrepresented by what previous commentators have offered
as its key sentence:

> And the poignant grip of the past, the grandiose, violent past of
> the Middle Ages, when blood was strong and unquenched and life
> was flamboyant with splendours and horrible miseries, took hold
> of me till I could hardly bear it. (p. 318)[13]

That by itself would verge on purple prose, the only moment
when L approaches M's facile gush. But the focus of the
paragraph as a whole is the present, in which 'the Middle Ages

live on in a sort of agony, like Tithonus', a relic of a past for which L yearned 'and yet [knew] that I was myself, child of the present'; a present, however, seen on the plain below with 'tiny people swarming like flies' and its straight metalled ways leading as it were to time future,[14] which feels even more alien. We are left with an agonizingly dual tug, 'almost a violation to my soul . . . almost a wound' (pp. 318–19).

Midway between this passage and the third comes a brisk moment which in many writers would have been final:

> We looked at the ancient cell away under the monastery, where all the sanctity started. We looked at the big library that belongs to the State, and at the smaller library that belongs still to the abbot. I was tired, cold, and sick among the books and illuminations. I could not bear it any more. I felt I must be outside, in the sun, and see the world below, and the way out.   (p. 320)

This could cut through the dilemma while tying together the intricate strands of thought: L, who has just said 'I was an outsider' compared with M (although 'the monks were rather brief' with M's 'yearning to be admitted'), now wants out; out of the cold, into the world.[15] The judgment, the rejection, comes straight as the metalled ways below. But the piece – dare I say it? – resists such closure. Just as his eyes keep moving out, around and beyond, L's mind swoops and circles, and the episode works itself up into a more intense crisis of torn feelings, pulled equally for and against both the monastery and the world below.

The power of the resulting passage does not come simply from emotional intensity, piling on the agony and vacillation. There is an energy of thought, and an increase in the range of factors to be balanced. Above all it has behind it L and M's last walk (pp. 321–5) with its closer encounter with the peasants whom L from his arrival has constantly noticed out of the corner of his eye and who are the other half of the medieval system. 'The monks keep their peasants humble', L observes, precipitating a comic-painful non-conversation which is a classic representation of the difficulties of working out what you feel in the face of cocksure opposition and, worse, superficial agreement. ('It is terrible to be agreed with, especially by a man like M. All that one says, and means, turns to nothing' (p. 323)). But if L prefers the peasant to M's 'glib talk and more glib thought', the very lack of mental consciousness makes it equally impossible to converse with the old peasant they encounter, who speaks to him 'as a tree might speak'. L thinks of him as 'the hard, fixed tissue of the branch or trunk', a static persistence of a past way of life, and a form of 'living in the present moment' which entails being 'cut off from all past and future'. This helps L see that, to be the live wood and a 'growing tip' of the race, one has to carry forward. The conclusion for himself is that 'one's got to go through with the life down there – get somewhere beyond it. One can't go back'. As for 'up here', the monastery is still live wood, despite its dependence on serfdom and despite its being almost only a shell of meaning. For the meaning it carries forward, L now reaches for a root word: not the mind, as M would have it, not simply the spiritual, the medieval spirit, or the Christian, but as root of these, the *sacred*. This root is at the centre of the culminating paragraph, behind which all those rejections reached on the walk form a shadow-presence:

> We went slowly back. The peaks of those Italian mountains in the sunset, the extinguishing twinkle of the plain away below, as the sun declined and grew yellow; the intensely powerful mediæval spirit lingering on this wild hill summit, all the wonder of the mediæval past; and then the huge mossy stones in the wintry wood, that was once a sacred grove; the ancient path through the wood, that led from temple to temple on the hill summit, before Christ was born; and then the great Cyclopean wall one passes at the bend of the road, built even before the pagan temples; all this overcame me so powerfully this afternoon, that I was almost speechless. That hill-top must have been one of man's intense sacred places for three thousand years. And men die generation after generation, races die, but the new cult finds root in the old sacred place, and the quick spot of earth dies very slowly. Yet at last it too dies. But this quick spot is still not quite dead. The great monastery couchant there, half empty, but also not quite dead. And M and I walking across as the sun set yellow and the cold of the snow came into the air, back home to the monastery! And I feeling as if my heart had once more broken: I don't know why. (pp. 325–6)

Two footnotes will not, I hope, be officious. 'The new cult finds root in the old sacred place': the monastery just manages to continue nurturing fresh growths of the sacred (*root* draws out the root-meaning of *cult*). In the felicitous word *couchant*, the physical shape of monastery on the mountain-top prompts a precisely apt comparison with a medieval heraldic beast, more emblem than reality, lying with head raised, half-dormant and half-alert.

It might sound as if M has been elbowed entirely out of the picture. But the passage also has as under-presence that preceding showdown, the abortive conversation. M has said that '*mental* friendships last for ever', L thinks them 'trash': M goes yellow and cold, terms L now also applies to the sunset. M has his dilemma: as L sees it, he has a 'fear of life' and (despite that defiant remark in Florence) a 'fear of the world' (p. 308), but he is 'too worldly' to be a monk. The dilemma is in this way close to L's in its factors if different in the way M perceives it; hence L feels no contempt, and so the paragraph can end with the delicately balanced apartness-in-closeness of these two sentences:

> And he seemed to walk so close to me, very close. And we had neither of us anything more to say.   (p. 326)

'Straight as judgment'; 'straight as thought' (pp. 320, 325). These similes for the roads and rails of the plain below Monte Cassino may at first appear fleeting and perhaps odd. In view of my analysis, which suggests that many apparently casual words (e.g. *little*, *cold*, *world*) are used very deliberately, those phrases may now well seem to have been dropped in quietly to remind us by contrast of the very mode and strategy of the whole piece. For (to borrow from more explicit passages elsewhere in Lawrence) in its thoughts and judgments the 'Introduction' 'makes curious swoops and circles. It touches the point of pain or interest, then sweeps away again in a cycle . . . yet . . . swoops and stoops again, until at last there is the closing-in, and the clutch of a decision or a resolve'; 'every natural crisis in emotion or passion or understanding comes from this pulsing, frictional to-and-fro, which works up to culmination'.[16]

These swoops and sweeps continue after the potential conclusion I have just been discussing, when L's heart was broken and he and M have no more to say. Most immediately comes the mundane relief of eating spaghetti with fat modern Italians in the steamed-up dining-car taking him away from the monastery; then, on the steamer to Sicily, an exultant renewal of himself and the world, 'like the dawn of our day, the wonder-morning of our epoch' ('the sun rose with a splendour like trumpets every morning, and me rejoicing like a madness in this dawn, day-dawn, life-dawn, the dawn which is Greece, which is me') – and then 'into this lyricism suddenly crept the serpent' in the shape of M, with something to say ('a terrible thing has happened . . . I came straight to you') which turns the Ionian sea black (pp. 328–30). There are to be many such swoops and circles, returns to fellow-feeling and then recoil, before a conclusion to thought about M arrives; which is why what would otherwise be a sum-mary judgment at that conclusion can be offered as what Lawrence calls 'deep, true justice' (p. 359).

III

But now I pull back from Lawrence's conclusion, re-approaching it from an angle that will draw selectively on the later episodes as well as make brief returns to Florence and Monte Cassino. The angle is prompted by comparing that phrase 'deep, true justice' with Lawrence's two claims for the 'Introduction' with which this chapter began. Does 'true' simply mean 'deep'? In Lawrence's second claim for the piece, truth was tied to exactness ('the exact truth'), even to facts. Has precision, even facts, no say in the mat-ter of justice? Is there no independent way of checking Lawrence's account?

One could doubtless bustle around researching. Magnus's let-ters to Lawrence may be somewhere; and what about that suitcase of his papers which (Douglas says) was confiscated in Malta, not to mention the ones left in the monastery? Or could one trace through other witnesses the 'facts' about Magnus which Lawrence said darkly were much worse than he'd revealed?

Facts in themselves, however, have played remarkably little part in the actual controversy. Douglas claimed he had proof (an official statement of debts) that Magnus borrowed £55 in Malta, not £100 as Lawrence alleged (*Experiments*, pp. 242–3). Lawrence claimed to quote a letter from Douglas giving him a free hand in publishing the *Memoirs* and telling him to '*pocket all the cash*'.[17] This kind of stuff is both tangential and unproven (appealing to documents not available for checking). And beyond these, virtually no facts were even alleged that can be disentangled from interpretation. To take one trivial point which has nonetheless much exercised commentators: Lawrence's suggestion that Douglas's meanness was indicated by his getting the cost of undrunk wine taken off his restaurant bill. *A Plea for Better Manners* leads off by retorting that it just shows Lawrence's ignorance of the facts of accepted Italian practice (*Experiments*, pp. 223–4). But here Douglas is less concerned with facts than with his main theme (and the subsidiary one about literary bad manners): 'friend Lawrence's idiosyncrasies in the matter of portraiture', his distortingly selective *leitmotif* method, what in a later passage (which is one of many) he links to

> a failure to realise the profundities and complexities of the ordinary human mind; it selects for literary purposes two or three facets . . . and disregards all the others . . . The facts may be correct so far as they go, but there are too few of them; what the author says may be true, and yet by no means the truth. That is the novelist's touch. It falsifies life. (*Experiments*, p. 246)

Thus 'facts' give way to 'facets', fullness and depth ('profundities and complexities') as the basis of the critique. Furthermore the *Plea* gives added encouragement to the way I have approached the 'Introduction' in the preceding parts of this chapter, in that it offers itself principally not as discursive critical prose but as a rival 'piece of writing' in a similarly hybrid form, challenging comparison with Lawrence's and aiming to supplant it. Although it adopts a framework of general points, rather than Lawrence's overall narrative form, its positive work is done by the sequence of vignettes thus framed, the fully dramatized anecdotes. True, it appeals to a Magnus who existed outside his or Lawrence's portrait, but only by out-writing Lawrence does Douglas feel he can represent that Magnus more fully and fairly.

The little matter of the rebate on undrunk wine also illustrates the slipperiness of facts if we see how later commentators reacted to Douglas's defence. 'Well yes', rejoined Aldington, 'if there is a litre or more remaining, but if there is less you leave it as part of the waiter's tip, the over-worked waiter whom Lawrence shows Norman treating so "callously" and the servitor was collapsing with fatigue and malaria!'[18] But the situation is circular in that, in order to confirm Lawrence, the second point depends upon him ('. . . Lawrence shows Norman . . .'). And when Aldington draws on his independent impressions of

Douglas as selfish, greedy, mean and envious, this is still 'his Douglas' which merely coincides with Lawrence's without thereby proving it correct. In any case Aldington's Douglas, or rather his Lawrence, changed sharply when he introduced volume three of Nehls's *Composite Biography*. So that instead of using Aldington as an independent check on Lawrence and Douglas, we are thrown back on the question, which of his accounts is more convincing?

An answer would, I think, take the form of the observation that his earlier account is fuller, with the kind of fullness that gains our confidence because it consists largely of anticipating and dealing with many points in the later account. Now it is remarkable how far consideration of this kind of advantage will also take us in comparing Lawrence's and Douglas's pieces.

First, Douglas on himself. He complains that Lawrence seizes on the obvious *leitmotif* of 'blustering railer of the old school' with 'wicked red face' and 'bluff, grandiose manner' (*Experiments*, pp. 247, 223). Yet he himself plays this *leitmotif* throughout. He adopts a genially booming *de haut en bas* towards 'my young friend Lawrence' and a swashbuckling manner towards lesser breeds:

> Duelling would soon put an end to these caddish arts . . . there would be no more low-class allusions to living people in novels or newspapers or memoirs if their authors realised that by next morning they might have half a yard of cold steel in their gizzards. (*Experiments*, p. 259)

Differing from Lawrence's self-portrait in degree of subtlety, Douglas's nonetheless manages to be inconsistent, particularly in veering between righteous indignation and swaggering hints of wickedness. He wants to make Magnus an injured innocent but 'like all persons of sound health, not inaccessible to coarser impulses at times. And thank God for that; else . . . I should soon have dropped his acquaintance' (*Experiments*, p. 236).

As for whether Douglas exploited that acquaintance: such a character as Lawrence makes me, goes on Douglas, could never 'feel anything but contempt for an "effeminate little bounder" as Magnus is described' (*Experiments*, p. 247). Quite apart from the fact that I have shown earlier that the phrase does not

represent Lawrence's entire view of M, the *Plea* goes far to confirm Lawrence's view of D's attitude.

> I had prodigious fun with him. He used to bring breakfast to my
> bedside at a reasonable hour — say, 7.30 — on a wonderful little
> tray, and then look round despondingly and remark:
>   "Rather a mess in here. I'd like to tidy the room a bit."
>
> (*Experiments*, p. 234)

The ensuing scene, with Magnus bustling and Douglas grumbl-
ing, although more longwinded and monotonous, echoes those
in the 'Introduction' with M supervising the cooking or organizing D's appointments. 'So it always was', says Lawrence; 'M in-
dulged D, and spoilt him in every way. And of course D wasn't
grateful' (p. 305). 'There was nothing he would not do for me,'
confirms Douglas, 'he seemed to delight in anticipating my
smallest wishes' (*Experiments*, p. 230). Whether ungrateful or
not, he is unashamed: 'I think it creditable to myself. Lucky the
man, I say, who can inspire such a deep and lasting affection'
(*Experiments*, p. 230). But this doesn't dispose of Lawrence's
claim that M resented, even while he masochistically permitted,
being used. And Douglas's bighearted gratitude does not go well
with a later comment, that Magnus was 'one of those people
who are never happy, never quite happy, unless they are obliging
others — for which, of course, they get the devil's thanks'
(*Experiments*, p. 249). Who was the devil in Florence? Douglas
also calls Magnus *fussy* (the very word Lawrence attributed to
D), 'finicky and fussy', 'far too fastidious' and 'fastidious to a
degree' (*Experiments*, pp. 236, 233): it is to enforce this *leitmotif*
that he recommends Lawrence's own description of M 'in
matutinal garb'.

Lawrence claims that, at Florence at least, D and not M was
the sponger, and his recurring qualifications include: 'one could
never dismiss him [M] just as a scoundrel' (p. 342). This under-
mines in advance Douglas's case that 'Lawrence had made up
his mind that Maurice was to be classed as a sponger' and had
therefore wiped out all conflicting evidence (*Experiments*, p.
252). What counter-evidence does Douglas himself give?

Douglas has a story of Magnus noticing an old man in a bar,
waiting for hours till he left, following him, giving him money
and walking away before the man could refuse or thank him
(*Experiments*, pp. 250–1. This is Douglas's one telling story

because it records Magnus's *manner* of giving on that occasion, and the manner counts more than would the number-count, which Douglas would like heaven to record, of Magnus's spongings offset by his givings. But does Douglas have a real dispute with Lawrence over this? In the lines immediately following those Douglas quotes in order to argue that Lawrence's Magnus was nothing but a mean sponger, Lawrence agrees — 'Not that he was mean, while he was about it. No, he would give very freely' — but goes on to describe a habitual manner of giving which harmonizes with Magnus's frequent manner of taking:

> he would give very freely: even a little ostentatiously, always feeling that he was being a *liberal gentleman.* Ach, the liberality and gentility he prided himself on! *Ecco!* And he gave a large tip, with a little winsome smile. But in his heart of hearts it was always himself he was thinking of, while he did it. (p. 357)

This partly draws on something Lawrence noticed in Valetta:

> The waiter, a good-looking Maltese fellow, appeared with two syphons. M was very much the signore with him, and at the same time very familiar: as I should imagine a rich Roman of the merchant class might have been with a pet slave. (p. 348)

The particular case of sponging from which Douglas says Lawrence generalizes wildly, is really Magnus borrowing from Lawrence himself; this, Douglas suspects, is what produces the anger of 'the novelist-creditor' on behalf of the Maltese creditor, Mazzaiba. This is Douglas's nearest hit and he knows it, saving it for the end of the piece. But if, towards the end of *his* piece, Lawrence does fly off from particulars to generals and also wish his own feelings on Mazzaiba, what angers him is not swindling people in their pockets but swindling them in their feelings.

> The worst thing I have against him, is that he abused the confidence, the kindness, and the generosity of unsuspecting people like Mazzaiba. He did not *want* to, perhaps, But he did it. And he leaves Mazzaiba swindled, distressed, confused, and feeling sold in the best part of himself. What next? What is one to feel towards one's strangers, after having known M? (p. 354)

He gives (p. 349) a first-hand description of M arousing esteem and affection in several Maltese which Douglas, not knowing them, can't counter. That Mazzaiba paid for the body to be moved from the public grave to the Mazzaiba family grave, doesn't, as Douglas thinks, refute the idea of his feeling 'sold', but does confirm, as in advance Lawrence points out, that Mazzaiba's affection had been aroused.

But, says Douglas, it was Magnus whose affection was aroused, and by the more generous of those people he turned to for help. The first of what I have called the vignettes in the *Plea* dramatizes Douglas's first encounter with Magnus (the second, which immediately follows, shows Magnus later fulfilling his promise that 'I will never forget your kindness'):

> 'My dear Sir', I said, 'you have just come to the right person for a loan. And who is the damned idiot that recommended you to apply to me?' . . .
>   'I wish the devil I didn't look so kind. Anyhow, you won't get me to lend you money; I never do. It makes enemies.'
>   'Dear, dear – '
>   'But I have been known to give, on occasion. Let me see – ' pulling out my pocketbook grumblingly and counting up all I could spare – 'would thirty-seven francs meet the case?' . . .
>
> (*Experiments*, pp. 228–9)

This is certainly the touch of which some novels are made, although – as Henry James once murmured in response to a blanket distrust of fiction equivalent to that which Douglas inconsistently professes a page or two further on – there are good novels and bad novels.[19] As biography-cum-autobiography the episode is offered as illustrating the borrower, but if this were a novel we would complain that he gets scant 'realization': it shows little curiosity about his feelings and pushes to centre-stage a naively self-congratulatory performance by the giver, who gets the best lines under a thin veneer of grumpy reluctance – 'What a fool I am to be so kind-looking and soft-hearted'. It is one distinction of Lawrence's piece that he explores all the tactics of giving as well as of taking, and in this respect as in others his self-portrait is self-scrutiny. A brief instance is the exchange of letters between the meetings at Florence and Monte Cassino. When L senses in M's first letter a curious appeal, an unspoken trouble, he sends money, but does so 'partly out of revenge' as 'he despised me a little for being careful'. M's third letter appeals more openly and 'rather cockily, as if he had a right to it. And that made me not want to give him any'; that and the carefulness for which M despised him ('besides, as my wife said, what right had I to give away the little money we had . . .') (pp. 311–12). The same fluctuation of response and frank impurity of motives are central to the Sicily episode when M throws himself on L's money. That episode deserves the space of a separate section.

I V

Rather than analysing the episode sequentially and thoroughly, however, let me identify the elements which it brings into balance; or, if you like, its related lines of force.

First and foremost, it is no part of the narrative to offer L as Mr Clean. What gets prominence is a frank admission of what one really feels in a situation like this, and not an attempt to justify reactions morally. So the instinctive reaction is that 'I detest terrible things, and the people to whom they happen' (p. 329), and 'first thing I knew was that I could not have him in the house with me' (p. 331). Later, he looks away at the Ionian sea and 'felt M then an intolerable weight and like a clot of dirt over everything' (p. 337) – especially shocking and brutal as M has just accepted quietly L's refusal to retrieve his compromising papers from the monastery. Equally, the narrative nowhere plays down M's plight, panic and part-claim on L as a fellow human being and acquaintance, if not a friend. Another of L's flinchings away to the Ionian sea is prompted by this:

> 'I came here,' he said, 'thinking you would help me. What am I to do, if you won't? I shouldn't have come to Taormina at all, save for you. Don't be unkind to me—don't speak so coldly to me——' He put his hand on my arm, and looked up at me with tears swimming in his eyes. Then he turned aside his face, overcome with tears. I looked away at the Ionian Sea, feeling my blood turn to ice and the sea go black. I loathe scenes such as this.
> (p. 334)

L, despite himself, feels the plight and acknowledges the claim, so that two characteristically complicated summaries are:

> I spent a week avoiding him, wondering what on earth the poor devil was doing, and yet *determined* that he should not be a parasite on me. (p. 338)

and:

> And I with my bowels full of bitterness, loathing the thought of that journey [to Monte Cassino] there and back, on such an errand. Yet not quite sure that I ought to refuse. And he pleaded

> and struggled, and tried to bully me with tears and entreaty and
> reproach, to do his will. And I couldn't quite refuse. But neither
> could I agree.   (p. 336)

But this last quotation makes me look back at my claim that
M's plight is nowhere played down and add 'Well, hardly ever'.
It also suggests why I cannot quite maintain *tout court* that the
episode inspects impartially both would-be asker and won't-be
giver, and eschews any moral frame of reference to vindicate the
instinctive reactions of the latter. For although the quotation
offers itself as sheer brute opposition of *ought* and *won't*, with
the *won't* winning ('I decided in the day I would *not* go. Without
reasoning it out, I knew I *really* didn't want to go. I plainly
didn't want it. So I wouldn't go' (p. 336)) there is a blur in the
middle which smuggles in 'moral' reasons for refusing. These
insinuated reasons are M's emotional bullying, and perhaps an
element of facile or contrived intensity implied in 'tears and
entreaty and reproach'. And these hints are amply if intermittently reinforced throughout the episode. The reinforcement
comes partly in distancing, diagnostic generalizations about
'your modern rogue', 'these modern parasites' and 'the modern
creed' (pp. 338, 342, 333), and in particular this on the 'terrible
insolence of the humble. It is the humble, the wistful, the would-
be-loving souls today who bully us with their charity-demanding
insolence' (p. 336). It comes also in the recurrence of *leitmotifs*:
the tears welling up, and two of M's little habits. At first, when
saying Don Bernardo didn't know everything, he 'laughed a
little, comical laugh over the *everything* as if he was just a little
bit naughtily proud of it: most ruefully also' (pp. 329–30). That
is still L curious about the curious, but a few lines later it is simply called 'his little jerky laugh' and, a few lines later, 'his little
laugh', as if it is a music-hall hall-mark or catch-phrase. It
becomes as frequent as M's other habit, his *sweating blood*;
which phrase achieves a crescendo of three appearances on one
page (p. 344).

I cannot suggest that all this is part of a disinterested portrayal
of how, in the typical case of L, we selfishly seek to detach and
distance ourselves from people who press on us with demands
and even with real obligations. We have rather the kind of
authorial *ex cathedra* and anticipation of the final judgment
which I noted at one moment in the Florence episode. Where by

contrast one can find here that purity of relation between narrator and L which prevails in nearly all of the Florence episode, is in the uninterrupted stretches of dialogue, and in the visual element, which together provide what we are told was missing in the draft of the *Memoirs of the Foreign Legion*: 'sharp detail and definite event' (p. 321).

For *visual* read *spatial*, often territorial space and manœuvre. If a chapter of *Women in Love* is called 'Gladiatorial', this episode could be entitled 'Territorial'. I mean this not simply in the general sense of being crowded by obligation, compromised by M using L's address, or the pervasive sense of M 'looming in the village, waiting' (p. 337). The episode is a small drama, in the sense that anyone adapting it for the stage would seize on the conversations and also on L's house, which M eyes and appraises with a view to estimating the size of the guest wing, on the outside stairs of which L looks down on him and bars his way. 'My wife' then holds the steps which L goes up in order to change so that they can escort M safely away from the house and back to the village. On his next visit 'my wife would not see him' (p. 332) so L meets him on the fairly neutral territory of the terrace; but a further − or rather, nearer − touch of personal space-invasion is M's hand on L's arm (p. 334). He then calls while L is out and

> my wife found him on the stairs. She was for hating him, of course. So she stood immovable on the top stairs, and he stood two stairs lower, and he kissed her hand in utter humility. And he pleaded with her, and as he looked up to her on the stairs the tears ran down his face and he trembled with distress.   (p. 334)

Theoretically, this last passage is one effective way of filling out the study of asking and giving by comparing L's reactions to those of others. M's 'utter humility' gains power over L's wife by giving her a sense of power over *him*:

> And her spine crept up and down with distaste and discomfort. But he broke into a few phrases of touching German, and I know he broke down her reserve and she promised him all he wanted. This part she would never confess, though. Only she was shivering with revulsion and excitement and even a sense of power, when I came home. (p. 334)

In practice this is somewhat contaminated by the kind of authorial irony I detected earlier. The work of comparison comes in more effectively when M's unpaid landlord, Pancrazio Melenga, calls on L. Territory enters again with L caught in his pyjamas and old straw hat by this Sicilian, 'handsome, in the prime of life, and in his best black suit, smiling at me and taking off his hat!' (p. 338) This is a case of courtesies entirely ruled by questions of cash: Melenga smiles amid the cushions until he finds M is broke. 'Then Pancrazio exploded on the sofa.' When he calls M a *mezzo-signore*, L feels implicated and vulnerable but also thereby almost roused to M's defence. For the insult 'was so true. At the same time it was so cruel, and so rude.' And Melenga – 'there I sat in my pyjamas and sandals – probably he would be calling me also a mezzo-signore, or a quarto-signore even' (pp. 340–1). So that when cash seems after all in the offing and Melenga restores M's status as a *bravo signore* who is welcome to stay on, L replies 'I'm afraid he is offended', almost taking M's part.

The contrast heightens the fluctuations in L's feelings. In encounters with M that follow (on the boat to Malta and during L's short stay there) the tone is comic as well as detached – because L is as relieved as M at the escape. This is swept away by news of the suicide: 'now I *realized* what it must have meant to be the hunted, desperate man: everything seemed to stand still'. And finally, 'after a year has gone by, I keep to my choice. I still would not save his life' (p. 354). Whatever we think of the reasons for this last resolve, there is no doubt about the deepest disturbance and self-scrutiny caused by M's death as well as his life. Nothing equivalent is reflected in Douglas who, getting Magnus's final letter describing his desperation, wrings his hands with the comment, 'Surely a pathetic state of affairs!' (*Experiments*, p. 241)[20]

V

Having recalled Douglas, we can now ask: what, according to the *Plea*, were those complexities in Magnus's character which the 'Introduction' missed?

They cannot be to do with his religion, central to Lawrence's Monte Cassino episode, for Douglas professes genial scorn for it:

> Sometimes, again, he interrupted his work in order to attend early Mass, since he felt utterly wretched without such periodical

doses of anthropomorphism. Then he would return home, beaming all over, and say:

'I prayed ten minutes for your happiness just now.'

'Very thoughtful of you, my dear boy. Though I can't say I feel any the better for it.'

'You will, you will.'

Possibly. But I always prefer to take these things in ready cash. Then you know where you are.'

'You can't imagine how it hurts me, when you talk like that.'

(*Experiments*, pp. 232–3)

Douglas sees Magnus's conversion to Catholicism as one of the 'sundry dichotomies of his nature' caused by his being 'an only son, brought up by an adoring mother and almost continually in her company to the day of her death . . . – that is, up to his own *thirty-sixth* year . . . her death was the tragedy of his life' (*Experiments*, p. 235). But this is an explanation of character, not a complication of it. And far from going beyond Lawrence, the paragraph which I have just quoted appears to be borrowed from Lawrence himself. Douglas blames Magnus's 'refinements', 'reckless expenditure' and psychological 'twists' on his being the only son of a doting and adored mother, and on his consciousness of having royal blood (his mother being the illegitimate daughter of a German Kaiser): Lawrence says that 'part of his failings one can *certainly* ascribe to the fact that he was an only son . . . in whose veins the mother imagined only royal blood' (p. 360).

The mother's-lover explanation is always in danger of overuse. It has been pressed too hard, and with a reductive rather than a complicating effect, in dozens of biographies including those of Lawrence and Douglas themselves. (On the latter Aldington argues, as Douglas does with Magnus, that his brusque manner covered and protected an oversensitive nature which, together with his extravagances and sexual 'twist' – in his case, young boys – came from being brought up exclusively by women.)[21] Here again the main difference of the 'Introduction' lies in the degree to which it works by 'sharp detail and definite event'. That L does not get close to M or talk far with him is central to the moment when he glimpses M's deep feelings; when

he showed me a wonderful photograph of a picture of a lovely lady—asked me what I thought of it, and seemed to expect me to be struck to bits by the beauty. His almost sanctimonious

expectation made me tell the truth, that I thought it just a bit cheap, trivial. And then he said, dramatic:
'That's my mother.'
It looked so unlike anybody's mother, much less M's, that I was startled. I realized that she was his great stunt, and that I had put my foot in it. So I just held my tongue. Then I said, for I felt he was going to be silent forever:
'There are so few portraits, unless by the really great artist, that aren't a bit cheap. She must have been a beautiful woman.'
'Yes, she *was*,' he said curtly. And we dropped the subject.
(pp. 317–18)

The picture does stand for a deep feeling but is, like the way M produces it, a little cheaply theatrical. Yet it *is* a real feeling and L's innocent insult does hurt; yet again, though he sees he has hurt M, L sees no way of making amends or talking further about it. No such definite event and complexity of reaction appears in the *Plea*. Douglas borrows Lawrence's phrase 'his great stunt'. What he calls his 'regrettable incuriosity' about Magnus's pedigree seems to have stiffened into distaste about the mother: 'he began to talk about her once or twice, but his voice at once took on such tremulously tender accents that I lost no time in changing the conversation' (*Experiments*, p. 235).

It continues to be no part of my intention to imply any moral comparison of Lawrence and Douglas as friends of Magnus. I think my foregoing quotation is yet another instance of Douglas's attempt to portray Magnus being thwarted by the impulse to ink in heavily a simple self-caricature. Whatever the cause, it gives no support of definite event for the attempt, a few lines later, to report Magnus's prevailing sadness, so that the pity sounds empty and pious. As for pity and praise in the *Plea*:

Poor M.M. 'What (he) aspired to be, and was not, comforts me'. For him 'the high' indeed 'proved too high'; 'the heroic for earth too hard', but these he was 'worth to God', and to his sorrowing, remembering, understanding friends, one of whom I am proud to subscribe myself. (*Experiments*, pp. 245–6)

This is cheating slightly as it is not Douglas but an ally of his, one Irene M. Ashby Macfadyen, a lady unknown to Douglas (and myself). Her letter to the *Spectator*, protesting at Lawrence's 'Introduction', came to hand as Douglas wrote the *Plea*, and he quotes it in full. I cheat only slightly, because Douglas brings her in as a worthy counter to Lawrence in the interests of humanity and truth, and because she contributes an extreme but extremely clear example for my general question: what serves the interests of truth and humanity, what do these qualities look like, in biography? Mrs Macfadyen contributes less subtly what Douglas does: evasive general praise and, more than praise, pity and 'understanding' forgiveness. Douglas follows her letter with that attack on 'the novelist's touch'. What is Mrs Macfadyen's touch? – The postmortem kiss of death. It is terrible to be agreed with, understood and forgiven, especially by people like Mrs Macfadyen. We are confronted by the fact that there can't be any humanity in a biography if it doesn't first have truth in the form of attentive detail, frankness and impartial justice. To face another of Lawrence's inescapable brute choices: if I had to be remembered by Mrs Macfadyen's pious forgiveness and Douglas's sweeping generosity, or by Lawrence's justice (even in an introduction to my own posthumous book!), I would, as Lawrence argues one would, choose the latter. His argument to that effect gains part of its persuasiveness by again answering Douglas and Mrs Macfadyen in advance:

> Even the dead ask only for *justice*: not praise or exoneration. Who dares humiliate the dead with excuses for their living? I hope I may do M justice . . . Forgiveness gives the whimpering dead no rest. Only deep, true justice. (p. 359)

We have every reason to be concerned only with truth and justice for the M internal to the piece. For who now cares about Magnus himself, never mind reads him? Fifty years ago, with the grave still unquiet, Catherine Carswell had a more delicate task in praising the piece. Yet she gives us our cue by saying that 'the man whom Douglas defends . . . does not command the outside reader's sympathy in anything like the same degree as does the man whom Lawrence condemns'.[22] There never was some reliable access to an actual Magnus: we can only compare the man in Lawrence's piece and the other man in Douglas's. And she ends by suggesting that the quality of Lawrence's justice depends on the quality of his writing: 'the Lawrence production will stand as a creative, and the Douglas one as a pious effort'.[23]

6 Verse or worse: the place of 'pansies' in Lawrence's poetry

In his 'Introduction to These Paintings', Lawrence attacks Roger Fry for giving support to the view then current that Cézanne couldn't draw, that – as he cites Fry as putting it – 'With all his rare endowments, he happened to lack the comparatively common gift of illustration, the gift that any draughtsman for the illustrated papers learns in a school of commercial art'. It was not at all, Lawrence retorts, because Cézanne was incapable of drawing well that he failed in his early pictures, but because of a discrepancy between his '*notion* of what he wanted to produce, and his other, intuitive knowledge of what he *could produce*'.[1]

Very often, the claim that the original artist could have done the conventional thing had he wanted to is irrelevant, or a sop to conventional opinion. It is often irrelevant because, as Lawrence partly implies, the artist in question usually *can't want*: is too distracted by his originality to spend the requisite time perfecting traditional skills. But in any case, the power and interest of what he does produce will make futile the hypothetical question of what he might have achieved in a more familiar manner.

These points are worth making because of their bearing on Lawrence's own career as a poet. His first two volumes – *Love Poems and Others* (1913) and *Amores* (1916) – show a surprising degree of metrical ambition and, more than anything else, are a reminder of the Lawrence who, for a party piece at Garsington, was fond of reciting Swinburne. Reviewers of them tended to suggest that there was a discrepancy between the poems' subject-matter, or the temperament of their author, and the complicated stanza forms in which he chose to write. One could take up this hint and ask whether, by continuing to work hard at the more 'technical' aspects of his verse, Lawrence could eventually have become, if not a virtuoso like Swinburne, then at least an important figure within the bounds of traditional

146

forms; or whether his decision in his third volume – *Look! We Have Come Through!* (1917) – to commit himself to free verse was no more than his way of making a virtue of necessity. Yet since it is only after this decision that Lawrence really begins to matter as a poet, the question has about as much relevance as whether or not Cézanne could draw properly.

In a review of the edition in two volumes of Lawrence's *Collected Poems* published in the *Observer* in October 1928, J. C. Squire noted how typical it was of their author that the second volume should be entitled 'Unrhyming Poems' and nevertheless contain a considerable number of poems in rhyme.[2] Certainly, nothing in Lawrence's career as a poet is straightforward. Not all of the poems in *Look! We Have Come Through!* are in free verse, for example, and although Lawrence's famous rationale for its adoption appeared as the preface to the American edition of his next volume (*New Poems*), it is very much out of place there when the poems it precedes were in general not new but old: examples of Lawrence's early manner (they include 'Piano'). After characterizing all poetry before Whitman as concerned with either the past or the future and incapable of rendering 'the instant, the immediate self', Lawrence ends his preface by saying that it should have appeared with *Look! We Have Come Through!*.[3] Yet the very high claims he makes for free verse in it mean that it would have been a more appropriate forerunner to *Birds, Beasts and Flowers* (1923) since it is only in that volume that they are fully justified.

Commentators on Lawrence have always been inclined to assume that the *New Poems* preface was, in part at least, a response to the review of *Look! We Have Come Through!* by Conrad Aiken which appeared in an August number of the *Dial* in 1919. At first sight this appears unlikely, since the *Dial* was a New York periodical and we now know that August 1919 was also the date for the composition of the preface (a letter to Thomas Moult in volume 3 of the Cambridge *Letters* suggests that Lawrence must have finished it by 29 August 1919).[4] But the *Dial* was a fortnightly publication, the number in which the review appears is dated 9 August 1919 and the postal service across the Atlantic was scarcely less quick in Lawrence's time than it is in ours.

Aiken's concern in his review is less with *Look! We Have*

Come Through! than with the whole issue of free verse. He cites
as the members of a new school of free-verse writing John Gould
Fletcher, H.D. and Richard Aldington; and he indicates their
lineage by suggesting that the place to look for the most 'complete lack of musical unity or integration' in poetry is in 'the vast
majority of Whitman's poems'. For Aiken, poetry is not poetry
unless it appeals to 'our sense of the musically beautiful'. The
title of his review is 'The Melodic Line' — a phrase repeated in
it several times.[5] The same phrase occurs in Lawrence's preface
when, after a lyrical defence of free verse as the 'poetry of the
sheer present' and of Whitman as its best exponent, he writes,
'It is no use inventing fancy laws for free verse, no use drawing
a melodic line which all the feet must toe. Free verse toes no
melodic line, no matter what drill-sergeant.'[6]

All the surrounding circumstances make it likely that
Lawrence is here referring directly to Aiken; and this link between his preface and the review makes it reasonable to point out
others which, in a different context, it would be best to attribute
to coincidence. As his illustration of 'perfect musical unity', for
example, Aiken cites Keats's 'Ode to a Nightingale'. Although
he never mentions it by its title, it is absolutely clear that with
its 'perfect symmetry, the rhythm which returns upon itself like
a dance where the hands link and loosen and link for the
supreme moment of the end', Keats's poem represents for
Lawrence an encapsulation of 'perfected bygone moments' just
as — much less obviously, as far as his readers are concerned —
Shelley's 'To a Skylark' encapsulates 'perfected moments in the
glimmering futurity'. These two 'treasured gem-like lyrics of
Shelley and Keats' provide Lawrence with his points of reference
as he argues that perfect form in verse can only be associated
with the past or future. Forgetting that in the 'Ode to a
Nightingale' Keats is only '*half* in love with easeful Death',
Lawrence detects in its beauty, its 'exquisite finality', the in-
sidious appeal of nostalgia. To immortalize perfect moments in
the past or, presumably, perfect imagined moments in the
future, may leave one with 'crystalline, pearl-hard jewels, the
poems of the eternities' but it is a distraction from living in 'the
moment, the immediate present, the Now' and 'the seething
poetry of the incarnate Now is supreme, beyond even the
everlasting gems of the before and after'.[7]

Lawrence's impassioned evocation of the immediate present suggests another possible link with the Aiken review which begins, 'It has been said that all arts are constantly attempting, within their respective spheres, to attain something of the quality of music . . .'. Lawrence would have known as well as anyone who it was that claimed, 'All art constantly aspires towards the condition of music', but he sets against the Pater of that famous remark the equally well-known celebrator of the moment: the writer who, in the 'Conclusion' to *The Renaissance*, described physical life as, 'but a combination of natural elements to which science gives their names'; claimed that, 'This at least of flame-like our life has, that it is but the concurrence, renewed from moment to moment, of forces parting sooner or later on their ways'; and asked, 'How shall we pass most swiftly from point to point, and be present always at the focus where the greatest number of vital forces unite in their purest energy?'[8] With its implied appeal to science for confirmation that, 'The perfect rose is only a running flame, emerging and flowing off, and never in any sense at rest, static, finished', and for all the inevitable differences of emphasis, the first part of Lawrence's preface especially is, in both subject and manner, an updating of Pater's 'Conclusion', the great difference being that its concern is not only with appreciation of the momentaneity of life, but also its expression in free verse. Of course, the elusiveness and value of what T. S. Eliot called the 'intersection time' between past and present is a preoccupation of several important writers in the first decades of this century and very many influences, in addition to Pater's, help to explain its popularity (in the case of Virginia Woolf, for example, that of Bergson). When he was reading Burnet's *Early Greek Philosophy* in 1915, Lawrence himself told Russell that he would 'write out Herakleitos, on tablets of bronze'.[9] Yet it is reasonably certain that, well before this date, he would have known at least the fragment from Heraclitus which, in *The Renaissance*, Pater uses as the epigraph to his 'Conclusion' and which he translates as, 'All things give way; nothing remaineth'. Lawrence's aesthetic of 'the Now' is a characteristically individual and distinctive version of ideas which were current in his time. If the form they take in the *New Poems* preface is nevertheless reminiscent of Pater, and more reminiscent of him than of anyone else, it may well be because Lawrence had been reminded of *The Renaissance* by the opening of Aiken's review.

When 'the seething poetry of the incarnate Now is supreme' and necessarily associated with free verse, then Whitman's importance is inevitable since, like Aiken, Lawrence implicitly acknowledges Whitman as the first modern poet to develop free verse successfully. It is hard to think of another writer about whom Lawrence is more complimentary than he is about Whitman in the *New Poems* preface, or in the article on Whitman which he published in the *Nation and Athenaeum* in July 1921. His admiration is partly ideological: a matter (that is) of the stimulus which Whitman's concept of comradeship and manly love gave to Lawrence at a crucial stage in his struggle to elaborate a satisfactory account of sexual relations. But it is also admiration for Whitman's manner as a poet. At its best, he writes at the end of the *Nation and Athenaeum* article, Whitman's verse 'springs sheer from the spontaneous sources of his being. Hence its lovely, lovely form and rhythm: at the best . . . It is not, like Swinburne, an exaggeration of the one part of being. It is perfect and whole. The whole soul speaks at once, and is too pure for mechanical assistance of rhyme and measure.'[10] These phrases, and others like them in the *New Poems* preface, confirm the feeling that – although he had of course been a reader of Whitman's poetry since his youth – it was above all through Whitman that Lawrence eventually discovered what kind of poet he could be.

Even after the reservations Lawrence had always had about certain attitudes in the *Leaves of Grass* had been developed in a way which makes the total effect of the Whitman essay in *Studies in Classic American Literature* unfavourable, Whitman's influence on Lawrence's work, and on his poetry especially, remains very strong. In the *Studies* essay, Lawrence protests against Whitman's confusion of genuine sympathy with the undiscriminating urge to have the same feelings as the negro slave, the leper or the syphilitic; and in the jaunty manner he developed so effectively for the final version of the *Studies*, he complains of Whitman's efforts to be at one or merge with all the elements in his environment. 'As soon as Walt *knew* a thing, he assumed a One Identity with it. If he knew that an Eskimo sat in a kyak, immediately there was Walt being little and yellow and greasy, sitting in a kyak.' But

Walt wasn't an Eskimo. A little, yellow, sly, cunning, greasy little Eskimo. And when Walt blandly assumed Allness, including Eskimoness, unto himself, he was just sucking the wind out of a blown egg-shell, no more. Eskimos are not minor little Walts. They are something that I am not, I know that. Outside the egg of my Allness chuckles the greasy little Eskimo. Outside the egg of Whitman's Allness too.[11]

Although they describe relations with the non-human world only, it is no accident that one of the strengths of several of the best poems in *Birds, Beasts and Flowers* (published in America less than two months after the *Studies*) is their definition of the limits of human understanding of and participation in other manifestations of life. There are negative as well as positive ways in which one poet can help another to (the phrase is appropriate) find himself. As far as Lawrence's merely poetic development is concerned, Whitman's negative aid must have been particularly important because the most striking weakness of the early volumes is an extravagant anthropomorphism. For someone who must have known well the chapter in *Modern Painters* in which Ruskin discusses the pathetic fallacy, Lawrence has a surprising tendency – in *Amores* especially – to produce effects for which the only appropriate word is grotesque. If the opening image of 'At The Window' —

> The pine-trees bend to listen to the autumn
>   wind as it mutters
> Something which sets the black poplars
>   ashake with hysterical laughter

– is just about at the limit of what is possible in the anthropomorphic line, the seventh stanza of 'The Wild Common' (much altered when this poem appeared in Lawrence's 1928 edition of his *Collected Poems*) seems to me to go unequivocally beyond it:

> Over my sunlit skin the warm, clinging air,
> Rich with the songs of seven larks singing at once,
>   goes kissing me glad.
> And the soul of the wind and my blood compare
> Their wandering happiness, and the wind, wasted in
>   liberty, drifts on and is sad.

The large number of passages from the early volumes which fall into the same general category as this last quotation make it hard to dismiss what they represent as no more than the exaggeration of a bad stylistic habit of the period. Although they are partly that, the passages are also indicative of the same narcissistic tendency to ignore the inevitable boundaries of the self which Lawrence attributes to Whitman. To say that this tendency is triumphantly resisted in *Birds, Beasts and Flowers* is true but requires careful definition. In the first place, when 'otherness' is being established in that volume it is usually in relation to other *inhabitants* of the environment (rather than to landscapes like the ones on to which Lawrence so often projects his feelings in the early poems). Secondly, it is established most frequently through those inhabitants most people have an instinctive tendency to regard as alien: bats, snakes, mosquitoes and − perhaps most obviously − fish. But even these creatures are largely defined by analogy and contrast with human life, and through the controlled and often playful attribution to them of human feeling.

In his 'Introduction to These Paintings', Lawrence praises Cézanne for his still-lifes and his heroic struggle to 'let the apple exist in its own separate entity, without transfusing it with personal emotion. Cézanne's great effort was, as it were, to shove the apple away from him, and let it live of itself.'[12] This aspiration − more valuable as a protection against solipsism than because it could ever be fully realized − is perhaps easier for a painter to be inspired by than for someone who works in the inescapably anthropomorphic medium of language. More obviously than a daub of a paint, the use of any *word* is a human appropriation of whatever is being described so that it is as true in detail as it is in general that the non-human can only be described effectively and intelligibly in human terms. In Lawrence's great sequence of tortoise poems, the life-cycle of the tortoise and the peculiarities of its mating habits are continually compared with and measured against human experience.

> On he goes, the little one,
> Bud of the universe,
> Pediment of life.
>
> Setting off somewhere, apparently.
> Whither away, brisk egg?
>
> His mother deposited him on the soil as if he were no
>   more than droppings,

And now he scuffles tinily past her as if she were an old
     rusty tin.

A mere obstacle,
He veers round the slow great mound of her –
Tortoises always foresee obstacles.

It is no use my saying to him in an emotional voice:
'This is your Mother, she laid you when you were an egg.'

He does not even trouble to answer: 'Woman, what have I
     to do with thee?'
He wearily looks the other way,
And she even more wearily looks another way still,

Each with the utmost apathy,
Incognizant,
Unaware,
Nothing.[13]

This is the beginning of the poem Lawrence calls 'Tortoise
Family Connections'. The convincing impression it conveys of
someone in the immediate process of observing tortoise behaviour
('Whither away, brisk egg?') is characteristic of all six poems in
the sequence; but its title is an indication that in order to make any
sense this behaviour will have to be measured against distinctively
human notions of family feeling. By this stage in his career, the
awkwardness of Lawrence's early verse has been left so far behind
that it is hard to remember it ever existed, and his control of both
tone and the related phenomenon of pace is so effortless that he
can incorporate without incongruity the most famous occasion in
history when family feeling was decisively rejected. Later in the sequence, he will even succeed in obliging his readers to associate in
their minds a 'crucifixion into sex' with the thought of the male
tortoise spread-eagled on the 'great mound' of the female in the
act of copulation. As he describes how the sexual urge obliges the
young tortoise to abandon the animal indifference or independence illustrated here, he will also be led into talking at one
moment of its 'adolescence'. But the flagrant anthropomorphism
of that reference is very different from what one finds in *Love
Poems* or *Amores*. In comparing another form of life to his own,
Lawrence never loses sight of how distinctive and different from
human beings that form is. (In this passage, the sense of difference
is partly sustained by humour but partly also by the strategically
placed remark from a putative zoological text book that

'Tortoises always foresee obstacles'.) The appearance and habits of tortoises are observed with a flair and sharpness which act as a continual reminder that, however much their behaviour may be a stimulus to thought about human life, they have ways of being which can never be fully accessible to human understanding and which help to make them unalienably 'other'. In Lawrence's poems on the beasts in his collection especially, there is both reflection on human life and that recognition of otherness which prevents any single beast becoming no more than the reflection's excuse.

'Otherness' is by no means the only avenue of approach to *Birds, Beasts and Flowers*; and it doesn't much help towards an account of the wit in a poem such as 'Peach' or explain the success of those like 'Sicilian Cyclamens', 'Cypresses' or 'Humming-Bird' in which — despite his remarks on nostalgia in Keats's 'Ode to a Nightingale' — Lawrence charms the reader with his evocations of the world in a pristine state. There are almost as many features to explain the strength of the volume as there are poems between its covers. No collection of verse published in the twentieth century is more uniformly successful or has more genuine variety (despite the constrictions implied by its title). To try to do it justice would need more than this chapter and might in any case prove pointless when it can speak so powerfully for itself. What happened to Lawrence as a poet after its publication is less self-evident. In his last years, Lawrence began writing a kind of poem which was on the whole different from the kinds he had been concerned with before and which, by side-stepping the issue of 'Verse Free and Unfree' (the title Lawrence gave to his preface to *New Poems* when it appeared in the magazine *Voices* in October 1919),[14] raises again the question of quite what sort of animal a poem by Lawrence might be and thus the issue of genre with which this book has had to be concerned.

Knowing that the name for one of the commonest of English flowers is what the *OED* calls a 'fanciful application' of the French world for thought, Lawrence described his new kind of poems as 'pansies' and he offered rationales for them in the short introductions to two collections published under that title in 1929. In the second of these introductions, he retains from the *New*

Poems preface the emphasis on immediacy by contrasting his bunch of 'pansies' – called such 'because they are rather "Pensées" than anything else' – with a 'wreath of *immortelles*'. This last reference is the equivalent to his description in the *New Poems* preface of the lyrics of Shelley and Keats as 'gem-like'. But whereas previously he had spoken ambitiously of the 'pure present' as a realm to be 'conquered', through free verse, now he only asks the reader to recognize the paradox that 'A flower passes, and that perhaps is the best of it . . . the same with the pansy poems; merely the breath of the moment, and one eternal moment easily contradicting the next eternal moment.'[15] There is a lowering of sights here, conveyed as much in the tone of the later piece as in its arguments. The author of the *New Poems* preface knew that, as a poet, he had it in him to break important new ground. There were certainly moments, on the other hand, when Lawrence asked himself whether his *Pansies* could be called poetry at all. Announcing them in a letter to the Huxleys in December 1928 he wrote, 'I have been doing a book of Pensées, which I call pansies, a sort of loose little poem form; Frieda says with joy: real doggerel. – But meant for Pensées, not poetry, especially not lyrical poetry.'[16] The joyful intervention of Frieda is shown here obliging Lawrence to withdraw from his tentative assertion that his 'pansies' were after all poetry of some kind; and in a draft for the introduction to the first volume he wrote that they were 'not offered as a collection of poems'.[17] This defensiveness is characteristic of the Lawrence who subscribed to that hierarchy of literary form which accords poetry an especially privileged position and might well cause its supporters to look askance at poetry's inclusion in the general category of 'non-fiction' (even though this is demonstrably one of the things it is). But the less conventional, more characteristic Lawrence reappears in the introduction to the second volume with the claim that not only are his 'pansies' poetry but it is crucial that they should be so. This is because in the 'pansies' or pensées of prose writers – Lawrence refers to La Bruyère and Bacon, as well as Pascal – 'There is a didactic element . . . which makes them repellent, slightly bullying'. 'It has always seemed to me', he writes, 'that a real thought, a single thought, not an argument, can only exist easily in verse, or in some poetic form.'[18]

This second introduction is a better because more appropriate one than the first where, with his mind on recent legal difficulties over *Lady Chatterley's Lover*, Lawrence moves from the idea that pansies have their roots in 'earth and manure' to English prudery and prejudice over the use of the so-called obscene words. Since he very naturally uses a couple of the latter in his earnest denunciation of the way people shy away from any thought of the natural functions, it is as if he were anticipating and partly inviting the trouble which the first typescript of *Pansies* ran into. Sent to England by post at the beginning of 1929, this typescript was held by the Post Office at government request and only returned to Lawrence after the intervention of a barrister. When *Pansies* appeared in July of that year, Lawrence had had to agree to a nervous publisher's request for the exclusion of fourteen poems. It was for the expurgated edition that Lawrence wrote what I have called his second introduction (he called it a 'Foreword'): second from the point of view of composition although in fact published first. His original introduction appeared in the unexpurgated, 'subscribers only' edition of *Pansies* which came out in August 1929.

With only one or two exceptions, the poems which Lawrence was forced to omit from the July edition of *Pansies* were no great loss. He is rarely at his best when he is jeering at the sexual preferences and inadequacies of his younger contemporaries or attempting to make robust, bawdy fun of English prudery; and the natural desire he felt − not being a 'Willy Wet-Leg' − to revenge himself on his censors was not always consonant with the nature of his gifts. After his legal difficulties had increased with the seizure of the paintings he was exhibiting in the Warren Gallery in July 1929, Lawrence gathered together about thirty poems which were mostly related to the issue of censorship. These were published in England under the title *Nettles* in the same month as his death (March 1930) and make up the most feeble volume for which Lawrence can be held responsible. If it didn't suggest such total botanical confusion, it would be convenient to regard Lawrence's 'pansies' as the species within which 'nettles' constitute an unsuccessful but influential variety. Their influence has been in promoting the idea that 'pansies' are predominantly works of jeering social satire when, even in the minority of the poems which are satirical, the tone is by no means consistently aggressive or contemptuous. 'How Beastly

the Bourgeois is' and 'The Oxford Voice' (from *Pansies* of
course, not *Nettles*) have done well in the anthologies but 'Intimates' (a poem from the notebook which Aldington dubbed
MsB) deserved to do better.

> Don't you care for my love? she said bitterly.
>
> I handed her the mirror, and said:
> Please address these questions to the proper person!
> Please make all requests to head-quarters!
> In all matters of emotional importance
> please approach the supreme authority direct!
> So I handed her the mirror.
>
> And she would have broken it over my head,
> but she caught sight of her own reflection
> and that held her spell-bound for two seconds
> while I fled.

The tone here is light and affectionate and the joke elegantly
managed, more elegantly than if the same words had been written out in prose. This is satire of the personal kind, but on graver
issues of social life Lawrence is very far from always being what
Aldington called − in reference to both *Pansies* and *Nettles* but
allowing the latter to distort his judgment − 'like a little Blake
raving, but without the fiery vision'.[19] 'Wages' is well-known
but I quote it here in conjunction with 'Intimates' in order to illustrate how varied Lawrence's manner can be when he turns his
attention to the shortcomings of contemporary society.

> The wages of work is cash,
> The wages of cash is want more cash.
> The wages of want more cash is vicious competition.
> The wages of vicious competition is − the world we live in.
>
> The work-cash-want circle is the viciousest circle
> that ever turned men into fiends.
>
> Earning a wage is a prison occupation
> and a wage-earner is a sort of gaol-bird.
> Earning a salary is a prison overseer's job,
> a gaoler instead of a gaol-bird.
>
> Living on your income is strolling grandly outside the prison
> in terror lest you have to go in. And since the work-prison covers
> almost every scrap of the living earth, you stroll up and down

> on a narrow beat, about the same as a prisoner taking his
> exercise.
>
> This is called universal freedom.

The relentless succession of statements, relieved only by
Lawrence's humorous side-glance at his own solemnity in
'viciousest'; and the grim ingenuity which allows for the inclusion
of the beneficiaries of unearned income in the total picture, make
this 'pansy' a minor masterpiece: a classic statement of quite what
money means to the twentieth-century's 'free world'.

As the last paragraph was partly meant to suggest, there is in
Lawrence's *Pansies* nothing like the uniform quality of *Birds,
Beasts and Flowers*. To appreciate best the many successes, the
reader has to accept the implicit invitation in the introductions to
the two 1929 volumes and turn over some pages rapidly. But the
standards set by the successes make it clear that neither the 1929
volumes nor the 'More Pansies' section in Orioli and Aldington's
edition of the two notebooks of poetry left unpublished at
Lawrence's death (*Last Poems*) are the only places where good
'pansies' can be found. Difficult as the genre is to define, poems
like 'Peace' and 'Southern Night' in *Birds, Beasts and Flowers*
show that Lawrence had been writing 'pansies' before he published his two rationales for them; and Aldington and Orioli's decision to mark a firm separation between the two notebooks they
edited by calling one 'More Pansies' and the other 'Last Poems' is
arbitrary and misleading. In his introduction to the edition,
Aldington says that he and Orioli believe the two notebooks
'represent two different books, one a continuation of *Pansies*, the
other a new series leading up to the death poems for which
Lawrence had not found a general title'. He supports this claim by
suggesting that the pieces in the 'Last Poems' notebook (he calls it
MS A) are more 'pondered and *soignés*' than those in the
notebook he calls MS B.[20] What they certainly are (as far as they
go – MS A is only a quarter full) is more consistently serious in
theme, but not therefore immediately and necessarily
distinguishable from the 'pansies' in MS B. The final seventeen
entries in MS A are related to death or rather to Lawrence's
pondering of what he calls 'oblivion'; but before that, and
therefore before 'The Ship of Death', which introduces this final
series, the poems deal with a great variety of topics: the nature

of evil, for example, the futility of the search for self-knowledge, the sea, the world of the ancient Greeks or − a familiar preoccupation this − the foolishness of supposing that the idea of any being could precede its material incarnation. The last of the poems associated with this topic is 'The Rainbow'.

> Even the rainbow has a body
> made of the drizzling rain
> and is an architecture of glistening atoms
> built up, built up
> yet you can't lay your hand on it,
> nay, nor even your mind.

If there is such a thing as a 'pansy', then this is undoubtedly one, as are in fact most of the poems which follow 'The Ship of Death' in Ms A. Aldington's error lies in implying that 'a pansy' is defined by its relatively trivial subject-matter when several of the poems in the notebook which, with considerable justification,[21] he called 'More Pansies' deal with death and there are clearly no restrictions on what 'pansies' can be about. They can range from 'Willy Wet-Leg', at one end of a possible scale,

> I can't stand Willy wet-leg,
> can't stand him at any price.
> He's resigned, and when you hit him
> he lets you hit him twice.

to 'Sea-Weed' at the other:

> Sea-weed sways and sways and swirls
> as if swaying were its form of stillness;
> and if it flushes against fierce rock
> it slips over it as shadows do, without hurting itself.

'Sea-Weed' is a reminder of a number of short poems Lawrence wrote near the beginning of his career which encouraged people in the mistaken belief that he was an Imagist. (It is not surprising that six poems from the 'More Pansies' notebook were published in the Imagist Anthology for 1930.) But it is not its brevity alone − nor that of 'Willy Wet-Leg' and 'The Rainbow' − which make it a 'pansy'. 'Pansies' are recognizable by some idea of scale which the reader infers was in the author's mind; but that does not mean they can have no development. A 'real thought' may need space to work out, even if the longer a 'pansy' becomes the more it is in danger of degenerating into argument and the more it pushes therefore against the limits of the genre.

The question of what precisely 'pansies' are is so difficult to answer conclusively that it is not surprising to find it evaded by acquiescence in Aldington's specious invention of a category – 'Last Poems' – from which they can be distinguished. If the reference in that title were *solely* chronological (as it may be taken to be in the title of the edition as a whole), there could be no quarrel with it. Keith Sagar is one of the several critics to assume that, having filled Ms B, Lawrence began writing down his verse in Ms A and that the entries it contains therefore belong to the last months of his life.[22] But joining with other possible evidence the fact that Ms B concludes with the 'Prayer' which is 'unfinished and written in a very uncertain hand', Aldington himself decides that the two notebooks must 'have been in progress simultaneously'.[23] Explaining the decision to print Ms A first in the 1932 edition he writes, 'Believing as we do that there are two unfinished books of poems represented in these Mss, we have kept them separate. Ms A comes first, as being obviously the more important and we have supplied the title, "Last Poems". We abandoned the idea of calling the book "The Ship of Death", as we once thought of doing, since we felt we had no right to give a fancy title without Ms authority.'[24] If the two notebooks which Aldington is discussing were 'in progress simultaneously', 'Last Poems' must be for him a fancy title: a compromise formation between some entirely neutral phrase and 'The Ship of Death'. His introduction makes clear that it refers not only to the poems in Ms A having been written towards the end of Lawrence's life but also and more importantly to the fact that they deal with 'the last things'. Both the introduction and the title have been unfortunate in suggesting that it is because the poems in Ms A – the significance of the lettering will now be clear – show Lawrence contemplating his own death that they are 'obviously the more important' (in the paragraph in which Aldington calls the Ms A poems more 'pondered and *soignés*' than those in Ms B, he also refers to them as 'more serious'); and both may have been influential in attracting to 'The Ship of Death', for example, an attention which is disproportionate to its merits. What Aldington's title and introduction certainly do is tempt readers into ignoring the variety in subject and manner of the poems in MS A. But for my present purposes, their main disadvantage is of course the creation of a false distinction between the 'obviously more important' and 'more serious poems' which deal with death on the one hand, and 'pansies' on the other. It is a distinction which, joined to the effect of *Nettles*, has led to *Pansies* being misrepresented in Lawrence criticism and (I think) undervalued. The two critics who have written best about Lawrence's poetry in recent times are Sandra Gilbert and Keith Sagar but although both make interesting and appreciative comments on individual 'pansies' they are apologetic about the genre. Sandra Gilbert tends to write as if 'real doggerel' were Lawrence's considered estimate of it rather than an off-hand remark of Frieda's,[25] and in *D. H. Lawrence: Life into Art* Keith Sagar denies the relevance of Lawrence's appeal to the example of Pascal.

> But, rather than any sense of debt to or affinity with Pascal, it was probably more [Lawrence's] need to write what could be produced without taxing imaginative effort, his desire to communicate with a larger audience than that which 'art' poetry commands, and his need, time being short now, to encapsulate his ideas, which led him to jot down loosely versified thoughts, the poetic equivalent of the newspaper articles he was writing at the same time.[26]

The last of these explanations ('encapsulation') is no doubt valid, but the way it is expressed and the two which precede it seem to me to have too much in common with the tradition of thought Orioli and Aldington inaugurated.

To criticize Orioli and Aldington too severely — or even at all — for confusing the issues would be foolish given the date of their edition and the public service it performed. What is suprising is not that they proposed a false category but that no-one seems to have challenged it since.[27] It appears to be a case of making do with what's there because of a wholly understandable lack of something better. If they are not 'last poems', what other name is one going to give to all those pieces Lawrence wrote in his final period which are clearly not 'pansies'? Just how far can a 'pansy' be expanded until it becomes something unequivocally different, and quite how long can a 'pansy' be? These last questions wouldn't be difficult if they could always be answered with a ruler. In the 1929 editions of *Pansies*, there are five 'elephant poems', three of which are very short: 'Plod! Plod!/' writes Lawrence in one of them, 'And what ages of time/the worn arches of their spines support'. The better of the other two is longer, but no more so than many of those 'pansies' where the thought has needed room to develop.

> *The Elephant is Slow to Mate*
>
> The elephant, the huge old beast,
>   is slow to mate;
> he finds a female, they show no haste
>   they wait
>
> for the sympathy in their vast shy hearts
>   slowly, slowly to rouse
> as they loiter along the river-beds
>   and drink and browse
>
> and dash in panic through the brake
>   of forest with the herd,
> and sleep in massive silence, and wake
>   together without a word.
>
> So slowly the great hot elephant hearts
>   grow full of desire,
> and the great beasts mate in secret at last,
>   hiding their fire.
>
> Oldest they are and the wisest of beasts
>   so they know at last
> how to wait for the loneliest of feasts
>   for the full repast.
>
> They do not snatch, they do not tear;
>   their massive blood
> moves as the moon-tides, near, more near,
>   till they touch in flood.

It isn't because this is longer than the other poems I have quoted that it doesn't have the feel of the more characteristic 'pansies', and the question it raises has clearly nothing to do with a point at which it might be in danger of changing its nature. The issue is rather how far that nature was ever 'pansy'-like in the first place. (As I have already said, nothing in Lawrence's poetic career is straightforward.) To suggest that 'The Rainbow' belongs with 'More Pansies' rather than 'Last Poems' is not difficult when the responsibility for both those titles lies with Orioli and Aldington. But 'The Elephant is Slow to Mate' appears in the 1929 collections which Lawrence himself called *Pansies*. A 'pansy', he tells us, is above all a thought and the difference between 'Willy Wet-Leg' and 'Sea-Weed' demonstrates how flexible that definition can be. Whether it is flexible enough to include this poem is problematic, but what differentiates it most from other 'pansies' is the 'pondered' quality which Aldington – allowing the presence of 'Bavarian Gentians' and 'The Ship of Death' too much dominance – wrongly attributes to all the Ms A poems. Of course, 'ponderousness' (in the best sense) is very much in keeping with the subject and it is encouraged here by the comparative regularity of the verse form and rhyme-scheme. The poem entitled 'Elephant' in *Birds, Beasts and Flowers* is at least equally about Edward VII when he was Prince of Wales and is based on detailed observations Lawrence was able to make whilst he was living in Ceylon.[28] 'The Elephant is Slow to Mate' is more in the manner of 'Humming-Bird': a form of reverie around one or two striking peculiarities of a non-human life-form (and in that sense at least it constitutes one single 'thought' about elephants). There is no narcissistic incorporation into the human sphere because the poet's own feelings are only very indirectly present and the poem never offers itself as either more or other than a soothing imaginative speculation. Its success as such is closely related to the regularity of its form but in abandoning free verse it runs the risk of having that static or fixed quality which Lawrence attributes to poems of the past or future in his *New Poems* preface. Certainly it is not a poem which corresponds in spirit to his ambition for *Pansies* in his second introduction, or 'Foreword': 'I should like [these poems] to be as fleeting as pansies, which wilt so soon, and are so fascinating with their varied faces, while they last'.[29] But then, it would have been hard for Lawrence to make the mating of elephants appear fleeting, and foolish of him to try. 'Pansies' cannot be defined by their subject-matter but, in this special case, subject-matter may help to explain why 'The Elephant is Slow to Mate' feels less like a 'pansy' than most of its companions in the 1929 editions.

If the longer, more argumentative 'pansies' strain against the limits of the genre in one direction, 'The Elephant is Slow to Mate' – by being so much more what is traditionally thought of as a poem – does so in another. Yet since short pieces like

'The Rainbow', 'Willy Wet-Leg' and 'Sea-Weed' become difficult to read if they continue to follow on from each other, those longer ones which suggest the likely limits of the 'pansy' form are a guarantee of variety, and variety is a crucial feature of Lawrence's *Pansies*. When in the introduction to the July 1929 volume Lawrence encourages his readers to think of them as above all 'thoughts' he says that 'thoughts' in prose are 'slightly bullying'; but it is rather that their effect is more in danger of becoming monotonous than when they appear as squibs, solemn Whitmanesque declarations, imaginary dialogues, ballads, aperçus, and even (assuming 'The Elephant is Slow to Mate' to be in fact a 'pansy') poems of a comparatively conventional kind. Introducing the August 1929 *Pansies*, Lawrence says that 'at least, they do not pretend to be half baked lyrics or melodies in American measure'.[30] This may well be a final glancing blow at Conrad Aiken. 'The Elephant is Slow to Mate' shows that although Lawrence would no doubt have distinguished true musical quality from 'melodies in American measure', he was capable of satisfying Aiken's expectations of poetry on occasions, or rather when it was musical quality – what Aiken had called 'the melodic line' – which the occasion required. More than any other of the collections of verse Lawrence published, *Pansies* conforms to the Lawrentian ideal of allowing the subject of a poem to determine its form. And when that subject is meant to be some thought about the world which is self-contained and relatively non-sequential, so that the collections as a whole offer themselves as modern day equivalents of Bacon or Pascal, then the choice of verse, or even of what Lawrence himself disarmingly refers to as 'some poetic form', allows for a variety difficult to achieve in prose.

'Pansies' may not be sequential in any strict sense but a cluster of them will often deal with the same subject nevertheless. In a well-known remark quoted elsewhere in this book, Lawrence talks of the 'emotional mind' making 'curious swoops and circles' (see p. 132). Thus in certain small groups of 'pansies', he comes back several times to old age or to memories of the dead; and he writes a group of remarkable poems in which swans feature prominently. One of the other subjects which preoccupies him is self-sufficiency. How varied the related results can be is clear from these three examples of his swooping down upon it.

> *Desire is dead*
>
> Desire may be dead
> and still a man can be
> a meeting place for sun and rain
> wonder outwaiting pain
> as in a wintry tree.
>
> *Man reaches a point*
>
> I cannot help but be alone
> for desire has died in me, silence has grown,
> and nothing now reaches out to draw
> other flesh to my own.
>
> *Delight of Being Alone*
>
> I know of no greater delight than the sheer delight of being alone.
> It makes me realise the delicious pleasure of the moon
> that she has in travelling by herself: throughout time,
> or the splendid growing of an ash-tree
> alone, on a hill-side in the north, humming in the wind.

This is my grouping rather than Lawrence's, just as it was my decision to associate 'The Elephant is Slow to Mate' with the other elephant poems.[31] There are poems which either his published collections or his notebooks suggest he thought of as going together, and others which make a group in the reader's mind. Although the mood of these three moving pieces is so different — celebratory in the last but either grimly hopeful or flatly dejected in the others — and although this difference is matched by a sharp alteration in poetic manner between the third poem and the first two, their family relationship is evident enough. The 'pansy' which it seems to me could fairly be called their complement is 'We Die Together'.

> Oh, when I think of the industrial millions, when I see
>   some of them,
> a weight comes over me heavier than leaden linings of coffins
> and I almost cease to exist, weighted down to extinction
> and sunk into a depression that almost blots me out.
>
> Then I say to myself: Am I also dead? is that the truth?
> Then I know
> that with so many dead men in mills
> I too am almost dead.

I know the unliving factory-hand, living-dead millions
is unliving me, living-dead me,
I, with them, am living-dead, mechanical enslaved at the
   machine.

And enshrouded in the vast corpse of the industrial millions
embedded in them, I look out on the sunshine of the South.

And though the pomegranate has red flowers outside the window
and oleander is hot with perfume under the afternoon sun
and I am 'il Signore' and they love me here,
yet I am a mill-hand in Leeds
and the death of the Black Country is upon me
and I am wrapped in the lead of a coffin-lining, the living death
   of my fellow men.

Lawrence had criticized Whitman for his belief in the 'one identity' of all mankind. ('His poems, "Democracy", "En Masse",
"One Identity", they are long sums in addition and multiplica-
tion, of which the answer is MYSELF.')[32] In a general manner
but certainly not a mood which is Whitmanesque, he reluctantly
acknowledges here identification with his compatriots, recognizing the impossibility of living a life independently, with no
responsibility for others. With its effective reference to lead
coffin-linings to evoke a living-death and its striking but finally
cheerless contrast between the 'Black Country' and 'the sunshine
of the South', 'We Die Together' demonstrates (as do the best
parts of *Lady Chatterley's Lover*) how futile it is for us to think
that we can 'escape our origins'; how earnestly concerned
Lawrence always continued to be with what had been known in his
youth as 'the condition of England question'; and how essentially
English he remained during all his years of self-imposed exile.

Whereas Whitman regards every human being's common
humanity with the leper, the syphilitic and the negro slave with
jubilation, Lawrence – more understandably – is depressed by
the realization that in some sense he too is 'a mill-hand in
Leeds'. But however indirect, unwilling or ambivalent his return
to Whitman in this late poem, it can be taken as an appropriate
recognition of the influence that poet continued to have on
Lawrence throughout his career. In the later years the influence
had usually taken the form of repudiation. In *Birds, Beasts and
Flowers* there is a poem about a dog called Bibbles which
Lawrence acquired on his first visit to New Mexico. It is a piece

remarkable for the vividness with which the habits and appearance of the dog are made present to the reader and for the complexity of attitude which Lawrence is able to convey through changes of pace and tone. His chief complaint is against Bibbles's undiscriminating friendliness. 'You love 'em all/', he writes at one moment, 'Believe in the One Identity, don't you,/You little Walt Whitmanesque bitch'; and later he reviles the dog for being willing to eat excrement, ' "Reject nothing", sings Walt Whitman./So you, you go out at last and eat the unmentionable,/In your appetite for affection.' In 'More Pansies' the debate continues when Lawrence retorts to Whitman's 'And whoever walks a furlong without sympathy walks to his own funeral dressed in his own shroud', with 'And whoever walks a mile full of false sympathy/walks to the funeral of the whole human race'. In spite of which, the work closest to Lawrence's non-rhyming 'pansies' is the section of 'Inscriptions' at the beginning of *Leaves of Grass*.

Whatever the influence, negative or positive, which by the time of *Pansies* Whitman continues to have on Lawrence, it is no longer associated with the commitment to free verse, as it had been in the *New Poems* preface ('The quick of all time is the instant . . . Poetry gave us the clue: free verse; Whitman. Now we Know'),[33] so that with *Pansies*, that comparison with Cézanne with which I began this account breaks down. Its usefulness was in suggesting how the question of whether Lawrence could have been a great poet in traditional forms is made irrelevant by his achievements in free verse. In arguing for free verse, Lawrence would often claim that it was a more exacting medium in which to write poetry than any other.[34] Whether or not it is would probably have not seemed very important to him by the time he was writing the 'pansies'. The analogy between their author and Cézanne breaks down not only because there is no longer the same point in trying to find an equivalent term for 'drawing' but also, perhaps, because of a much increased sense of comparing great things with small. Yet just as no-one would complain if Cézanne had been as prone to quick sketches or instant art-work as Picasso, so the best of Lawrence's 'pansies' are a part of his total output it would be impoverishing to be without. 'When a man *lives*', wrote Henry James's father to Emerson in 1849, 'that is lives enough, he can scarcely write . . . All his writing will be algebraicised, put into the form of sonnets and proverbs and the community will feel deeply insulted to be offered a big bunch of pages, as though it were stupid and wanted tedious drilling like a child.'[35] It wasn't fullness of life but a diminution consequent on illness which led Lawrence to 'algebraicise' some of his writing in his last years; but in certain moods, the *best* of the results (and that qualification is as important to anyone writing about Lawrence's poetry as it was to Lawrence himself in writing about Whitman's) can seem to offer a distillation of experience preferable to very many more elaborate workings-through. They represent, that is, not a feeble tailing-off of Lawrence's poetic career but a genuine new development in a writer from whom it was always futile to expect the same thing twice.

Lawrence's familiarity with the great Victorian writers must have helped to form his elevated notion of the responsibilities of the literary artist or confirm him in the feelings which lie behind such frequently quoted remarks as that he wrote so that English folk would have more sense, or 'for the race, as it were'.[36] It would have seemed self-evident to him that a creative writer should feel impelled to convey his thought to the public in addition to telling it stories. Lawrence knew of course that thought of the kind which interested him most was conveyed most effectively *through* stories – 'art-speech' in one meaning of that term; but in the 1920s especially he found it more and more difficult to reconcile his novel-writing (the novellas and short stories raise different issues) with the expression of his views on major social and religious questions. He was much less successful than Proust or Mann at converting the novel form into a hold-all. When he abandoned the experimentation of *Kangaroo* and *The Plumed Serpent* in order to return to a far more traditional manner and setting in *Lady Chatterley's Lover*, it was at the cost of having to give to Mellors what sounds, in the consequently more traditional context he had created, uncomfortably close to the male equivalent of curtain lectures.

In part because they were so often the consequence of major physical *effort*, novels were at the top of Lawrence's literary hierarchy. His readers can agree that his reputation is rightly and soundly based on three great novels he published in the first two-thirds of his writing career without believing that novels are always and inevitably at the top of theirs. In the final third, he published only the three novels I have just mentioned – not many for someone whom Catherine Carswell called the most prolific writer in English since Scott. How he occupied his time between their composition is partly a consequence of economic factors (as of course is all his literary production); but it can also be represented accurately as Lawrence's search for appropriate literary forms in which he could express his views on the world. They had to be appropriate because, as well as being as aware as anyone of how 'thought' is inseparable from the means which convey it, Lawrence had his own ideas as to what real thought was. There is a resounding declaration of these in one of the better-known 'pansies'.

> *Thought*
> Thought, I love thought.
> But not the jaggling and twisting of already existent ideas
> I despise that self-important game.
> Thought is the welling up of unknown life into consciousness
> Thought is the testing of statements on the touchstone of the
>   conscience
> Thought is gazing on to the face of life, and reading what can
>   be read,
> Thought is pondering over experience, and coming to
>   conclusion.
> Thought is not a trick, or an exercise, or a set of dodges
> Thought is a man in his wholeness wholly attending.

One way of considering the texts with which this book has been principally concerned is as part of a life-long effort to find the literary form which would best allow for precisely this kind of thought. 'Pansies' themselves are a consequence of the realization that it is often the need to organize individual thoughts into an argument which distorts them into a 'trick, or an exercise, or a set of dodges'. The strength of the conception would perhaps only be fully obvious in a selection where one could choose the best of Lawrence's several 'thoughts' on the same subject, and *Pansies* would also need to be thinned out in order to show most effectively how, in spite of his popular reputation for being interested in only one thing (hugely encouraged by those curtain lectures), Lawrence remained until the very end of his life extraordinarily diverse in interests, moods and concerns. I have noted elsewhere how remarkable it is that in 1921 he should have written works as different in both manner and subject as *Sea and Sardinia*, *Fantasia* and *The Captain's Doll*. Many other years in his writing life reveal a similar variety. A selection of his 'pansies' would − in the precise sense of the word − epitomize this undervalued aspect of Lawrence's literary personality. It would also illustrate the last but by no means least satisfactory of his attempts to reconcile a restlessly enquiring mind and a passion for discovering the truth of things with the feeling conveyed in the 'pansy' he called 'All-knowing'.

> All that we know is nothing, we are merely crammed waste-paper baskets
> unless we are in touch with that which laughs at all our knowing.

It is not certain that Lawrence was as interested in this reconciliation when he was occasionally tempted to make his 'philosophy' complete or perfect, around the time of the 'Study of Thomas Hardy', as he clearly was in writing *Pansies*. If age and sickness made him less energetically fervent towards the end of his life, it also gave him that degree of sceptical caution traditionally thought to be a component of wisdom. But since the caution did not prevent him from remaining one of those people able to commit themselves to an enterprise with total absorption, it left him with that difficulty of simultaneously recognizing the same enterprise's insignificance in the total scheme of things which is dramatized by the threatening presence of obsession at one possible extreme and weary or cynical indifference at another. As his introductions to the 1929 volumes suggest, Lawrence's conception for 'pansies' provides an answer to this problem − 'One eternal moment easily contradicting the next eternal moment'. To look through the best of them is to dispel any suspicion that a strong conception − what Lawrence would, throughout his career, have referred to pejoratively as a mere 'idea' − is all that is involved.

Notes

Introduction

1 Catherine Carswell, *The Savage Pilgrimage: A Narrative of D. H. Lawrence* (reprinted Cambridge, 1981), p. xxxvii.

2 Henry James, 'Anthony Trollope' (1883), reprinted in *The House of Fiction*, edited by Leon Edel (London, 1957), p. 90.

3 Carswell, *Savage Pilgrimage*, p. xxxvii.

4 *'Fantasia of the Unconscious' and 'Psychoanalysis and the Unconscious'* (Harmondsworth, 1971), p. 209.

5 *Apocalypse*, reprinted in *Apocalypse and the Writings on Revelation*, edited by Mara Kalnins (Cambridge, 1980).

6 Helen Corke, 'Lawrence and *Apocalypse*', reprinted in *D. H. Lawrence: The Croydon Years* (Austin, Texas, 1965), pp. 57–132.

7 Helen Corke, 'D. H. Lawrence's "Princess": A Memory of Jessie Chambers', reprinted in *D. H. Lawrence: The Croydon Years*, p. 40. (Original italics.)

8 Rebecca West, *D. H. Lawrence* (London, 1930), pp. 34–6. Jessie Chambers's ground for complaint is thus viewed as a matter for congratulation.

9 T. S. Eliot, *After Strange Gods* (London, 1934), p. 58.

10 F. R. Leavis, *Thought, Words and Creativity: Art and Thought in Lawrence* (London, 1976), pp. 40–1.

11 *Studies in Classic American Literature* (Harmondsworth, 1971), p. 8.

12 D. H. Lawrence, *Phoenix II: Uncollected, Unpublished and Other Prose Works*, edited by Warren Roberts and Harry T. Moore (London, 1968), p. ix.

13 Frank Kermode, *Lawrence* (London, 1973), pp. 27, 30.

14 Mark Kinkead-Weekes, 'Lawrence on Hardy', in *Thomas Hardy after Fifty Years*, edited by L. St J. Butler (London, 1977), p. 90. It should be stressed that the remark quoted is a convenient summary of the approach which Kinkead-Weekes sets out to supplement: his aim is to indicate the value of the 'Study' 'to the student of the Wessex novels' (p. 90.). The first chapter of our book has a similar aim.

15 Carswell, *Savage Pilgrimage*, p. 117. (See below, p. 120.)

16 Matthew Arnold, 'Count Leo Tolstoy', reprinted in *The Complete Prose Works*, edited by R. H. Super, vol. 11, *The Last Word* (Michigan, 1977), p. 284.

17 Matthew Arnold, 'The Function of Criticism at the Present Time', reprinted in *Complete Prose Works*, edited by Super, vol. 3, *Lectures and Essays in Criticism* (Michigan, 1962), p. 259.

18 'Foreword' to *Pansies*, reprinted in *The Complete Poems of D. H.*

Lawrence, edited by Vivian de Sola Pinto and Warren Roberts, 2 vols. (London, 1964), vol. 1, p. 423.

19 Paul Delany, *D. H. Lawrence's Nightmare: The Writer and His Circle in the Years of the Great War* (Sussex, 1979), p. 31. The same sentence applies the remark not only to the war years but the 'long series of speculative works' which followed the 'Study of Thomas Hardy', 'from *The Crown* in 1915 to *A Propos of Lady Chatterley's Lover* in 1929'.

20 *The Letters of D. H. Lawrence*, edited by James T. Boulton and Andrew Robertson (Cambridge, 1984), vol. 3, p. 224. (Hereafter referred to as '*Letters* 3'.)

21 'Foreword' to *Fantasia of the Unconscious*, p. 15.

22 'They come to me, and they make me talk, and they enjoy it, it gives them a profoundly gratifying sensation. And that is all . . . They then say, I – D.H.L. am wonderful, I am an exceedingly valuable personality, but that the things I say are extravaganzas, illusions. They say I cannot think'. (*The Letters of D. H. Lawrence*, edited by George J. Zytaruk and James T. Boulton (Cambridge, 1981), vol. 2, p. 380. Hereafter referred to as '*Letters* 2'.)

23 Ibid., p. 448.

24 *Letters* 3, p. 163.

25 *Study of Thomas Hardy and Other Essays*, edited by Bruce Steele (Cambridge, 1985), pp. 86–7, 84, 87.

26 *Etruscan Places*, in *D. H. Lawrence and Italy*, introduction by Anthony Burgess (Harmondsworth, 1978), p. 25; 'Pictures on the Walls', reprinted in *Phoenix II*, edited by Roberts and Moore, pp. 608–15.

27 Samuel Johnson, 'Alexander Pope', in *Lives of the English Poets*, 2 vols. (London, 1968), vol. 2, p. 211.

28 *Phoenix II*, edited by Roberts and Moore, p. 616.

1. 'Slightly philosophicalish, mostly about Hardy': 'Study of Thomas Hardy'

1 All references are to the Cambridge Edition: *Study of Thomas Hardy and Other Essays*, edited by Bruce Steele. In quotations I omit the editorial brackets around conjectural readings, all of which are convincing.

2 'The Future of the Novel' ['Surgery for the Novel—Or a Bomb'], reprinted in *Study of Thomas Hardy*, p. 154.

3 John Worthen, *D. H. Lawrence and the Idea of the Novel* (London, 1979), p. 58.

4 This passage echoes 'Ashes to ashes, dust to dust'; these chapters also debate the idea that 'all is vanity' from Ecclesiastes, and draw on the Book of Job. These are Hardy's favourite biblical texts.

A link between the images of the war and Lawrence's own fiction: when telling Edward Garnett that 'I have done a third' of the 'Study', he asked of the stories making up the *Prussian Officer* volume: 'Shall they be called "The Fighting Line". After all, this is the real fighting line, not where soldiers pull triggers' (*Letters* 2, pp.

221–2). The dust-jacket description of *The Rainbow* (probably written by Lawrence) announced that Ursula was to be thrust into 'the advance-post of our time and blaze a path into the future'.

5 In this and all further references, *The Return of the Native* is abbreviated as *RN* and quoted from the New Wessex Edition (London, 1975).

Incidentally, without these words of Hardy's, Lawrence might not have written that Tom Brangwen 'balked the mean enclosure of reality' after the encounter with the girl and foreign man at Matlock 'set fire to the homestead of his nature' (*The Rainbow*, edited by John Worthen (Harmondsworth, 1981), p. 60).

6 'Note' (Preface to *Collected Poems* (London, 1928)), reprinted in *Complete Poems*, edited by Pinto and Roberts, vol. 2, p. 28.

7 Herbert Spencer, *Education: Intellectual, Moral and Physical* (London, 1861), pp. 9, 10.

8 Jane Harrison, *Ancient Art and Ritual* (London, 1913), p. 50. I have been unable to trace the quotation from Frazer.

9 John Stuart Mill, *Collected Works*, vol. 7 (Toronto, 1977), pp. 265–6.

10 Walter Pater, 'Winckelmann', in *The Renaissance: Studies in Art and Poetry*, reprinted in Fontana Library (London, 1961), p. 196.

11 *The Life and Work of Thomas Hardy, by Thomas Hardy*, edited by Michael Millgate (London, 1984), p. 222. This work combines *The Early Life* and *The Later Years* published over the name of Hardy's second wife.

12 David J. De Laura, ' "The Ache of Modernism" in Hardy's Later Novels', *ELH*, 34 (1967), p. 380.

13 *D. H. Lawrence and the Idea of the Novel*, p. 56.

14 Kinkead-Weekes, 'Lawrence on Hardy', p. 102.

15 I pick up a phrase of Hardy's: 'my pages show harmony of view with Darwin, Huxley, Spencer, Mill, and others, all of whom I used to read more than Schopenhauer' (cited in W. F. Wright, *The Shaping of The Dynasts* (Lincoln, Nebraska, 1967), p. 38).

16 *The Collected Letters of D. H. Lawrence*, edited by Harry T. Moore, 2 vols. (London, 1962), vol. 2, p. 827.

17 Ian Gregor, *The Great Web: The Form of Hardy's Major Fiction* (London, 1973), p. 228.

18 Kinkead-Weekes, 'Lawrence on Hardy', p. 102.

19 My summary quoted two of the few critics who discuss Lawrence, and particularly the 'Study', as well as Hardy: an earlier, outstanding and slighted example is Richard L. Swigg, *Lawrence, Hardy and American Literature* (London, 1972); more recent are Roger Ebbatson's *Lawrence and the Nature Tradition: A Theme in English Fiction, 1859–1914* (Sussex, 1980) and *The Evolutionary Self* (Sussex, 1982). But equally to my purpose are those critics of Hardy (and some of Lawrence) who write of the novelist's fictional technique and/or intellectual context without making the connections with the other author. Of these, particularly relevant to Hardy's relation

to Darwinism, but (except for a few asides in the second) ignoring the parallel aspect of Lawrence, are Gillian Beer's *Darwin's Plots* (London, 1983) and Bruce Johnson's *True Correspondence: A Phenomenology of Hardy's Novels* (Florida, 1983).

20 John Bayley, *An Essay on Hardy* (Cambridge, 1978); Ebbatson, *The Evolutionary Self*, p. 3.

21 Preface to *Poems of the Past and Present* (London, 1902); *Life and Work of Thomas Hardy*, edited by Millgate, p. 235.

22 Swigg, *Lawrence, Hardy and American Literature*, p. 14.

23 Kinkead-Weekes, 'Lawrence on Hardy', p. 93.

24 Ibid., p. 93.

25 Gregor, *Great Web*, p. 32.

26 For 'universal pagan sentiment' see above, p. 14 and note 10. 'The ache of modernism' is what Angel sees in Tess: *Tess of the d'Urbervilles*, edited by J. Grindle and S. Gattrell (Oxford, 1983), p. 177 (ch. 29). Pater also speaks of the modern urge 'to contend for a perfection that makes the blood turbid, and frets the flesh, and discredits the actual world about us' (*The Renaissance*, p. 212). Equally influential on *The Return of the Native* was Arnold's essay 'Pagan and Mediaeval Religious Sentiment' (*The Cornhill Magazine*, April 1864; reprinted in *Complete Prose Works*, ed. Super, vol. 3, *Lectures and Essays in Criticism*) which Hardy read just before revising his manuscript version of the novel's first two books.

27 J. Paterson, *The Making of 'The Return of the Native'* (Berkeley, 1963), p. 65.

28 Bayley, *Essay on Hardy*, p. 113.

29 Swigg remarks that 'the artist can pattern his work in such a way that it excludes from view the very terms by which his surrender to fatalism can be questioned or contested', and that in such cases the main task of the critic is 'to discover the missing terms and put them back in the argument' (*Lawrence, Hardy and American Literature*, p. 2).

30 This point (without examples) is also made in R. Langbaum's 'Lawrence and Hardy', in *D. H. Lawrence and Tradition*, edited by Jeffrey Meyers (London, 1985), p. 69.

31 Johnson, *True Correspondence*, p. 70.

32 *Sea and Sardinia*, in *D. H. Lawrence and Italy*, p. 99.

33 *Lawrence, Hardy and American Literature*, p. xi.

34 One of these, retrospectively relevant to Clym, is the need to escape the maternal matrix, to be 'born, detached from the flesh and blood of our parents' and to be reborn in early manhood from 'the parent womb' (p. 44).

35 For this paragraph I acknowledge a general debt to Swigg, *Lawrence, Hardy and American Literature*, especially pp. 59–60 and 67.

36 *D. H. Lawrence and the Idea of the Novel*, p. 61.

37 See especially his *Greek Studies* (London, 1895).

37 See especially his *Greek Studies* (London, 1895).
38 It further underlines Lawrence's and Hardy's common background to point out that Hardy knew well Arnold's theological writings.
39 *Life and Work of Thomas Hardy*, edited by Millgate, p. 225.
40 Ibid., p. 192.
41 Ibid., p. 118.
42 *Tess of the d'Urbervilles*, pp. 90 and 88.
43 *Essays in Criticism*, 25 (July 1975), pp. 304–28.
44 *Essays in Criticism*, 30 (October 1980), pp. 326–45.
45 Ibid., p. 327.
46 It is also far preferable to the headlong diatribe on Angel ('the only one of Hardy's characters who is genuinely odious') in Lascelles Abercrombie's *Thomas Hardy: A Critical Study* (London, 1912), pp. 98–100.
47 Jacobus, 'Sue the Obscure', p. 307.
48 Ibid., p. 307.
49 Ibid., p. 321.
50 It is therefore too simple a dismissal of Lawrence's critique to say that 'Hardy wrote a fiction which presumed a commission to write about the world as he found it' whereas Lawrence 'felt under no such obligation' (Gregor, *Great Web*, p. 232).

   On *Jude* as in its earlier general discussion of tragedy, it is ironic that the 'Study' invokes against Hardy a distinction that Hardy himself had expounded: between the 'essential laws' which confront the protagonists of Greek and Elizabethan tragedies, and the 'social expedients . . . without a basis in the heart of things' which in modern tragedy cause 'the triumph of the crowd over the hero, of the commonplace majority over the exceptional few' ('Candour in English Fiction', reprinted in *Thomas Hardy's Personal Writings*, edited by J. Orel (Lawrence, Nebraska, 1966), p. 127).
51 The last phrase is used by F. R. Leavis for our reaction to Samuel Johnson's fear of death and damnation: see *'Anna Karenina' and Other Essays* (London, 1967), p. 37. It could also describe Johnson's attitude to Swift's last years in his 'Life'. Both 'cases' have analogies with Sue's.
52 Langbaum, 'Lawrence and Hardy', p. 85.
53 Jacobus, 'Sue the Obscure', p. 325.
54 Ibid., p. 304.
55 Ibid., p. 325.

2. 'Full of philosophising and struggling to show things real': *Twilight in Italy*

References in the text are to *Twilight in Italy*, in *D. H. Lawrence and Italy*.

1 Reprinted in *Study of Thomas Hardy*, edited by Steele, pp. 171–6.
2 I invoke Macbeth's line, and the speech it concludes, because although Lawrence's wartime letters occasionally affect a Hamlet-like shrug at the unreality of this world (e.g. *Letters* 3, p. 305),

Lawrence is more often shaken by what Macbeth called 'horrible imaginings', by what Lawrence himself calls 'the terrible things that are real, in the darkness' and 'the entire unreality of these things I see' (*Letters* 2, p. 307).

3 Three 'Italian Studies', written in late 1912 or early 1913, appeared in the *English Review* for September 1913 but have never yet been reprinted; two 'German Impressions' and 'Christs in the Tirol', originally in the *Westminster Gazette* during August 1912 and March 1913, reappeared in *Phoenix: The Posthumous Papers of D. H. Lawrence*, edited by Edward D. McDonald (London, 1936), pp. 71–86. Of the other, still unpublished, German sketches, two were recently rediscovered and are in the possession of George Lazarus. There is no firm evidence for Keith Sagar's claim that Lawrence wrote more Italian pieces in April 1913 (see *D. H. Lawrence: A Calendar of His Works* (Manchester, 1979), p. 37).

4 *The Prussian Officer and Other Stories*, edited by John Worthen (Cambridge, 1983), pp. 196 and 198.

5 J. C. F. Littlewood, 'D. H. Lawrence's Early Tales', *Cambridge Quarterly*, 1 (1966), p. 123.

6 For the first phrase, see 'Odour of Chrysanthemums' in *The Prussian Officer*, edited by Worthen, p. 198. The second comes from a couplet in Eliot's 'The Dry Salvages' which is very relevant to my present theme: 'We had the experience but missed the meaning, /And approach to the meaning restores the experience'.

7 'Spinner and the Monks', *English Review*, 15 (1913), pp. 204–6.

8 From the 'Preface to Shakespeare': *Works*, edited by A. Sherbo (Yale, 1968), vol. 7, p. 65.

9 'Spinner and the Monks', p. 206.

10 Ibid., p. 204.

11 Ibid., p. 206.

12 Ibid.

13 One small aspect of this: the negative forms of thin, neutral words in *not in existence* and *colourlessness* have the effect of Hardy's *existlessness*. The next chapter speaks of the tiger's *sightlessness* (a word which could have been used of the spinner's eyes which 'had no looking in them').

14 Many readers are reminded of Wordsworth's leech-gatherer, on which the author thus commented: 'What is brought forward? ''A lonely place, a pond'' ''by which an old man was, far from all house and home'' – not stood, not sat, but *was* – the figure presented in the most naked simplicity possible'. In another sense the presentation is not so simple, because in the approximation of stone, sea-beast and old man 'the conferring, the abstracting and the modifying powers of the imagination . . . are all brought into conjunction'. (Letter, 14 June 1802; Preface to Poems, 1815).

15 For the first phrase, see *Kangaroo* (London, 1950), introduction by Richard Aldington, p. 308; for the second, Worthen's introduction to *The Rainbow*, p. 32.

16 'The Two Principles', in *Phoenix II*, edited by Roberts and Moore, p. 227.

17 *D. H. Lawrence and Italy* and other recent editions misprint 'I' as 'It'.

18 Distinguished examples are Florizel's praise of Perdita ('What you do . . .') in *The Winter's Tale*, Keats's 'Ode on a Grecian Urn' and Eliot on the Chinese jar in 'Burnt Norton'.

19 In his introduction to Heinemann's Phoenix edition (London, 1956).

20 *D. H. Lawrence and Italy*, pp. x–xi.

21 Months after finishing the book he still felt 'utterly at a loss for a title' (*Letters* 2, p. 524) and appealed to friends for bright ideas. Not until May 1916 did he refer to it as *Twilight in Italy* (*Letters* 2, p. 606).

22 Lawrence perhaps echoes *Macbeth*'s apprehension of darkness not as a negative, an absence of light, but as a thick substance. There is also a similar feel for sun-substance and an element of near-synaesthesia in describing it (night strangles the sun and entombs the earth, while living light kisses it).

23 *Study of Thomas Hardy*, edited by Steele, pp. 86, 82.

24 Ibid., p. 83.

25 Cf. Lawrence's poems 'Sicilian Cyclamens' and 'Cypresses' in *Complete Poems*, edited by Pinto and Roberts, vol. 1, pp. 310–12, 296–8. For those interested in tracing parallels with the fiction, see *Women in Love*, edited by David Farmer, Lindeth Vasey and John Worthen (Cambridge, 1987), pp. 13–14: 'the sunshine fell brightly into the churchyard, there was a vague scent of sap and of spring, perhaps of violets from off the graves. Some white daisies were out, bright as angels.' This strengthens the suspicion of wordplay in the phrase 'grave violets' in the opening of 'San Gaudenzio' (p. 82). Michael Black, in his *D. H. Lawrence: The Early Fiction* (London, 1986), pp. 60–1, draws attention to a precursor in *The White Peacock*, edited by Andrew Robertson (Cambridge, 1983), p. 130.

26 This contains an implicit reply to both Wordsworth's 'Immortality Ode' and the notion that Lawrence's experience lost its vividness in reminiscence and revision.

27 I owe the final part of this point to Paul Eggert (unpublished Ph.D. thesis, University of Kent, 1981).

28 The phrase occurs in his well-known letter rejecting 'the old stable ego of the character' (*Letters* 2, pp. 182–4).

29 Lawrence is not simply saying 'they struck sparks off each other'. In marrying his idea of human marriage with the marriage of opposites in the universe and with the Holy Trinity, he combines Greek season-myth with Easter symbolism. Mrs H. Jenner's *Christian Symbolism* (London, 1910), which he read enthusiastically in late 1914, explains that 'the lights have all been extinguished in the church on Good Friday . . . the Light of the World is dead upon the Cross'. Then 'the new Fire is struck by a flint and steel in the porch of the Church' (pp. 16–17).

30 *Study of Thomas Hardy*, edited by Steele, p. 89; see above, p. 14.
31 See especially Mark Kinkead-Weekes, 'The Marble and the Statue: The Exploratory Imagination of D. H. Lawrence', in *Imagined Worlds: Essays on Some English Novels and Novelists in Honour of John Butt*, edited by Maynard Mack and Ian Gregor (London, 1968), pp. 371–418. (This essay does not, however, discuss *Twilight in Italy*, identifying rather 'The Crown' as an influence on *Women in Love*.)
32 The suggestion is implicit in Barzini (New York, 1964), explicit in Nichols (London, 1973), pp. 148–9.
33 London, [probably 1919]. Lawrence's letters refer to her as Mrs Anthony.
34 Often the work is for very little cash. For forty days (and nights) tending silk-worms, the family gets £9.
35 This puts one in mind of Lawrence's 1913–14 letters from the Gulf of Spezia. The procession he describes (*Letters* 2, pp. 163–4) is allowed to be religious. But his account of the destruction of the olive trees by a snowstorm (*Letters* 2, pp. 140–1) is realistically economic in point.
36 *Women in Love*, edited by Farmer, Vasey and Worthen, p. 57.
37 See below, pp. 131–2.
38 *Phoenix II*, ed. Roberts and Moore, p. 321: see below, pp. 141, 143.
39 Gregor, *Great Web*, p. 232: above p. 36 and p. 175 n.50.
40 Antonia Cyriax gets the better of Rosina: other people she gets to know make her realise the full potentialities of her status as *padrona* and encourage her to call Rosina's bluff about overcharging. Rosina has respect for her match and the two become intimate confidantes and gossipers. The narrator's acceptance by the community is underlined by contrasts (the fashionable lady visitors, 'hedged in with artificiality, and brought up in an atmosphere of false values, they had little experience of things that matter – of real life. No wonder they understood the peasants as little as the peasants understood them' (p. 239)) and by public acclaim (a grand speech paying tribute to 'a signora who is so beautiful and intelligent, and who has been the friend of every one' (p. 246)).
41 *Etruscan Places*, in *D. H. Lawrence and Italy*, pp. 62–70; *Phoenix*, edited by McDonald, pp. 582–4.
42 The small degree to which this needs qualifying indicates an element of disunity in the book. In instances too obvious for me to waste space enumerating, 'Italians in Exile' and even more so 'The Return Journey' do anticipate *Sea and Sardinia* and the 'Introduction' to Magnus's *Memoirs*. This results in some risky juxtapositions even within these chapters. A reversion to the note of 'The Crucifix Across the Mountains', a mountain summit imagined as 'the very pure source of breaking-down', follows a Chekhovian episode with two little old ladies and their delicate dog (pp. 147, 153).
43 *The Letters of D. H. Lawrence*, edited by James T. Boulton (Cambridge, 1979), vol. 1, p. 428.

44 The body of the letter ends: 'But now I feel like a blind man who would put his eyes out rather than stand witness to a colossal and deliberate horror' (*Letters* 2, p. 415). I might add in parenthesis that this is not a self-absorbed letter. The feelings I have quoted don't eclipse what is their immediate prompting, Cynthia Asquith's loss. So it is in the letter he has to write to Else Jaffe five days later about the death of her young son.

45 For 'real', see pp. 124 and 145.

46 I speculate, more hesitantly, that there is some connection between Lawrence's flinching from the exiles' pamphlets and his misgivings about the enterprise of lectures and of *The Signature*. Not that the political views were in any way similar: but there was in both enterprises some contradiction between wanting to resurrect one's nation and standing away from one's fellow-countrymen as from leprosy, or at very least separating oneself from and partly despising them.

In ending this section of my chapter, I have touched on the book's 'double time-scheme' or chronological double-exposure, which is analogous with that posited by the 'Foreword' to *Women in Love*: 'This novel was written in its first form in the Tyrol, in 1913. It was altogether re-written and finished in Cornwall in 1917. So that it is a novel which took its final shape in the midst of the period of war, though it does not concern the war itself. I should wish the time to remain unfixed, so that the bitterness of the war may be taken for granted in the characters.' (reprinted in *Women in Love*, edited by Farmer, Vasey and Worthen, p. 485).

Although *Twilight* makes terse references to the war (e.g. the end of 'San Gaudenzio'), and the first general passage in 'The Lemon Gardens' has the war in mind, the main effect is to let it be taken for granted as colouring the narrator's concerns. At the same time the book preserves that feeling of Life Before the Fall, of what was for Lawrence and Frieda 'the first morning', 'the start of Creation', which he must have rediscovered as he re-read 'Italian Studies'.

47 'Foreword' to *Fantasia of the Unconscious*, p. 15.

48 The passage is attacked – appropriately I think – in John Middleton Murry's *Son of Woman* (London, 1931), and is an important piece of evidence for Colin Clarke's *River of Dissolution* (London, 1969).

49 See above, p. 8.

50 An interviewer asked him 'what made a writer write'. 'You don't write for anybody', replied Lawrence: 'you write rather from a deep moral sense – for the race, as it were.' (Frieda's answer was 'Egotism' – 'And to let everybody know how clever you are'.) See *D. H. Lawrence: A Composite Biography*, edited by Edward Nehls, 3 vols. (Wisconsin, 1958), vol. 2, p. 414.

51 *Apocalypse*, edited by Kalnins, p. 149.

3. Poetry and science in the psychology books

Page-numbers after my quotations from the psychology books refer to the Penguin edition (Harmondsworth, 1971).

1 *Letters* 3, p. 466.
2 Ibid., pp. 473; 477.
3 Ibid., p. 400. The analyst who had gone to Vienna was probably Ernest Jones. In the next sentence of his letter Lawrence refers both to him and to David and Edith Eder. He knew Jones reasonably well but was a close friend of the Eders and of Barbara Low, Edith Eder's sister and another pioneer analyst.
4 For details see Armin Arnold, *The Symbolic Meaning: The Uncollected versions of 'Studies in Classic American Literature'* (Arundel, 1962). Lawrence's phrase may have been prompted by revisions he had made to the published essays by September 1919.
5 There is a typescript of the original 'Foreword' (most of which Seltzer must have found it 'politic not to publish') in the Harry Ransom Humanities Research Center in Austin, Texas. For my quotation from the 'Epilogue' see the Viking Press edition of the psychology books (New York, 1960), p. 222. This epilogue was dropped from the English editions, probably because it addresses itself so directly to American readers.
6 *The Letters of D. H. Lawrence*, edited by Warren Roberts, James T. Boulton and Elizabeth Mansfield (Cambridge, 1987), vol. 4, pp. 57 and 104. (Hereafter referred to as *Letters* 4.)
7 Some of this enthusiasm can be found reprinted in J. M. Murry's *Reminiscences of D. H. Lawrence* (London, 1933), pp. 237–42.
8 See *The Rainbow*, edited by Worthen, p. 491. Both Ursula and Lawrence are vitalists who cannot believe that life merely consists – to quote one of Ursula's teachers – 'in a complexity of physical and chemical activities, of the same order as the activities we already know in science'.
9 'It all hung together, in the deepest sense', thinks Birkin in *Women in Love*, edited by Farmer, Vasey and Worthen, p. 26. For a comparison of Lawrence's approach with Freud's see my 'Lawrence and the Biological Psyche', in *D. H. Lawrence: Centenary Essays*, edited by Mara Kalnins (Bristol, 1986), pp. 89–109.
10 See Evelyn Hinz's 'The Beginning and the End: D. H. Lawrence's *Psychoanalysis* and *Fantasia*', *Dalhousie Review*, 52 (1972), pp. 251–65.
11 *Letters* 4, p. 97.
12 In accusing Lawrence of having 'mixed those babies up' the reviewer in the *Pittsburgh Dispatch* is recalling an episode from Owen Wister's very popular novel, *The Virginian* (New York, 1902). (I am grateful to Don L. Cook for this identification.)
13 This chronology emerges from remarks Lawrence makes in *Letters* 4 (see pp. 83, 86, 93, and 103, amongst others).
  Two copies of the typescript of *Fantasia* exist, one in the Austin library and another in the University of California at Berkeley

collection. Both have hand-written additions to the beginning of chapter 4 but although the addition in the Berkeley typescript is similar in substance to the Austin version, there are many differences in wording. Since the Austin typescript is in accord with the published text it might be that Lawrence used the Berkeley typescript for a first draft of the amended typescript he sent to Seltzer on 22 October. Several other of its features support this supposition, including chapter headings which are different from those in the Austin typescript and the first edition; but supposition is all it could be without very detailed comparison of the two documents concerned.

It is in the Austin typescript only that Lawrence bothers to link his new opening for chapter 4 to the original typed text with, 'Excuse my digression, gentle reader. At first I left it out . . .' etc. It is possible, although not, I think, very likely, that this last phrase points to there having been some version of the present opening of chapter 4 which Lawrence wrote in the Black Forest but didn't give to his Florence typist. Even if that is so, the differences between the openings in the two typescripts we now have, and the fact that they both begin with a reference to a review Lawrence didn't see until September, indicate that it would have been no more than 'a version', i.e. that Lawrence would have been amending or enlarging it in the Austin typescript and writing of being 'here in Ebersteinburg', therefore, when he wasn't.

14 Lawrence writes very well when he is describing the world around him or, one might say (given the note above), when he is describing the world which he remembers having been around him. Many of the poems in *Birds, Beasts and Flowers* (London, 1923) are made more effective by the impression they convey of a Lawrence who is observing 'Nature' *sur le vif*. So he usually was but, as Keith Sagar has pointed out, in one of the best and most famous poems from the collection – 'Humming-Bird' – Lawrence was probably relying on neither immediate observation nor memory but on descriptions of humming birds which he had read in various travel writers. See Sagar's *D. H. Lawrence: A Calendar*, pp. 102–3.

15 Hinz, 'The Beginning and the End', p. 257.

16 Ibid., p. 252.

17 Ibid., p. 265.

18 John Burnet's *Early Greek Philosophy* was a favourite book of Lawrence's. It needs to be said, however, that encouragement to express non-scientific ideas in a quasi-scientific idiom must also have come from theosophy. It seems relatively certain that Lawrence first took the hint for his biological psyche from John M. Pryse's extravagantly theosophical *The Apocalypse Unsealed* (New York, 1910) and in Madame Blavatsky's books – which Lawrence knew – an attempt is often made to put the latest scientific knowledge at the service of her idea of religion.

19 See I. A. Richards, *Poetries and Sciences* (London, 1970), pp. 72–4.

20 *The Letters of D. H. Lawrence*, edited and with an introduction by Aldous Huxley (London, 1932), p. xv.

21 The one specific reference in this section of the 'Foreword' is to Thomas Belt whose popular book, *The Naturalist in Nicaragua*, first appeared in 1874 and was praised by Darwin. On pp. 206–10 of the Everyman edition (London, 1911), which Lawrence may have used, Belt explains why he thinks the 'fabled Atlantis' may have been a reality and ends by talking of a 'noble enquiry, an unexplored region of research, at the entrance of which I can only stand and point the way of abler and stronger minds; an inquiry that will lead to the knowledge of the lands where dwelt the peoples of the glacial period who lived before the flood'. These pages show that Evelyn Hinz is wrong to take the reference in the 'Foreword' to what she, but not Lawrence, calls the 'myth of Atlantis' (p. 261) as a sign of his abandonment of science for poetry. In Lawrence's time, Atlantis was a topic for scholarly debate amongst anthropologists and geologists.

22 'Introduction to These Paintings' in *Phoenix*, edited by McDonald, p. 575.

23 'Pollyanalytics' can be traced back to John V. A. Weaver who in his 'Personally Conducted' column in the *Brooklyn Daily Eagle* (28 May 1921) writes, 'And now, after a steady perusal of three Lawrentian theses, we are Pollyanalysitic enough to want to go and read some nice clean Rabelais'. Weaver's column has the subtitle, 'The Sex-obsessed Mr. D. H. Lawrence'.

24 F. R. Leavis, *D. H. Lawrence: Novelist* (London, 1955), pp. 197–224.

25 *Kangaroo*, p. 195.

26 *Apocalypse*, edited by Kalnins, p. 68.

27 *Kangaroo*, p. 325.

28 No one has yet been able to name any one book or article by Freud which it is even reasonably certain Lawrence read. His opportunities for hearing about Freud came not only from Barbara Low, Jones and the Eders but also from Frieda. Before meeting Lawrence, Frieda had had a long affair with Otto Gross, an important if eccentric figure in the early days of the psychoanalytic movement. See Martin Green, *The Von Richthofen Sisters* (London, 1974).

That there are no records of Lawrence having read Freud cannot be conclusive, especially when he was quite often in houses where work by Freud, in either German or English, was available. But the depth of his knowledge is called into question by a letter he wrote to his sister-in-law in May 1921. He asks her if she knows of a German family with whom Edith Eder's son (by her first marriage to Haden Guest) could spend the holidays. 'The Eders', he explains, 'were the great Freudians in London: he practised as psychoanalist: and they translated Freud's *Traumdeuting*' (*Letters* 3, p. 716). If the Eders had translated Freud's *Traumdeutung* information about them would not be so hard to come by. A translation of Freud's short *Über den Traum* appeared under David Eder's name in 1914.

The massive *Interpretation of Dreams* was translated by A. A. Brill (Mabel Luhan's analyst) and published in England in 1913.

29 Leavis, *D. H. Lawrence: Novelist*, pp. 147, 150, 310 and *Thought, Words and Creativity*, pp. 21, 22.

30 See James C. Cowan, *D. H. Lawrence's American Journey: A Study in Literature and Myth* (Cleveland, 1970), p. 20.

31 John Wisdom, *Philosophy and Psycho-analysis* (Oxford, 1953), p. 182.

32 Leavis, *Thought, Words and Creativity*, pp. 23 and 49.

33 Ibid., pp. 82–3.

34 See 'Morality and the Novel', in *Study of Thomas Hardy*, edited by Steele, p. 172.

35 *'Mornings in Mexico' and 'Etruscan Places'* (Harmondsworth, 1960), p. 12.

36 Earl and Achsah Brewster, *D. H. Lawrence: Reminiscences and Correspondence* (London, 1934), p. 48.

4 Here and now in Sardinia: the art of Lawrence's travel writing

1 Mabel Dodge Luhan, *Lorenzo in Taos* (New York, 1932), pp. 256–7.

2 Compare, 'To her I was a piece of the environment. That was all. Her world was clear and absolute, without consciousness of self. She was not self-conscious, because she was not aware that there was anything in the universe except *her* universe.' *Twilight in Italy*, in *D. H. Lawrence and Italy*, p. 24. The meeting with the fellow Englishman is on pp. 148–9.

3 *D. H. Lawrence and Italy*, pp. 6–7. Page numbers for all the other quotations from *Sea and Sardinia* are included in my text.

4 As Howard Mills points out, the decision 'not to be' is given many different shades of meaning in *Twilight in Italy*. What I am thinking of here is Lawrence's claim that Hamlet decides 'not to be King, Father, *in the Self supreme*' (my italics), p. 70.

5 Jeffrey Meyers, *D. H. Lawrence and the Experience of Italy* (Philadelphia, 1982), p. 15.

6 This is the unintelligible expression in the first edition of *Sea and Sardinia* as well as the one I am using, but the typescript has 'drum-roaring'. I am grateful to Mara Kalnins for this information.

7 Billy T. Tracy Jnr, *D. H. Lawrence and the Literature of Travel* (Michigan, 1983), p. 44.

8 The description of the Cagliari market is on pp. 71–2. If Lawrence did work from detailed notes at this stage in his career, it is surprising that none have survived and that there is no reference by Frieda, or by anyone else close to him, of a Lawrence busily engaged in taking them.

9 Luhan, *Lorenzo in Taos*, p. 4. Mabel Luhan's letter of invitation to Lawrence pre-dates by a few weeks the American publication of *Sea and Sardinia* in December 1921. (She had read extracts from the coming book in the *Dial*.)

10 *Letters* 3, p. 688.
11 Sagar's *D. H. Lawrence: A Calendar* establishes that the two accounts were written within a few days of each other in August 1924 (see p. 138). The first sketch appeared in the number of *Laughing Horse* for September 1924.
12 Emile Delavenay, *L'homme et la genèse de son Œuvre* (Paris, 1969), p. 236.
13 See 'John Galsworthy', in *Study of Thomas Hardy*, edited by Steele, p. 209.
14 See 'Abysmal Immortality', in *Last Poems*, edited by Richard Aldington and Giuseppe Orioli (Florence, 1932), p. 28.
15 Compare, from Lawrence's preface to his translation of Verga's *Cavalleria Rusticana*, 'A third law is that the naive or innocent core in a man is always his vital core, and infinitely more important than his intellect or his reason. It is only from the core of unconscious naivete that the human being is ultimately a responsible and dependable being', or from the essay on John Galsworthy, 'While a man remains a man, a true human individual, there is at the core of him a certain innocence or naivete which defies all analysis, and which you cannot bargain with, you can only deal with it in good faith from your own corresponding innocence or naivete' (*Phoenix*, edited by McDonald, p. 245 and *Study of Thomas Hardy*, edited by Steele, pp. 210–11).
16 The original titles of the first four pieces in *Mornings in Mexico* indicate the order which Lawrence originally had in mind for them, 'Corasmin and the Parrots' was once 'Friday Morning'; 'Walk to Huayapa', 'Sunday Morning'; 'The Mozo', 'Monday Morning'; and 'Market Day', 'Saturday Morning'. 'Indians and Entertainment', 'The Dance of the Sprouting Corn' and 'The Hopi Snake Dance' relate to Lawrence's *New* Mexican experiences and were written in the spring and summer of 1924. For further details see Ross Parmenter's introduction to the Peregrine Smith edition of *Mornings in Mexico* (Salt Lake City, 1982).
17 It was Martin Secker who, by volunteering to select and arrange the material himself, overcame Lawrence's initial reluctance to offer the public a number of previously published 'half-baked essays in volume form'. See Parmenter's introduction to the Peregrine Smith edition, pp. x–xi.
18 The phrase comes in a letter written to Curtis Brown on 23 June 1925. See *Letters of D. H. Lawrence*, edited by Huxley, p. 637.
19 *Etruscan Places*, in *D. H. Lawrence and Italy*, p. 93.
20 *Phoenix*, edited by McDonald, p. 343.
21 See *Studies in Classic American Literature*, p. 147.
22 Brewster, *D. H. Lawrence: Reminiscences*, p. 237.
23 *D. H. Lawrence: A Personal Record* by E. T. (reprinted Cambridge, 1980), p. 198. Jessie Chambers's memoir was first published in 1935.
24 'Though I am glad to see them [i.e. his sister Emily and her nineteen-year-old daughter Margaret], it worries and depresses me

rather. I am really not "our Bert". Come to that, I never was. And the gulf between their outlook and mine is always yawning, horribly obvious to me'. See Harry T. Moore's *The Intelligent Heart* (Harmondsworth, 1980), pp. 569–70.

25 *Letters of D. H. Lawrence*, edited by Huxley, p. 762.
26 West, *D. H. Lawrence*, p. 35.

5 'My best single piece of writing': 'Introduction to *Memoirs of the Foreign Legion* by M.M.'

1 T. S. Eliot, at the start of his essay on Marvell, speaks of bringing the poet back to life.
2 This remark, which my title adapts into direct speech, was made to Catherine Carswell: see *Savage Pilgrimage*, p. 117. The italics are hers, perhaps representing Lawrence's own emphasis.
3 The phrase quoted is from p. 283 of Keath Fraser, 'Norman Douglas and D. H. Lawrence: A Sideshow in Modern Memoirs', *D. H. Lawrence Review*, 9 (1976), 283–295; see also Meyers, *D. H. Lawrence and the Experience of Italy*, pp. 29–49. While both refer in passing to the artistic qualities of the 'Introduction', they treat it primarily as a historical document or a legal affidavit, seeking to determine whether Lawrence or his disputant Douglas is 'more nearly correct' and who in real life 'comes out of the dispute more soiled' (Fraser, p. 287). The more sensitive comments of Carswell (*Savage Pilgrimage*, pp. 117–34) and Edward Nehls ('D. H. Lawrence: The Spirit of Place', in *The Achievement of D. H. Lawrence*, edited by Frederick J. Hoffman and Harry T. Moore (Norman, Oklahoma, 1953), pp. 268–90) take the piece rather too trustingly as a direct piece of autobiography.
4 *Memoirs* came out in 1924, as did *D. H. Lawrence and Maurice Magnus: A Plea for Better Manners* which was reprinted with small variations in pamphlet form and in his *Experiments* (London, 1925). My references are to *Experiments* (hereafter given in text as '*Experiments*') and to the reprint of Lawrence's 'Introduction' in *Phoenix II*, edited by Roberts and Moore (hereafter given in the text). In quotations I omit Lawrence's dash after the abbreviations M and D.
5 *Collected Letters*, edited by Moore, vol. 2, p. 841. A similar phrase occurs in his letter to the *New Statesman* on 20 February 1926 (ibid., pp. 889–91).
6 'Genres are essentially contracts between a writer and his audience' (Frederic Jameson, 'Magical Narratives: Romance as Genre', *New Literary History*, 7 (1975), p. 135).
7 The invitation is not that new. Aldington suggested in 1966 that 'what Lawrence wrote was a short imaginative novel about a possible (not necessarily the real) Magnus, and that his grave error was to publish this as a biography'. He sees himself in what is the present-day reader's position in that 'As I knew nothing of Magnus, I can easily read the thing as a short novel, and as such I find it

extremely interesting' (Introduction to *Apocalypse* (New York, 1966), p. xv). As we will see later, Aldington did not always adopt this approach.

8 From the 'Preface to Shakespeare': *Works*, edited by Sherbo, vol. 7, p. 88.

9 The phrase comes from a relevant context in James's 'The Art of Fiction' (1884), reprinted in *House of Fiction*, edited by Edel, p. 33.

10 *Aaron's Rod* (Phoenix edition, London, 1954), ch. 12, especially pp. 137–9.

11 Fraser, in 'Douglas and Lawrence: A Sideshow', working with a similar distinction between literal and 'substantial' truth, is much too unwary of the pitfalls of the latter.

12 Douglas, *Experiments*, p. 249; see also pp. 223, 256 and 252–3.

13 Picked out by Nehls (in *Achievement of D. H. Lawrence*, p. 284), and by Meyers (in *D. H. Lawrence and the Experience of Italy*, p. 34) who offers it more broadly as L's attitude in the episode as a whole, on which Meyers writes only two paragraphs.

14 This phrase comes from a part of 'Burnt Norton' which, with its similarly repeated word 'world', it is illuminating to place next to the monastery episode.

15 Lawrence makes the apparently casual word *cold* reverberate. It is first attached to 'the world', then applied (about thirty times in a few pages) to the monastery, later to M's voice at a moment of absolute disagreement with L, and finally to the sunset.

16 'Preface' to *Cavalleria Rusticana*, in *Phoenix*, edited by McDonald, pp. 249–50; *Phoenix II*, edited by Roberts and Moore, p. 276.

17 *Collected Letters*, edited by Moore, vol. 2, p. 890.

18 Richard Aldington, *Pinorman* (London, 1954), p. 192.

19 'The Art of Fiction', *House of Fiction*, edited by Edel, p. 28.

20 Douglas wrings his hands. Frieda washes hers:

> Magnus . . . came [to Taormina] almost taking for granted that we would be responsible for him, that it was our duty to keep him. This disturbed Lawrence.
>
> 'Is it my duty to look after this man?' he asked me.
>
> To me it was no problem. Had I been fond of Magnus, had he had any meaning, or purpose – but no, he seemed only anti-social, a poor devil without any pride, and he didn't seem to matter anyhow. With the money Lawrence had lent him, he stayed at the best hotel in Taormina, to my great resentment, we who could not afford to stay even in a second-rate hotel. I felt he made a fool of Lawrence, and afterwards, when we went to Malta, crossing second class from Palermo, whom should I discover gaily swanking and talking to an English Navy officer but Magnus on the first-class deck! The cheek of the man! He had written to Lawrence: 'I am sweating blood till I am out of Italy.' I know his sort, people always sweating blood and always going to shoot themselves.' (Frieda Lawrence, *"Not I, But the Wind . . ."* (New York, 1934), p. 99)

This is the average sensible-selfish attitude, allowing easy ways of not feeling disturbed, responsible or compassionate. It puts into perspective my criticism of L's intermittent knowingness.

21 Aldington, *Pinorman*, pp. 48, 55, 212.
22 Carswell, *Savage Pilgrimage*, p. 132.
23 Ibid.

6 Verse or worse: the place of 'pansies' in Lawrence's poetry

1 See *Phoenix*, edited by McDonald, pp. 571–3.
2 In *D. H. Lawrence: The Critical Heritage*, edited by R. P. Draper (London, 1970), p. 299.
3 *The New Poems* preface is reprinted in *Complete Poems*, edited by Pinto and Roberts, vol. 1, pp. 181–6. (Hereafter referred to as *Complete Poems*.) The responsibility for calling Lawrence's fourth collection *New Poems* lies with his publisher, not Lawrence himself.
4 *Letters* 3, p. 387.
5 *Dial*, vol. 67, no. 796, pp. 97–100.
6 *Complete Poems*, vol. 1, p. 184.
7 Ibid., pp. 182–3.
8 *The Renaissance* (London, 1901), pp. 233–4. Pater's remark about all art aspiring to the condition of music occurs in the section of this edition called 'The School of Giorgione' (p. 135).
9 *Letters* 2, p. 364.
10 *The Symbolic Meaning*, edited by Armin Arnold, p. 264.
11 *Studies in Classic American Literature*, pp. 174–5. The first edition of the *Studies* was published by Seltzer in August 1923.
12 *Phoenix*, edited by McDonald, p. 567.
13 *Complete Poems*, vol. 1, pp. 356–7. The tortoise sequence was published separately in America, in what Lawrence referred to as a 'chap-book' form; but then incorporated into the first English edition of *Birds, Beasts and Flowers*.
14 Vol. 2, no. 4, pp. 128–34. *Voices* was published in London and edited by Thomas Moult.
15 Both of the *Pansies* introductions are reprinted in *Complete Poems*. For this quotation, see vol. 1, p. 424.
16 *Letters of D. H. Lawrence*, edited by Huxley, p. 766.
17 The draft has been published by David Farmer in the *Review of English Studies*, 21 (1970), pp. 181–4.
18 *Complete Poems*, vol. 1, p. 423.
19 See *Last Poems*, edited by Aldington and Orioli, p. xviii.
20 Ibid., p. xiii.
21 Ms B has the title 'Pensées' on the opening page and is the draft Ms which supplied some of the later poems for *Pansies* as well as nearly all the *Nettles*.
22 Keith Sagar, ' "New, Strange Flowers": *Pansies, Nettles and Last Poems*' in *D. H. Lawrence: Life into Art* (Harmondsworth, 1985), pp. 324–54.
23 *Last Poems*, edited by Aldington and Orioli, p. xviii.

24 Ibid., p. xiv.
25 Compare, in Sandra Gilbert's *Acts of Attention: The Poems of D. H. Lawrence* (Cornell, 1972), pp. 245–6 and especially, 'Perhaps it is because of his growing preoccupation with deliberately transient art that just as the poems of *Birds, Beasts and Flowers* owed a good deal to the critical and travel essays Lawrence was composing when he wrote them, the doggerel of *Pansies* and *Nettles* is related to slighter journalistic pieces he was publishing in the last few years of his life'.
26 Sagar, *D. H. Lawrence: Life into Art*, p. 327.
27 Not only has Aldington's concept of *Last Poems* remained un-challenged but it has also become customary to accept his suggestion that the poems in MS A represent a new departure and ought to be read as a sequence. This is the approach of Sandra Gilbert in the last section of *Acts of Attention* and of Michael Kirkham in an article on *Last Poems* published in the number of the *D. H. Lawrence Review* for summer 1972. For my purposes therefore the tendency of several remarks in Gail Porter Mandell's *The Phoenix Paradox: A Study of Renewal Through Change in the 'Collected Poems' and 'Last Poems' of D. H. Lawrence* (Edwardsville, Illinois, 1964) is very welcome. 'In "More Pansies", as well as "Last Poems",' writes Dr Mandell, 'religion and poetry often merge. A surprisingly large number of poems in "More Pansies" have religious subjects' (p. 134); and of several poems in 'More Pansies' which are celebratory and 'recount specific epiphanies in human life', she says that they 'share both content and style with "Last Poems". It is tempting to conjecture that had he lived to publish them, Lawrence would have grouped all such poems together as his religious testament, the story of his covenant with the demon' (p. 136).
    The more the inter-relationship of 'More Pansies' and 'Last Poems' is recognized, the easier it becomes to insist that there must be 'pansies' in both.
28 It was while Lawrence was staying with the Brewsters in Kandy that he attended a ceremony in honour of the Prince of Wales. 'Elephant' describes this ceremony (Perahera) in detail and ponders the question of political authority. Although there are several vivid phrases about elephants, they are relatively incidental.
29 *Complete Poems*, vol. 2, p. 423.
30 Ibid., p. 417.
31 'Desire is dead' and 'Man reaches a point' are from *Pansies*, 'Delight of Being Alone' from the 'More Pansies' section of *Last Poems*.
32 *Studies in Classic American Literature*, p. 175.
33 *Complete Poems*, vol. 1, p. 185.
34 The claim is implicit in the famous letter to Edward Marsh (August 1913) in which Lawrence insists that, 'to get an emotion out in its own course' needs 'the finest instinct imaginable, much finer than the skill of the craftsmen . . . Sometimes Whitman is perfect.

Remember skilled verse is dead in fifty years' (*Letters* 2, p. 61).
35 See p. 352 of *Notes of a Son and Brother* in F. W. Dupee's edition of Henry James's autobiographical writings (London, 1956).
36 See *Letters* 2, p. 544 and *D. H. Lawrence: A Composite Biography*, edited by Nehls, vol. 2, p. 414.

Index

N.b. Works by Lawrence are in bold print.